T0323770

"*Tank Warfare* by Jeremy Black is an in-depth, analytical study of the tank as a weapon of war. While there have been many books on armored warfare before, not one has this scope or critical analysis. This book will be of interest to general readers as well as military historians."

—Glyn Harper, author of *The Battle for North Africa*

"*Tank Warfare* is a tour de force of the history of armored combat from the Battle of Cambrai till Syria. In scope and brevity, this book surpasses all other available works on tank warfare. Through his lucid prose, Black not only provides an incisive account of the great tank battles fought by the panzers and Israeli Defense Force but also engages with the existing debates in the field. As this monograph shows, the value of the tank in war depends not only on the state of art technology but also on non-material factors like command, tactical concepts, training, and doctrine. The author persuasively argues that though tanks will remain relevant to armies in the near future, their combat effectiveness is somewhat decreasing due to the nature of future battlefield and weapons. *Tank Warfare*'s exciting prose and intricate analysis will not only attract the general readers but will also be of great help to the specialists."

—Kaushik Roy, Guru Nanak Chair Professor, Department of History, Jadavpur University, Kolkata, India

"Jeremy Black succeeds in steering the reader through the entire history of the tank, traversing a remarkable range of wars, campaigns, machines, and technical developments. Beginning with the origins of the tank, he manages to take the narrative through all the major conflicts, and from one side of the globe to another, including the world after 1990, bringing the story right up to the present day. He takes a skeptical view of the future of the tank, one which will certainly spark controversy. I can think of no short history of the tank which covers so much ground so succinctly. It provides an excellent overview of the subject."

—Alaric Searle, author of *Armoured Warfare: A Military, Political and Global History,* Professor of Modern European History, University of Salford, UK

"This superb book tells the story of tank warfare since its inception. In his sweeping account, Jeremy Black covers all aspects of the tank and all conflicts in which it has been involved, displaying a rare knowledge and integrating that knowledge into a coherent whole that few are capable of. Black covers both the tank's limitations and defeats as well as its strengths and successes. He shows that its effectiveness depended on context. It was not the silver bullet of its proponents like Fuller and Liddell Hart: it was important but only as part of a mix of weaponry. This book is a tour de force and strongly recommended."

—Dr. John Peaty, FRGS, FRHistS

TANK WARFARE

JEREMY BLACK

INDIANA UNIVERSITY PRESS

TANK

WARFARE

This book is a publication of

INDIANA UNIVERSITY PRESS
Office of Scholarly Publishing
Herman B Wells Library 350
1320 East 10th Street
Bloomington, Indiana 47405 USA

iupress.indiana.edu

The paper used in this publication
meets the minimum requirements of
the American National Standard for
Information Sciences—Permanence
of Paper for Printed Library Materials,
ANSI Z39.48–1992.

Manufactured in the
United States of America

Library of Congress Cataloging-
in-Publication Data

Names: Black, Jeremy, 1955- author.
Title: Tank warfare / Jeremy Black.
Description: Bloomington : Indiana
   University Press, [2020] | Includes
   bibliographical references and index.
Identifiers: LCCN 2020016129 (print) |
   LCCN 2020016130 (ebook) | ISBN
   9780253049995 (hardback) |
   ISBN 9780253050007 (ebook)
Subjects: LCSH: Tank warfare—History. |
   Tanks (Military science).
Classification: LCC UG446.5 .B57445 2020
   (print) | LCC UG446.5 (ebook) |
   DDC 358.1/8409—dc23
LC record available at https://lccn.loc
   .gov/2020016129
LC ebook record available at https://lccn.loc
   .gov/2020016130

1 2 3 4 5   24 23 22 21 20

for

DUNCAN PROUDFOOT

CONTENTS

PREFACE

Really a fearsome sight. . . . The road was on a slope of the hill,
and the tanks just crawled up the slope, up the right bank nose
in air, down with a bump into the road and across it—almost
perpendicularly up the left bank, and down with a bump behind
it and so up the hill without a moment's pause or hesitation.

Edward Heron-Allen, 1918

EDWARD HERON-ALLEN'S ACCOUNT OF BRITISH TANKS CROSSING
a road on October 16, 1918, captured the physicality of tanks as well as their
apparent remorseless ability to subordinate terrain.[1] At this stage, the Allies
were successfully advancing against the Germans on the Western Front in
Belgium and France at the close of World War I (1914–18), and tanks were part
of the victorious equation.

Size, scale, firepower, mobility—the tank, and armored warfare as a whole,
seized the imagination of commanders and commentators concerned about
the constraints of its infantry counterpart. However, as so often with innovations and, in particular, movement, there could be a failure to see matters in
perspective at strategic, operational, and tactical levels. This book, therefore,
is a parallel to mine on air power, of which the same is true.[2] Indeed, there is
a closer link because the stress on armor could draw on the same roots as that
on air power while, conversely, an emphasis on aircraft could lead to a downplaying of operations on land, most obviously after World War II (1939–45).
As with air power, an account of armor is a tale of limitations and defeats, as
well as potential and achievements. This is that history.

There is a standard account of tanks, one of potential unlocked, but only
eventually so, and in the face of misunderstanding and misguided opposition.

This standard account focuses on innovation and eventual success. Both are seen in World War I, with the tank held responsible for surmounting the constraints of trench warfare in 1918. Then the theme is of brilliant thinkers and innovators in the 1920s and 1930s and a failure in Britain and France to heed their ideas but a willingness, instead, to do so in Germany and the Soviet Union. The latter willingness is then regarded as responsible for Germany's blitzkrieg triumphs in 1939–41 in the early stages of World War II only for German panzers (armor) to be overcome from 1941 by the scale, weather, and numbers of the Soviet Union, factors exacerbated by Hitler's foolish command innovations. Thereafter, the focus switches to other exponents of bold armor advances, from the American George Patton in 1943–45 to the victorious Israelis in the Six-Day War in 1967. Albeit with a discussion of the Cold War, the popular narrative then runs a bit dry before rising to a conclusion with US successes in the two wars in the Persian Gulf (1991 and 2003).

This book both explains that account and challenges it, adding depth, qualification, context, and criticism. In considering the subject, it is important at every turn to remember the danger risked by tankers. Anton Herr, a professional soldier serving in the Twenty-First Panzer Division in 1944, "was terrified to suffocate in my tank and burn alive."[3] He survived the war experience. Many did not. For a fictional account, the first few minutes of the 2012 Russian film *White Tiger* provide a view of the terrible fate of a trapped tank crew when hit.

As with other types of history, it is important to note issues with definitions, records, and historiography. In the first case, tanks may seem simply defined as manned, tracked armored fighting vehicles. However, that definition is too narrow. States in the 2010s tested unmanned tracked vehicles mounted with guns. In 2018, the British army tested Titan Strike, in effect a robot that could move autonomously in which the gun had to be operated remotely by a human. The extent to which this is a tank requires consideration.

In the case of records, the papers of the military commentator and historian Basil Liddell Hart as he struggled to provide historical precision for World War II are instructive. He pointed out: "To deduce correct lessons it is necessary, above all, to determine the tank strengths on either side in any important operations." Reconciling sources involved addressing issues such as how best to distinguish those tanks that were fit for action and also the treatment of light tanks that were only appropriate for reconnaissance duties.[4]

Brigadier C. J. C. Molony added that he was skeptical about strength returns (reports of the number of working tanks) "perhaps because of vague memories of conjuring rabbits out of hats, as an adjutant a long time ago!" while a memorandum on the variable tank strength of German armored (panzer) divisions in 1942–43 drew attention not only to casualties but also to fluctuating replenishment priorities.[5] That was separate to the general cut in the size of the panzer divisions in 1941 while in 1942 the size of units varied depending on location—they were larger in Army Group South, which was advancing and the center of the German offensive, than in Army Group Centre, where there was far less fighting from the spring. The general trend in the size of a panzer division was downward. Similarly, Lieutenant-General Elfeldt, Commander of the Eighty-Fourth German Corps, discussing German operations in Normandy, complained in August 1944 of "the madness at Mortain of thrusting towards Avranches with six Panzer Divisions which weren't Panzer Divisions any longer."[6] Such points are repeatedly the case. Elfeldt captured a reason for the failure of the German counteroffensive against the US breakthrough.

In the case of historiography, the account of tank warfare in the Anglophone world is strongly affected by the continued grip of a narrative and an analysis essentially derived from Basil Liddell Hart and given earlier. Both narrative and analysis are somewhat problematic. Moreover, they sit within a characteristic tendency to emphasize the role of the subject and, in general, to do so in a disproportionate fashion. That is an aspect of the "silver-bullet" approach to weaponry, an approach that emphasizes the significance of weaponry and therefore of developments in this field. The concept of "Revolutions of Military Affairs," past, present, and future, is involved in this approach. It is deeply problematic.

As this book will show, armor indeed was important but as part of a more general mix of weaponry. Furthermore, the effectiveness of tanks was set in the varied contexts of their use and, notably, with reference to doctrinal and command factors. Over all was the relationship between this use of tanks and the tasking derived from the strategy of individual conflicts. Tanks were employed not in the abstract but in specific locations and against particular opponents. That remains the case and affects discussion of their future value.

NOTES

1. B. W. Harvey and C. Fitzgerald, eds., *Edward Heron-Allen's Journal: The Great War: From Sussex Shore to Flanders Fields* (Lewes, UK, 2002).

2. J. Black, *Air Power: A Global History* (Lanham, MD, 2016).

3. P. Caddick-Adams, *Sand and Steel: The D-Day Invasion and the Liberation of France* (Oxford, 2019), 755.

4. Liddell Hart to Major-General Ian Playfair, January 23, 1954, October 27, November 12, 19, December 4, 1956, reply November 28, 1956, LH. Liddell Hart papers, 4/32.

5. Molony to Liddell Hart, October 5, 1958, Brian Melland to Liddell Hart, May 17, 1961, LH. Liddell Hart papers, 4/32, 4/31.

6. M. Cobb, *Eleven Days in August: The Liberation of Paris in 1944* (London, 2013), 33.

ACKNOWLEDGMENTS

I AM GRATEFUL TO THE LARGE NUMBER OF HISTORIANS WHO HAVE already written on aspects of warfare relating to tanks. I hope I have paid sufficient tribute in my footnotes and select bibliography. I am also grateful for the opportunity to teach military history since 1996 at the University of Exeter and to lecture at a range of other institutions and events, including the National World War Two Museum in New Orleans. Visiting military museums, notably the Australian Armour and Artillery Museum near Cairns, the British Tank Museum at Bovington, and the First Division Museum at Cantigny, has also been instructive, as has been seeing historic tanks at other sites, from Rabaul to Sevastopol. Repeatedly, I have had arresting conversations, most clearly in 1997 when a US tank colonel responded to my query about the possibility of conflict over Taiwan by remarking that Taiwan was too small for his unit to operate in.

The topic can be grim, so it is worth finding a moment of unintentional humor in the shape of the Bob Semple tank, allegedly the worst tank ever made. New Zealand has a brave and distinguished military history, including with tanks in the Armored Regiments that operated in the Pacific War with Japan during World War II. Concern about the risk of Japanese attack led Bob Semple, the minister of works, to have tanks built by his ministry from corrugated iron on a tractor base. They weighed 25.4 tons and were armed with six machine guns, but these inadequately designed and built tanks did not perform well and were never used in combat. Another New Zealand improvisation, the Schofield tank, was also not pursued.

I am grateful to Chiaki Akimoto, Alejandro Amendolara, Roberto Muñoz Bolaños, Tom Cross-Brown, Jonathan Fennell, Jacques Fremaux, Bernard Kelly, Tony King, Alan Knuth, Dennis Showalter, Gareth Stansfield, and Javier Veramendi for advice on particular points. I have benefited from the comments of Colin Baxter, Jason Belgrave, Pete Brown, Peter Caddick-Adams, Mike Cailes, Alexander Hill, Jan Hoffenaar, Paul Malmassari, Ciro Paoletti, John Peaty, Alexander Querengässer, Anthony Saunders, Rick Schneid, Mark Stevens, and Ulf Sundberg on all or part of an earlier draft. All errors are my responsibility. It is a great pleasure to dedicate this book to Duncan Proudfoot, a good friend and a great publisher.

ABBREVIATIONS

Add	additional manuscripts
AFV	armored fighting vehicle
ANZEC	Australian and New Zealand Army Corps
APC	armor-piercing capped
APC	armored personnel carrier
APDS	armor-piercing discarding sabot
APFSDS	armor-piercing fin-stabilized discarding sabot
AWM	Canberra, Australian War Memorial
BL	London, British Library, Department of Manuscripts
CAB	Cabinet Office papers
CHARM	Challenger armament
CIA	Central Intelligence Agency
EFP	explosively formed penetrator
FOFA	follow-on forces attack
GAM	Free Aceh Movement
GPS	Global Positioning System
HC	*Hansard, the Official Report of the House of Commons*
HEAT	high-explosive antitank
HESH	high-explosive squash head
HVAP	high-velocity armor-piercing
IED	improvised explosive device
IRA	Irish Republican Army
IS	Islamic State
JMH	*Journal of Military History*
KEP	kinetic energy penetrator

LANDCENT	Allied Land Forces Central Europe
LCT	landing craft tank
LH	London, King's College, Liddell Hart archive
LMA	London, Metropolitan Archives
LST	landing ship, tank
MBT	main battle tank
MCV	mechanized combat vehicle
MDAP	Major Defense Acquisition Program
Mk	Mark
MM	Montgomery-Massingberd papers
NA	London, National Archives
NATO	North Atlantic Treaty Organization
NGO	nongovernmental organization
OMG	operational maneuver group
PIAT	Projector, Infantry, Anti-Tank
PLO	Palestine Liberation Organization
REME	Royal Electrical and Mechanical Engineers
RHA	rolled homogeneous armor
RMA	Revolution in Military Affairs
ROAD	Reorganization of the Army Division
RPG	rocket-propelled grenade
RUSI	*Royal United Services Institute Journal*
SAM	surface-to-air missile
SLA	South Lebanon Army
TAM	Tanque Argentino Mediano
TOW	tube-launched, optically tracked, wire-guided
TRADOC	Training and Doctrine Command
TUSK	Tank Urban Survival Kit
UAV	unmanned aerial vehicle
UN	United Nations
UNPROFOR	United Nations Protection Force
WAM	wide area munition
WO	War Office papers
YPG	People's Protection Units

TANK WARFARE

ONE

THE START

DEFINITIONS

Combining mobility with firepower was a longstanding goal of command-ers. The tank added power in the shape of the internal combustion engine. It was a variant on the steam power of an armored train, itself potentially a source of great firepower. However, caterpillar tracks gave the tank much greater maneuverability due to its ability to cross different terrain as opposed to vehicles that were dependent on wheels, whether they moved on roads or rails. That helps offer a clear definition of the tank, one made readily appar-ent by the series of emblematic photographs that are used so often, whether showing scenes of the world wars or depicting Chinese tanks facing a lone protestor in Beijing in 1989, as reproduced, for example, in the London *Sunday Times* of April 21, 2019.

Guns, armor, internal combustion engine, and tracks. Of course, however, that definition encompasses many fighting vehicles not classically defined as tanks: tank destroyers and self-propelled guns, obviously, but also armored fighting vehicles carrying guns, including if one of their main functions is transporting infantry. In turn, the latter overlap with wheeled vehicles that do the same. Moreover, wheeled vehicles can do so more effectively. Mod-ern suspension systems, with the wheels individually suspended, offer major advantages in terms of the equations (or trade-offs) of coverable terrain ver-sus speed and maneuverability. Vehicles with these systems do not have the load-sharing characteristics of those with tracks, especially wide tracks, but otherwise can readily match the specifications of light tanks.

Light vehicles, whether with tracks or wheels, have been of particular sig-nificance from the 1990s due to greater interest in transportability by air, a product of the US engagement with worldwide interventionist capability.

To a degree, these vehicles return attention to the early tanks that were solely armed with machine guns, rather than also with a main gun, the latter being the usual modern view of a tank.

These points encourage a definition of tanks in terms of vehicles that are called tanks. That is helpful as a working premise but also faces difficulties. First, there are past definitional usages that pose issues, notably that of tank-ettes, or small tanks used mainly for infantry support in the 1930s, which were used in practice by all powers with tanks. Second, the term *tank* leaves unclear how best to handle tank destroyers, which in the American and German armies were operated by the artillery. On the one hand, they are armed and armored vehicles tasked with destroying tanks, but, on the other, they are tanks with a particular function and specifications accordingly. As such, they are on a continuum with tanks armed with flamethrowers. *Armor* itself as a term includes, for example, combat engineer vehicles, some of which are tracked and some not. Possibly, therefore, a tank is what could be tactically used as a tank employing twentieth-century technology.

A tank, after all, is defined more by its function than by its construction or constituent parts. The Swedish S-Tank had no turret while the US M10 tank destroyer had one. Not all tanks have conventional guns as their main arma-ment; the US M551 Sheridan, in service from 1969 to 1996, fired a wire-guided MGM-51 Shillelagh missile from its gun barrel as well as conventional ammunition.

Moreover, the term *tank* is something of a catchall that does not translate literally into other languages. The German is *panzer*, and the French *char d'assault*; neither means tank. The only reason they are called tanks in the English-speaking world is because the vehicles were referred to as water tanks in World War I to hide what they were intended for because they resembled water tanks.

A common approach is to see what is "properly" a tank as what is now called a main battle tank (MBT), with everything else as an armored fighting vehicle (AFV), and a light tank as essentially a reconnaissance vehicle. However, MBT was not a term in use until the 1960s, and hence everything prior to that was a tank, with modifiers being applied to define what sort of tank. Func-tional intentions and attributes affected weaponry. Thus, during World War II, tanks were multirole platforms and generally had a coaxial machine gun whereas, in most cases, tank destroyers or antitank guns did not have such a machine gun as their role was set. However, to argue that there is something "properly" a tank—so that, for example, a flamethrower tank of World War II was a specialized AFV and not a tank—is unhelpful. If an MBT engages in an assault role, so can other vehicles that are tracked, such as tank destroyers, or wheeled. More generally, for all forms of armored vehicle, there has been a seesawing among speed, protection, firepower, and reliability, rather than a fixed goal or means.

The value of a loose definition of tanks will probably become more apparent in the future as miniaturized tanks play a greater role in urban combat. Like drones, and building on the technology of unmanned mine and explosive-tackling vehicles, these tanks will be operated from a distance.

In consequence of these points, there is a need for considering a broader narrative, and more open-ended analysis, than has usually been the case. This approach involves readers testing their assumptions not only about tanks but also concerning what they think should have been the trajectory of their development. Best practice, whether in doctrine, procurement, tactics, or operational planning, appears different if wider definitions of tanks and armor are adopted.

HISTORICAL BACKGROUND

To consider the particular strengths and deficiencies of the tank, however defined, it is useful to go back and assess the potential and problems of other means of combining mobility with firepower, even if they were very different in type. The most significant means was the chariot, which came to be seen as a fundamental military element in parts of the ancient world. As with the tank and the internal combustion engine, a new power source and the working of metal were crucial for chariots. The domestication of animals—notably horses—was the key prelude to the use of chariots. Indeed, it was a precursor to the widespread expansion in the tactical, operational, and strategic flexibility of armies. This was denied to societies, such as those in the Americas, Australasia, and Oceania, that lacked the horse.

Elsewhere, the horse was the fundamental technology that opened up a range of possibilities, rather as the internal combustion engine was to do. Long before the development of stirrups, most of these possibilities had already been explored with success: the Scythians were feared horse archers, and the Sarmatians had heavy cavalry. This variety in cavalry prefigured later variety in armor. Nevertheless, there were important environmental constraints in the development of cavalry, particularly with disease and terrain. Thus, horses could not be used in the extensive tsetse fly belt of Africa or in the mountainous terrain of Norway.

CHARIOTS

The development of wheeled transport was closely linked to that of draft animals. The beginnings of the wheel are unclear and possibly stemmed from log rollers. Wheeled vehicles were in existence in Southwest Asia by about 3500 BCE. Bronze Age societies had horse-drawn carts; from about 1700 BCE, lighter chariots requiring only two animals were employed. Chariots were prominent in the Middle East in the Middle and Late Bronze Age while, in Mycenaean Greece and Iron Age Britain (700 BCE–50 CE), the powerful were buried with their chariot and spear.

Mentioned as an important background to the idea of a mobile fortress or battle car by J. F. C. Fuller in his *Tanks in the Great War, 1914–1918* (1920),[1] chariots proved effective as part of combined weapons systems. In China, the use of chariots, composite bows, and bronze-tipped spears and halberds developed in the second millennium BCE. By the third century BCE, however, the rise of mass armies, a product of population growth and the introduction of conscription, ensured that chariots no longer played an important role in China.

There was a similar trade-off with tanks. They appeared most necessary when manpower was in short supply, and they could act therefore as a replacement for manpower. Moreover, tanks, like other high-specification weaponry, also seemed able to overcome large numbers of troops. As such, they were a substitute in a very different fashion.

Firepower and mobility were important to chariots and later to tanks. The combination of the compound bow with the light, two-wheeled chariot, beginning in the seventeenth century BCE in the Middle East, has been seen by some commentators as a tactical revolution that, in the later Bronze Age, ushered in mass confrontations of chariots acting as missile platforms by carrying archers. At the same time, it is important to avoid an account of military history in which the nature of the weaponry determined success or, indeed, constituted a revolution. That is generally an overly simplistic approach.

The Egyptians learned chariotry from the Palestinian Hyksos, who conquered Egypt at the end of the Middle Kingdom (c. 2040–1640 BCE). Impressions of chariotry can be gained from Egyptian temple reliefs of the Late Kingdom (c. 1550–1070 BCE), which show a use of bowmen mounted on chariots. Their employment by Thutmose III over a Syrian coalition at Megiddo (in modern Israel) in about 1460 BCE helped win the day by giving force and speed to the device of enveloping attacks. Ramses II faced the Hittites at the battle of Kadesh in about 1285 BCE, with both sides employing large numbers of chariots. The bas-relief monument at Thebes in Egypt depicts Ramses as a chariot rider, indicating the prestige of the role, which is matched by photographs over the last century of leaders on, or reviewing, tanks.

The Assyrian Empire, founded in 950 BCE, benefited from its great ability to supply horses, on which chariot strength depended, rather as tanks were to depend on the availability of oil supplies. The Assyrian preference was for heavy chariots, with four rather than two horses and carrying four men rather than two, thus greatly increasing firepower.

A very different type of mobile firepower was provided by siege towers, although that again raises issues of definition. Attackers needed to come to close quarters with an enemy in order to seize a fortified position and, notably, offset the missile weapons used by the defenders. Siege towers, a form of fortified gantry, were developed. The dramatic stone reliefs from the palace of Nineveh, the Assyrian capital, depict the sieges of walled cities in the mid-seventh century BCE. The Assyrians used battering rams. As shown in carvings, men fought from the tops of the towers that protected the rams: these were siege towers with battering rams or vice versa. Siege towers were supported by catapults. As later with artillery, these had different purposes; large catapults were employed to inflict damage to the structure while small ones provided an antipersonnel capability to enable the use of siege engines close up against the walls. The corollary with tanks was armament with guns or machine guns.

The comparison with the use of tanks in World War I is interesting but not clear-cut. Tanks were not used to surmount or smash enemy fortifications, for it appeared clear from the outset that they could prevail against barbed wire but not against concrete walls. The former was an obstacle—an aspect of the field fortifications, including trenches and earth bastions—that infantry (and therefore infantry-support tanks) had to overcome. Walled fortifications, in contrast, were a matter for artillery.

From that perspective, there is a clear distinction between siege towers and tanks. The former primarily appear not as an ancient form of self-propelled heavy artillery but rather as a troop carrier: an armored mobile bridge or landing craft designed to carry and protect infantry until they could jump onto an enemy-held walled fortification. That might not appear to be the role of tanks, but the distinction is less clear in practice. It was the normal role of tanks in many contexts to carry infantry, especially Soviet tanks on the Eastern Front in World War II. Tanks, moreover, often have been used against structures—for example, in confronting the Iraqi insurrection after the Second Gulf War. In addition, siege towers could carry machines as well as individuals firing projectiles and thus could act as mobile artillery.

After the fall of the Assyrians in the seventh century BCE, chariots continued to play a role, but it was secondary to that of cavalry, which offered greater flexibility than chariots, not least in difficult terrains, and was less expensive. The Persians, who rose to far-flung regional power in the sixth century BCE, used chariots, but cavalry warfare was more significant for them.

The chariots provided a way to disrupt opposing battle lines; to that end, chariots equipped with scythes on their wheels were particularly successful, although the understanding of equestrian factors has led to questions about whether chariots charged en masse and therefore were really formidable in battle. Scythed chariots are first on record in the early fifth century BCE and were, like elephants, probably more of a scare tactic than an effective tactical option, or, at least, the former was very important. As such, there was an important similarity with the initial use of tanks in World War I.

Chariots were used by the Persians against the Macedonians when Alexander the Great invaded the Persian Empire. At Arbela (Gaugamela) in 331 BCE, the Macedonians thwarted the Persian chariots and cavalry in part by the use of javelin throwers. This reflected the extent to which mobile attacking forces could be weakened by defending missile throwers. Well-deployed, well-led, and well-prepared infantry therefore could fend off chariot attacks, if necessary by opening up gaps in their formation and channeling the chariots through them.

Alexander employed siege towers, such as at Halicarnassus in 334 BCE. After Alexander's reign, they became heavier and better armed. At the unsuccessful siege of Rhodes in 305–4 BCE, by Demetrius "Poliorcetes" ("the Besieger"), there was a massive iron-plated mobile tower carrying catapults. The Hellenistic rulers also used battering rams sheathed with iron and mounted on rollers—early versions of armored vehicles. However, battering rams were very short-range, line-of-sight, projectile weapons that had to come close to their targets. Both the Romans and the Han Chinese used siege engines.

In contrast, chariots by then were no longer central to military culture in Eurasia. The Romans, who did not rely on their use and preferred, instead, to focus on infantry, were able to defeat those who did emphasize chariots. Cavalry proved a more formidable challenge to the Romans, as with the Parthian mounted archers. Moreover, cavalry, not chariots, was the choice in the medieval world.

On the other hand, from Antiquity on, elephants were used. These were "tanks" in that they had a crew, carried weapons that were used by the crew, were armored, and were employed to smash opposing lines and pursue the enemy. As with chariots, the form was different from twentieth-century tanks, but that did not mean the function necessarily was.

Wheeled platforms still proved to have a role in warfare in the medieval world, most notably with siegecraft. Siege towers, however, were cumbersome and, with the rise of the cannon, proved vulnerable to counterbattery fire from cannon in the besieged fortresses. These towers, nevertheless, were used into the sixteenth century. In the successful siege of Kazan in 1552, Ivan IV "the Terrible" of Russia employed a wooden siege tower that carried cannon and moved on rollers. However, the breaches through which Kazan was stormed were made by sappers undermining the walls and filling the mines with gunpowder.

Separately, in battle, carts offered a base for archers, and later musketeers, and also an obstacle to cavalry charges. They were used widely in the fifteenth and sixteenth centuries—for example, in the Hussite wars in Bohemia in the early fifteenth century and by the Ottoman Turks, notably against attacking Safavid Persian cavalry at the battle of Chaldiran in 1514, in each case successfully. However, these were generally defensive wagon forts, as in the Turkish tactic of the *tábúr congí*, rather than attacking deployments.

There were ideas about using war wagons in an offensive manner. Enea Silvio Piccolomini, later Pope Pius II, wrote in his *Historica Bohemica* that the Hussites employed wagons to encircle their enemies and then slaughtered them within the wagon fort. This is definitely wrong, but it is interesting that their potential could be assessed thus: the idea resembles the later doctrine of using superior speed to surround an enemy from the flank. There is one case where they were used as mobile battering rams. In the battle of Maleschau (1424), Jan Žižka had wagons filled with stones rolled down a hill to break up the formation of his attacking enemies. His infantry charged down close behind and finished them off. This might be a unique occasion, but there is a picture in Konrad Kyeser's *Bellifortis* (c. 1405), which Žižka probably knew, that shows this: a stone-filled cart with spikes to the fore rolled down a hill into the ranks of enemy soldiers in a trench. The book also shows other war wagons. This use resembles the initial use of tanks in World War I in helping break through enemy ranks. However, these examples were not typical for Hussite warfare, where war wagons were employed, instead, as a kind of mobile field fortification.

Meanwhile, imaginative designers—most prominently Leonardo da Vinci—advanced ideas that could not have been manufactured at the time. His prototype armored vehicle for the duke of Milan, illustrated in about

1485, had a wooden covering strengthened by metal plates; the machine was powered by inside cranks operated by a crew of four while the vehicles were equipped with light cannon and a sighting turret. Designed to overcome defending infantry supported by artillery, this design, although presented with a model in the British Tank Museum at Bovington, was not viable mechanically or in military terms. Nevertheless, it reflected an interest in a combination of firepower, armor, and mobility.

The development of the locomotive steam engine in the early nineteenth century provided further potential. At first, this form of power was for armored trains and other railed vehicles.[2] In his "La Guerre de Railway," published in *La Caricature* on October 27, 1883, Albert Robida anticipated completely armored electric-powered gunned vehicles moving fast on rails. Subsequently, there was also interest in those operating freely off rails but still steam powered. The invention of the gasoline-powered internal combustion engine in the late nineteenth century greatly extended these ideas.

TANKS AND WORLD WAR I, 1914–18

Prior to World War I, at a time of considerable innovation in warfare and weaponry, there was military interest in the options offered by road vehicles as well as much nonmilitary speculation. In part, this reflected a commitment to operational mobility in order to give force to offensive strategies and, in part, the need to support the tactics of attack. Trains could not leave railways and move cross-country. In contrast, road vehicles could leave roads, provided the terrain was suitable. This capability brought a tremendous increase in maneuverability and mobility, as with the use of armored car units on the Western Front from 1915. The opportunities offered by such vehicles led to interest in enhancing off-road maneuverability. Alongside that were questions of protection (armor) and firepower.[3]

As with aircraft, there was a sense of potential, but it is unclear what would have happened but for the added inducements provided by the outbreak of the war and its subsequent development in an unexpected direction. In 1909, Colonel Frederick Trench, the perceptive British military attaché in Berlin, reported that the Germans were proposing to develop power traction vehicles "of a type suitable for military use."[4] The British were interested in a "motor-war car."

Such interest was taken forward greatly during the war as both sides sought comparative advantage and in response to the apparently intractable problems posed by trench warfare. In a task-driven approach, tanks had not seemed necessary in 1914, but the situation was different by the end of the year as it became clear that the war would continue. The process of "invention" was complicated, as the ideas that were advanced were not always viable, but, nevertheless, these ideas contributed to the development of a practical weapon. In December 1914, Maurice Hankey, the influential secretary to the British Committee of Imperial Defence, suggested: "Numbers of large, heavy rollers, themselves bullet proof, propelled from behind by motor engines, geared very low, the driving wheels fitted with 'caterpillar' driving gear to grip the ground, the driver's seat armored, and with a Maxim [machine] gun fitted. The object of this device would be to roll down the barbed wire by sheer weight, to give some cover to men creeping up behind, and to support the advance with machine gun fire."[5]

Tanks were invented independently by the British and their allies the French in 1915 as they took forward and sought to merge existing technologies and capabilities. Treads, multiple wheel and multiple axle assemblies, armored caprices (as in insect exoskeletons), and limited traverse sponsons appeared together in the form of the tank. Treads and multiple wheel and axle assemblies were a carryover from steam tractors, and armor, sponsons, and turrets were innovations from warships. Thus, tanks were the result of technological inputs from a variety of machines in both the civilian and military sectors—on land and at sea—and represented an ingenuously selective fusion of these machines, showing the strengths of industry and the flexibility of development processes.

Earl Kitchener, the secretary of state for war, was not a supporter of the idea of a "landship," but Winston Churchill, the innovative first lord of the Admiralty from 1911 to 1915 who was also an advocate of air power, was far more positive and backed the Landships Committee. The proposed vehicle was given the codename "Tank" because the initial design was like that of a water carrier. The first British tanks were built in January 1916.

There was disagreement over how soon to use these tanks and, in particular, whether to wait until the design was improved and a large force of them had been built up. Although they were indeed underdeveloped in both specifications and numbers, Field Marshal Douglas Haig wanted to employ them swiftly. As a result, tanks were first used by the British in the Battle of the Somme on September 15, 1916, when the rhomboid-shaped Mark I was used in an attack on the village of Flers.[6] Eleven days later, the use of a tank, as well as that of an aircraft, helped the infantry capture Gird Trench.

The tank seemed a fitting means to, and symbol of, the overcoming of the impasse of trench warfare, and the *Daily Sketch* on November 23 made much of publishing the "First Official Pictures of the Tanks," which were carried on the front cover. Intended as shock weapons, tanks could apparently be hit by rifle bullets and machine guns without suffering damage, and they could also smash through barbed wire and cross trenches. These advantages attracted attention and were magnified in reports.

The tank, however, had its disadvantages. Many tanks broke down before reaching the assault point. At Flers, only nine of the forty-nine Mark I tanks that took part reached the German lines. The others broke down or got stuck in the mud. Moreover, in conflict, tanks rapidly became unfit for service—understandably so given their technical problems. In addition, the maximum speed of tanks, which even for the later Mark IV was only 3.7 miles per hour, increased their vulnerability.

It was also unclear in 1916 how best to integrate tanks into British tactics and operations—in other words, what doctrine to employ. The number of tanks was too small to make much of a difference. For example, initially only one was provided with the 169th Infantry Brigade, the orders for which noted: "The tank is to be considered purely as an accessory to the attack, and the attack must on no account be allowed to check if the tank should fail to carry out its programme."[7] At this stage, British officers, such as Arthur Child-Villiers, were uncertain of the value of tanks.[8]

Nevertheless, the British employment of tanks was an aspect of their search for greater effectiveness during the lengthy Somme offensive. This search is underrated due to the habitual emphasis on the tactics of the first day of the Battle of the Somme—July 1, 1916—when British troops advanced in lines into devastating machine-gun fire, leading to heavy casualties. However, there were subsequently significant developments. These primarily focused on infantry tactics and the use of artillery but included an increase in the consideration and scale of tank use.

In the battle of Vimy Ridge in April 1917, an Allied success, only eight tanks were deployed. In the larger-scale third battle of Ypres (Battle of Passchendaele), which began on July 31, 1917, tanks were employed in a supporting role. However, as on August 22 and 27, they found themselves hampered by the Flanders mud, which, that year, was made more intractable by the heavy and persistent rain.

In contrast, the British use of 348 tanks en masse at Cambrai on November 20, 1917, was certainly a shock to the Germans. The impressive commander of the Third Army, General Julian Byng, organized an effective combination of infantry, tanks, artillery, and aircraft and drove the Germans back four miles, breaking through their lines and capturing a considerable number of prisoners. The tanks played an arresting role in the initial British success, but a heavy, well-planned artillery bombardment, reflecting recent developments in British artillery tactics, was also important in combining surprise and impact.

Nevertheless, celebrations and hopes in Britain proved premature, and effective German command led to the rapid movement of troops who sealed the breakthrough at Cambrai. The British tanks also took heavy losses. On November 20, thanks in part to German artillery fire, 179 were destroyed. When the attack resumed the next day, more tanks were lost as a result, in part, of inadequate infantry support. Harold Farmar, a British staff officer, informed his wife: "I am afraid the Germans have been able to stop our progress. Anyway it has been a nasty blow to them and we have got a nice bit of unspoilt country and a haul of prisoners and guns."[9]

Whatever its deficiencies, the tank opened up a clear difference between the Allies and the Germans. Tanks were first used by the French on April 16, 1917, when 128 FT tanks were deployed in the Chemin des Dames offensive, but they made no significant impact, instead breaking down or sticking in the mud. However, by 1918, France had three thousand tanks, including the Schneider-Creusot CA, which carried a powerful 75 mm gun but was not terribly maneuverable, and the faster and lighter-gunned Renault FT. Moreover, that November, France planned to deploy six hundred tanks to support an advance into Lorraine. In any event, the war ended first, but, by then, French infantry preferred to be supported by tanks if attacking.

Italy, from 1915 an ally of Britain and France, attempted to develop its own tank, the Fiat 2000 Model 17, a heavy forty-ton tank with an impressive 65 mm gun. However, the first prototype, ready for display in June 1917, included only a wooden model for the superstructure and was not finished until 1918. By the end of 1919, six had been made, but they did not see combat. Only two were actually used. The first was publicly tested in Rome in 1919. One was sent to Libya, where it remained, while the other stayed in Rome as a sort of monument to tanks until the 1930s.

Italy had asked for French tanks, but France was unenthusiastic about sending them. Neither Italy nor the British and French units sent to Italy used tanks. Instead, the Italians relied on their own armored cars, which they had produced since 1910 and successfully tested and employed in Libya from 1911–12. These armored cars were widely used in the second half of 1918 when the Italians attacked the Austrian forces. French FTs were the basis for the Italian Fiat 3000, of which 1,400 were ordered, delivery to begin in 1921.

Russia, an ally of Britain and France from 1914, experimented with tank designs, notably the Tsar "tank" of 1914–15, which used a tricycle design rather than caterpillar tracks. The prototype carried three cannon, but, in tests in

August 1915, it proved ineffective due to being insufficiently powered for its weight. This "tank" was followed by the Vezdekhod, which was a true tank but faced design problems relating to steering. Development was abandoned in December 1915. Subsequently, in response to British and French advances in tank development, work started on a second design in October 1916; although the government was supportive, no progress was apparently made before the revolution in 1917 stopped development. Later, the Soviet Union was to argue that the Vezdekhod was the first true tank in the world. It was not used in combat.

In contrast to Russia, Germany did deploy tanks in 1918, but it did so in far smaller numbers, and to less effect, than Britain and France. German tanks, of which about 170 were captured from the Allies, did not influence the outcome of the German Spring Offensives. German industry was unable to manufacture tanks in sufficient quantities, and fewer than sixty of the large German A7V tanks were in service. In part, this was because of the amount of metal plate required for this large tank and other more urgent requirements for the plate, alongside metal shortages. Opportunity costs were a key element. In the spring of 1917, the tank program was superseded by the submarine one.

As a reminder of the complexity of explanations, it was also the case that the German success at sealing the Cambrai breakthrough in November 1917 encouraged skepticism about the effectiveness of tank attacks—skepticism that had been present from the outset. At any rate, there were far more tanks on the Allied side throughout the war. German tanks also suffered from low ground clearance and large crew requirements.[10]

The failure of the German Spring Offensives in 1918 was largely due to a repeated lack of focus in attacking on any particular axis, rather than a shortage of a specific weapon system; in short, a failure of operational-strategic goals, rather than tactical-operations means. The shortage of tanks was certainly an aspect of a more general weakness of motorization and mechanization on the part of the Germans. This weakness indeed proved operationally significant, and the German ability to sustain breakthroughs and breakouts in the Spring Offensives was thereby limited.[11] Yet strong Allied resistance was far more important. This resistance was a matter of infantry supported by artillery, good morale, and an effective defensive doctrine. Even with the initial collapse of the front, German failures—including of command and logistics—undermined their achievements, while Allied resources were superior. The mobile defense that tanks could provide in World War II—for example, for the Germans against Soviet attack on the Eastern Front—was not yet an option.

The first tank battle was between several A7Vs and light Whippets and heavy Mark IVs on April 24, 1918, near Villers-Bretonneux during a German infantry attack. At least one A7V and one Whippet were knocked out by tank gunnery, and the Whippets retreated because they were outgunned, although they did not realize at the time that they had been engaged by enemy tanks. The A7V was a poor tank. The engagement was not indicative of its effectiveness but rather of the novelty of tank-versus-tank conflict and the inability of any tank of any nation to wage it. The tank was not designed to fight other tanks, and the concept of tank warfare had limited traction until well into the 1920s.

At the tactical level, tanks, utilizing cavalry doctrine, seemed to overcome one of the major problems with offensives against trenches: the separation of firepower from advancing troops and the consequent lack of flexibility. By carrying guns or machine guns, tanks made it possible for advancing units to confront unsuppressed positions and counterattacks. The latter repeatedly served to blunt the impact of break-ins into opposing trench lines and break-outs through them. Tanks also offered precise tactical fire to exploit the consequences of the massed operational bombardments that preceded attacks. Moreover, tanks could also survive bullet strikes, although these caused a spall of metal to fly off inside of the panel adjacent to the strike. The damage this could create ensured that tank crews wore chainmail visors to protect their eyes.

Commanders had to decide how best to employ tanks and combine them with infantry and artillery. This issue was made dynamic by the variety of tank types, actual and possible developments in the technology, and uncertainties about the likely moves of opponents. Tanks apparently offered mobility not only in breaking open a static battlefield but also in subsequent operations. Optimism was on offer, as in a memorandum of June 1918 from the British Tanks Corps Headquarters:

> Trench warfare has given way to field and semi-open fighting . . . the more the mobility of tanks is increased, the greater must be the elasticity of the co-operation between them and the other arms. The chief power of the tank, both material and moral, lies in its mobility, that is, its space, circuit, handiness, and obstacle-crossing power . . . whilst formerly [the tank commander] merely led the infantry on to their objective protecting them, as best he could, now he must manoeuvre his tank in advance of them, zig-zagging from one position to another, over-running machine-guns, stampeding away and destroying the enemy's riflemen, and all the time never losing touch with the infantry he is protecting. The increased power of manoeuvre of the Mark V Tank demands an increased power of manoeuvre on the part of the infantry. By this is not meant a higher rate of advance, but skill in the use of ground and formations suitable to the ground and the tactical situation . . . the effect produced by tanks leading forward infantry may be compared to that of the artillery barrage.[12]

Tanks were indeed important, but their value was lessened by their limitations—especially durability but also firepower and speed. The engines were underpowered and unreliable, as were the gearbox and drive chain. The British light infantry mortar, the 3-inch Stokes—in practice was more effective, reliable, and capable of providing flexible infantry support than the tank, which itself was consistently underpowered, undergunned, underarmored, and unreliable. Moreover, it was difficult for the tank crew to communicate with each other, let alone anyone outside the tank, and this drawback made it harder to get tanks to engage a target of opportunity and lessened their flexibility in contrast to the infantry. The British all-weapons platoons of 1917 and 1918, in which infantry had the means to engage many different kinds of targets without calling in artillery support, were very effective tools. In these platoons, Lewis guns, hand and rifle grenades, riflemen, and Stokes light infantry mortars were used together. Tanks, in contrast, had the potential for flexibility but often were unable to fulfill that potential. The new artillery and infantry tactics devised during 1916 and 1917, along with the use of aircraft for comprehensive photo reconnaissance, were effective enough without the tank, which added little.

One of the biggest problems with tanks was that the crews were subjected to heat and noise at almost unbearable levels. Tanks had poor ventilation, so clean air was also a problem. Every time tanks went over rough ground, the crew was thrown around. There were no toilet facilities. These factors helped ensure that operating tanks for long periods was difficult, unpleasant, and stressful. Although circumstances have eased, tanks are still difficult to use. This consideration, which affects the tactical proficiency of tanks, is, in turn, greatly influenced by terrain and climate. Heat was more of a problem for the tank crews sent to Gaza in 1917.

The value of tanks in World War I was also affected by the difficulty of providing them in sufficient numbers, which reflected their late arrival in wartime resource allocation and production systems. That was a key constraint, although not one that would have prevented development over the longer term. The major expansion of war production already had used much industrial capacity, as well as labor and resources, but the addition of the US economy from 1917 on as an ally (technically, an "associated power") and not simply a trading partner, would have greatly increased that capacity. Indeed, the Mark VIII tank, also called the Liberty or the International, was a collaborative effort designed to equip Britain, France, and the United States with a single heavy tank. It was designed in 1917, and 125 were built from 1918 to 1920. They carried two 57 mm guns and seven machine guns but were produced too late to serve in the war. For Britain and France, tank numbers rose rapidly in 1918, although they were still insignificant compared with the numbers of infantry and artillery. The British, moreover, suffered from a failure to produce sufficient spare parts, which was a major issue given the mechanical flaws of tanks.

The ability to devise antitank tactics was also significant; under the pressure of necessity, the Germans rapidly developed antitank measures. They quickly understood how tanks worked. Tanks—highly conspicuous targets—were vulnerable to other tanks, of which there were few, as well as to mines, direct-firing artillery pieces firing low-velocity shells, machine guns, and German M98 Mauser antitank rifles. Ordinary German field guns employing direct fire and firing high-explosive shells proved effective at knocking out the thinly armored tanks of the time while bullets with tungsten carbide cores inflicted damage.[13] Moreover, antitank mines—shells buried with the fuses just below the surface pointing up—were introduced. Wherever tanks met real resistance, they did not do nearly as well as anticipated, a pattern more generally true of all weapons. The use of artillery against tanks was particularly important in this respect and reflected the extent to which the incremental nature of improvements in artillery was a matter of tactics as well as of technology and numbers.

At Cambrai on November 20, 1917, sixty-five British tanks were destroyed thanks to direct hits by German artillery fire, although the majority of losses were due to mechanical faults and tanks stopped by ditches. This antitank capability had to be confronted for tanks to operate effectively, and tanks needed to support, and be supported by, advancing artillery and infantry, which was a problem at Cambrai on November 21.

A different impression was created the following summer when the British deployed the Mark V tank, which was quicker and more maneuverable than its predecessors and controlled, as the light tanks were, by one driver, which was a major improvement. These tanks were supported by the Medium Mark A Whippet, a faster tank equipped with four machine guns and able to go 8.3 miles per hour. The Whippet entered service on March 26, 1918, and two hundred were built. On July 4, the Australians attacked the village of Le Hamel supported by sixty British tanks—Mark Vs and Whippets—the noise of which was drowned out by artillery and bombers, thus preserving surprise. This attack proved a success, with fifty-seven tanks reaching their objectives. Impressed by the prebattle exercises, the Australian commander, Lieutenant-General John Monash, saw tanks as able to overcome obstacles, "much as a man's heel would crush a scorpion."[14] The limited goals of the operation aided in its success.

At a greater scale, at the Battle of Amiens on August 8, no fewer than 430 British tanks broke through the German lines near Amiens in an attack launched to drive the Germans from a key rail junction. In a battle that General Ludendorff described as the "Black Day" of the German army, the British captured twelve thousand prisoners in a surprise attack and advanced seven miles, a gain the Germans were unable to reverse. The Mark Vs proved better than the Mark IVs used at Cambrai, while the Whippets broke into the German rear and excelled at chasing the retreating Germans.

However, like initial readings of the Battle of Cambrai, Amiens provided a misleading example of the usefulness of allegedly invincible tanks because there was weak resistance at first and the British artillery played a key role. The surrenders reflected increasing war-weariness. Moreover, most of the tanks engaged at Cambrai or Amiens subsequently broke down or were otherwise immobilized within a few days. Indeed, the Amiens offensive ceased on August 11, with the Germans benefiting from the delays created by the war-damaged terrain.

In addition, by then there were few British tanks still in operation. Thomas Blamey, chief of staff to the Australian Corps, recorded that, on August 9, tank support was "with very reduced numbers owing to casualties suffered on the 8th. . . . Direct fire [on August 9] was responsible for considerable casualties among the tanks supporting the 1st Australian Division." It was clear that the Allies needed to resort to artillery at Amiens. On August 11, Blamey wrote: "Owing to the greatly increased enemy resistance in the Lihons Ridge and the fact that there were but few tanks available to support the advance, it was decided to employ a creeping artillery barrage."[15]

As was only to be expected of a weapon that had not had a long process of peacetime development and preparation, there were major problems with reliability. There were also serious structural issues. Guns fixed in the hull of the tank, the French pattern, proved poor at engaging with targets. The British location of guns in sponsons on the side of the tank was linked to the guns' ability to move laterally and vertically.

The strain of conflict, combined with technical weaknesses, ensured that British tank numbers fell markedly in September and October 1918 when the war became increasingly mobile. It was also clear that, whereas tanks were a siege tool—able, for example, to carry fascines to help them cross the defenses of the German Hindenburg Line—and were appropriate for infantry support against such defenses, they were not yet a fast-moving mechanized force. For these reasons, there was a reaction in British circles against the use of armor after August 1918. Tanks might have appeared valuable in strategic terms as a potential replacement for infantry because the numbers of available men had become a more serious issue for Britain and France, but there was only limited discussion of the issue.

French tanks operated in support not only of their own forces but also of the Americans. Thus, a squadron of French heavy tanks took part in the Battle of Cantigny in May 1918, assisting the US infantry attack. France, moreover, supplied 144 FTs to equip the US First Provisional Tank Brigade, which was commanded by Lieutenant-Colonel George Patton, who led the tanks at the Battle of Saint-Mihiel before being wounded in the Meuse-Argonne offensive. The British also provided the Americans with tanks and training. US tanks crew entered combat September 12, 1918, but were affected by the rain-soaked terrain.[16]

Allied help proved far more significant than the US Army Corps of Engineers' pursuit that year of a steam-powered tank. Weighing 50.8 tons and with a crew of eight, this tank was armed with a flamethrower and four machine guns and could travel at 3.7 miles per hour. Financed by Boston bankers, and using the expertise of the Stanley Motor Carriage Company that produced steam cars, the tank was based on the design of British Mark IV tanks but was powered by kerosene. Only one, named *America*, was completed. The prototype was demonstrated in April 1918, paraded on several occasions, and shipped to France in June for testing. Its value was simply as propaganda, although its proposed use as a flamethrower was seen on other occasions in tank history and reflected the need to overcome the challenge posed to advancing troops by pillboxes.

More significantly, the Americans had begun building the M1917, a version of the French FT; 4,440 were ordered, but the 950 completed were too late to see war service. The 7.25 ton tank had a 37 mm gun or a machine gun.

LOOKING TO THE FUTURE

Colonel J. F. C. Fuller, then serving as chief general staff officer of the British Tank Corps, observed in May 1918, in an item on "The Effect of the Medium D Tank on Strategy": "Strategy or the science of making the most of time for warlike ends, that is of opportunity, will practically cease for the side which pits muscular endurance against mechanical energy."[17] This was an aspect of his pressure to understand and support the new capability brought by tanks and, more particularly, his argument that this capability had strategic consequences, rather than simply operational and tactical ones. There was a comparable argument about aircraft, but they had been in use for longer and on a far greater scale and were more obviously different.

In practice, the Medium Bs, Cs, and Ds, the successors to the Whippet or Medium A, did not see service in World War I. Seven hundred Medium Bs were ordered, but none saw service due to the speedy ending of the war, and the Medium B was rapidly phased out in favor of the faster Medium C, which could go about eight miles per hour and had a range of 140 miles. Six hundred of these were ordered, and there was talk of six thousand for 1919 if the Medium D was not ready, but the Medium Cs were too late for the war. The Medium D was a failed project.

Fuller's "Plan 1919" was the first expression of a new operational idea for the employment of armor en masse supported by aircraft: it was a new operational concept that presented conclusions about the possibilities for warfare in 1919 once the Allies had time to build up a more powerful tank force.[18]

Had Allied tank production been at a greater level, tanks might have made a larger contribution in 1918, not least in countering the decline in available numbers of British tanks after the Battle of Amiens. However, the idea that massed tanks would have made a significant difference to Allied capability had the war continued into 1919, a difference planned for by Fuller, is contentious. Assuming that, in order to produce the huge numbers required, the tank could have been mass-produced, which had not been the case hitherto, the same basic problems of unreliability, slow speed, vulnerability to antitank measures and guns, undergunning, inadequate intercommunication capabilities, and poor obstacle-crossing capability would have remained. Moreover, these problems interacted and were cumulative in their consequences. For example, both slow speed and poor obstacle-crossing capability were made more serious by antitank guns. The provision of more tanks and crews would not have obviated these issues. Tanks still had not successfully surmounted the problem of crossing no-man's-land without occurring heavy losses by breakdown or enemy action.

There is little to suggest the tanks would have performed well in 1919. Moreover, despite the greatly increased use of trucks, resupply with ammunition and fuel across territory badly damaged by the war would have been a serious issue. If the British tanks of the 1920s and early 1930s are considered an extension of the line of development from World War I, it is difficult to see how they would have been decisive.[19] Reliability undermined anything tanks might have achieved. Without reliability, it is hard to develop a meaningful doctrine.

Furthermore, this approach ignores the antitank technologies that would have been developed by the Germans. Indeed, due to greater skill and experience in the manufacture and use of artillery and the relative ease of production, antitank guns in 1919 probably would have been superior to the tanks, which would have been slower and less maneuverable than those two decades later. Antitank guns were easier to supply and maintain than tanks.

These problems illustrate the extent to which there was a choice at the operational and tactical levels of war between maneuver supported by firepower and firepower supported by maneuver, each of which had advantages as well as more than one form. In practice, aside from the shortages and deficiencies of tanks and the less costly nature of artillery, for which the British and French were anyway well prepared in manufacturing, training, command, doctrine, and tactics, there were also key capability strengths of artillery both tactically and operationally.

The fighting in the last stage of the war certainly and repeatedly indicated the problems tanks faced. Of the attack on the German Hindenburg Line, the key German defensive feature, on September 2, 1918, Blamey recorded: "A number of the tanks supporting the 27th American Division were put out of action by enemy shell fire and by antitank mines, and, with this support gone, the infantry in this sector of the attack rapidly lost touch with the barrage. Enemy machine guns were thus free to harass the main weight of the attack with the result that only isolated parties were able to get forward."

On the front of the Third Australian Division, "the tanks detailed to assist . . . suffered considerably from hostile shell fire."[20] The tank support for the Australian forces was British. The situation continued to be difficult. As Blamey recorded on October 3: "Considerable opposition was met with along the Beaurevoir-Masnieres Line which was too wide on the front of the right brigade for the Whippet Tanks to cross. The heavy tanks encountered much antitank fire but a few reached the line of La Motte Farm and ably assisted the progress of the infantry."[21]

Elsewhere, tanks were used by the British in the second battle of Gaza with the Turks in April 1917. In this, eight Mark I tanks were deployed in widely separated pairs. They were intended to provide shelter to the infantry, but they became targets and only two reached the well-prepared Turkish defenses, which repelled the attack and caused heavy British casualties. Thus, on April 17, the leading tank attached to the 163rd Brigade was hit by three shells and put out of action. Other tanks also suffered from the attention of the Turkish artillery, which had not been silenced by British bombardment. On April 19, the tank accompanying the 163rd Brigade was able to storm a Turkish redoubt but was destroyed by artillery fire.

However, in World War I, tank use was restricted. Only at Gaza did the British use their tanks outside Europe. None were sent to Mesopotamia (Iraq), where the British were also fighting the Turks. Thus, the use of tanks was focused on the most concentrated front, the Western Front, the front also in which artillery was most available. This situation affected the capability of tanks and their relative effectiveness, probably considerably so, but it is unclear how best to assess this factor.

At the same time, the drama of tanks was such that they were much photographed, as well as employed to parade through cities in an attempt to raise war loans. At the start of 1918, there was a nationwide drive to get British communities to purchase tanks. Coventry, a major British manufacturing city, raised eighteen pounds, six shillings, and six pence per head. Alongside a local hero came Tank 119, Ole Bill, one of the four tanks touring the country. It got its name from a popular wartime cartoon character, Old Bill, a pipe-smoking, walrus-mustached Tommy (British soldier) who played a significant part in propaganda. The bank arrived in Coventry with a garland of artificial flowers, presented by a schoolgirl, draped over its front. The *Midland Telegraph* reported: "Ole Bill generated scenes unprecedented in Coventry's history." The Reverend Canon A. G. Robinson, standing on the tank, played the crowd, telling the women, "You can easily do without a new hat," and then the men, "A little less in the tankard and a little more in the tank." Dr. Brazil followed, pointed out Coventry's role in developing the tank, and told the crowd: "We are fighting for the sanctity of our homes, ruthlessly and foully invaded by the Germans in France and Belgium, and desecrated in ways too shameful to be mentioned. We are fighting for the honour of our wives and daughters against a nation so revoltingly foul that wifely virtue and virgin purity seemed to exist for them, only to be trampled under the heel of bestial passion, and that by official order and sanction."

Tanks captured the imagination of the public. Muirhead Bone, who, in July 1916, had taken up his post as Britain's official war artist, produced plates that December in the first part of *The Western Front*, a monthly, "published by authority of the War Office," dedicated to his work. He suggested of this issue that "it would make it 'go' like anything to have tanks in it." Bone's 1918 charcoal drawing "Tanks" makes the tanks appear particularly menacing by adopting a low viewpoint as if from a trench being attacked. The tank is shown being followed by others.[22] The potential of tanks seemed clear.

NOTES

1. J. F. C. Fuller, *Tanks in the Great War, 1914–1918* (London, 1920), 4, fn. 1.
2. G. Balfour, *The Armoured Train: Its Development and Usage* (London, 1981).
3. R. Ogorkiewicz, *Tanks: 100 Years of Evolution* (Oxford, 2015), 11–24.

4. M. S. Seligmann, "A View from Berlin: Colonel Frederick Trench and the Development of British Perceptions of German Aggressive Intent, 1906–1910," *Journal of Strategic Studies* 23 (2000): 131.

5. BL. Add. 49703 fols. 128–29.

6. T. Pidgeon, *The Tank at Flers* (Cobham, UK, 1995).

7. September 13 and 14, 1916, LMA. CLC/533/MS 90400.

8. Child-Villiers to his mother, September 26, 1916, LMA. ACC/2839/D/002.

9. Harold to Violet Farmar, November 26, 1917, K. S. Eady, *Cornerstones: The Life of H. M. Farmar* (Warwick, 2019), 422.

10. R. Raths, "From the Bremerwagen to the A7V: German Tank Production and Armoured Warfare, 1916–1918," in *Genesis, Employment, Aftermath: First World War Tanks and the New Warfare, 1900–1945*, ed. A. Searle (Solihull, UK, 2014), 80–107; M. Pöhlmann, *Der Panzer und die Mechanisierung des Krieges: Eine deutsche Geschichte 1890 bis 1945* (Paderborn, Germany, 2016).

11. D. T. Zabecki, *The German 1918 Offensives: A Case Study in the Operational Level of War* (Abingdon, UK, 2006).

12. AWM. 3DRL/6643, 5/27.

13. D. Showalter, *Instrument of War: The German Army 1914–18* (Oxford, 2016), 193–94.

14. J. Monash, *The Australian Victories in France in 1918* (London, 1920).

15. AWM. 3 DRL/6643, 5/27.

16. D. E. Wilson, *Treat 'Em Rough: Birth of American Armor, 1917–20* (Novato, CA, 1989); L. M. Kaplan, ed., *Pershing's Tankers: Personal Accounts of the AEF Tank Corps in World War I* (Lexington, KY, 2018).

17. A. Searle, ed., *The Military Papers and Correspondence of Major-General J.F.C. Fuller* (Stroud, UK, 2017), 120.

18. Searle, *Military Papers and Correspondence*, 96; A. J. Trythall, *Boney Fuller: The Intellectual General* (London, 1977).

19. T. Travers, "Could the Tanks of 1918 Have Been War-Winners for the British Expeditionary Force?," *Journal of Contemporary History* 27 (1992): 389–406.

20. AWM. 3 DRL/6643, 5/27.

21. AWM. 3 DRL/6643, 5/27.

22. K. Robinson, "Muirhead Bone: Britain's First Official War Artist," *Military History Monthly* (June 2017): 14; S. Bone, *Muirhead Bone: Artist and Patron* (London, 2009).

TWO

THE 1920s

World War I left a legacy of experience to consider and contest and posed the question of if another major conflict could be waged more successfully, not least in terms of achieving victory more rapidly and with fewer casualties. Discussion of these issues involved tanks. However, alongside considerable interest in their potential was much uncertainty over the extent to which they should play a part in force structure and doctrine. This was a problem that partly arose from differences over the assessment of tank capability and significance in 1918; this uncertainty was accentuated because Allied plans for a major role for tanks in 1919 were not brought to fruition.

In July 1918, Sir Henry Wilson, the British chief of the Imperial General Staff, proposed that the Allies coordinate plans for tank warfare.[1] Discussion and planning, then and for 1918, however, exaggerated the mechanical effectiveness of tanks and assumed an operational capability not merited by their specifications and tactical capacity. There was a parallel with optimistic Allied, particularly British, projections in 1918 about air power, notably concerning the potential for bombing Germany and the results that would arise.

In contrast to such assumptions, the lack of large-scale tank attacks in the last two months of the war encouraged British officers who emphasized the importance of more traditional weaponry, especially artillery.[2] The French also presented victory in the war as demonstrating the value of their existing military system.[3]

As a means of, and to, maneuverability, tanks were seen as the antithesis of the front line. Indeed, paintings produced in 1918—for example, George Matthews Harding's *Storming Machine Gun*, a vivid depiction of US success in the Meuse-Argonne offensive—made much of the use of tanks to break opposing positions. That approach, however, seriously underplayed the problems involved in achieving and sustaining mobility in the campaign of that year. Indeed, tanks in 1918—as both designed and used essentially as tools for operating on the front line—were suited more for assisting in transforming static into maneuver warfare by breaking through defenses, rather than for maneuver warfare itself. Harding's picture was one of break-in, not breakthrough or breakout. Nevertheless, their potential for maneuver warfare attracted attention, notably as a result of the British use of Whippets at Amiens.

J. F. C. Fuller presented the war as a development from mass toward machine fighting.[4] But, in reality, durability, firepower, protection, speed, range, mobility, command and control, reliability, and the combination of losses with limited production were all major problems, and there were no signs they would have been overcome in 1919.[5]

TASKING AND DESIGN

The concept of a "tank" was itself unclear, which was why there were so many different types considered by the British army of the 1920s and 1930s. At this stage, speed and maneuverability attracted more attention than the different considerations of firepower and armor. Linked to this, tank technology did not match the capabilities of opposing artillery. Moreover, in break-in terms, tanks did not match the firepower of supporting artillery, although they were more mobile than artillery that had to be moved and far more flexible than railway-mounted guns.

The tank was too undeveloped to realize the expectations of commentators such as Fuller and Liddell Hart. It was easier to suggest a role, for then or the future, near or distant, as Fuller wrote in 1920 about "land fleets" of armor in his *Tanks in the Great War, 1914–1918*, than to ensure the technology, tactics, and doctrine to make tanks effective on the battlefield. Liddell Hart liked the role of would-be influential critic, and Fuller came to have this role, rather than the rigors (and trade-offs) of institutional command. Fuller, who, unlike Liddell Hart, had relevant experience, was far from alone. Speaking at RUSI, the Royal United Services Institute in London, Major-General Sir Louis Jackson, the director of trench warfare and supplies from 1915 to 1918, argued that tracked vehicles offered the opportunity to dispense with any reliance on roads for logistics and thus would make a rapid advance possible.[6]

There were certainly improvements in capabilities; to that end, the tanks used to fight World War I were replaced. Initially, Britain had disbanded all bar five tank battalions and, instead, planned a new tank, the Medium Mark D. This, however, did not reach fruition, and the Tank Design Department was closed in 1923. In its place, Vickers-Armstrong, a major British military manufacturer that had already built prototypes of a new tank in 1921, came to the fore. The Vickers Light Tank was replaced by what was renamed the Vickers Medium Mark I, the first prototypes of which were sent for trial in 1923. Thirty were built from 1924, with fifty Mark IAs following. None saw action, but they, and other variants, helped Britain acquire familiarity with tanks. No other tank was built in these numbers in this period.

Specifications improved in the interwar period as capabilities were addressed. For example, the Mark I was the first British tank in service with a revolving turret. However, the ability to aim and shoot on the move was not really available until the 1950s and 1960s with the development of stabilized gun systems and fast-traversing turrets. The former made it easier to handle the consequences of uneven terrain.

Similarly, it was not until after World War II that multifuel engines were a focus of development so that, eventually, tanks could run on any fuel.[7] The availability of fuel was indeed significant as part of the way logistics were a key issue for breakthrough operations. Indeed, Soviet planning in the 1920s for breakthrough operations presupposed exploitation largely by cavalry, which was the pattern during the Russian Civil War (1918–21). Cavalry fueled up en route on forage.

Tank design was very dependent upon tactical doctrines, and, as with other innovations, both were pursued in the context of strategic tasking. Thus, in 1921, Lieutenant-General Sir Philip Chetwode, deputy chief of the British Imperial General Staff, wrote that "the tank would not prove to be such a formidable engine of war as people think and that before long it will have lost much of its terror" and argued that British tank specifications and tactics ought to focus on colonial commitments, rather than the possibility of conflict with other regular forces.

Indeed, the latter appeared unlikely. Germany then only had a limited and lightly armed army as a result of the disarmament terms of the Versailles Peace Treaty of 1919, and the Soviet advance into Europe had been stopped by the Poles outside Warsaw in 1920, and then driven back. Germany would help the Soviet Union establish tank production facilities in the late 1920s, but no challenge from either was apparent at the time. The Ten Year Rule adopted by the British government in 1919 argued that there would be no major conflict for ten years and that the British did not have to prepare for war on the

Continent. The Chiefs of Staff did not initiate the abolition of this rule until 1932; in the meantime, it greatly affected British force structure and operational doctrine.

IMPERIAL CONFLICT

Focusing on colonial commitments, Chetwode pressed accordingly for tanks to be armed with a machine gun, not a heavier gun, and for training in the use of tanks against opponents equipped with artillery and machine guns, but not tanks.[8] This reflected the tasks of the period. Chetwode's comments illustrate how the potential of tanks was understood by many in the 1920s. He also noted continued support in the military for cavalry—support, indeed, that helped shape attitudes to tanks not only in Britain but more generally. Commenting on "how much the apparent success of the cavalry in Palestine has mesmerized" the British cavalry, Chetwode added, in contrast, that if the Turks in 1918 had been equipped with gas, tanks, aircraft, and firepower, the cavalry would have achieved far less.[9] This was an important corrective to the standard habit of measuring capability in a one-sided fashion, a habit that continues to the present day.

Terrain and tasking were issues that were often linked. Field Marshal Douglas Haig pointed out in 1927, with reason, that it was unclear that mechanized forces were suitable on many terrains.[10] Referring to the dispatch of tanks and aircraft to assist operations against Mullah Sayyid Muhammad in Somaliland, the *Times* in its issue of February 17, 1920, commented: "Whether tanks will be of use in this form of warfare is doubtful. It will be like chasing a hornet with a steamroller. The aeroplanes, though, ought to be of immense assistance."

The use of tanks in imperial warfare certainly faced difficulties, although, in part, these arose from specific environmental circumstances, as well as from a lack of familiarity with tanks and tank warfare. Confronting serious opposition in Morocco in 1922 in the Rif Rebellion, Spain used light French tanks in the first deployment of tanks in Africa. In 1921, Spain had purchased from France eleven Renault FTs, each armed with machine guns; six heavier Schneider CA1 tanks; tank transport trucks; and tanker trucks, alongside aircraft and artillery. The light tanks were deployed in Morocco, but the infantry, unable to keep up, could not prevent three of the tanks from being disabled by Moroccans throwing stones, while many of the tanks' machine guns jammed due to faulty ammunition.

Yet, in turn, improved mechanical reliability and better ammunition led to enhanced performance. As so often, it is necessary to note both aspects of

the situation.[11] In 1925, again using these tanks, Spain launched an amphibious assault in the Bay of Alhucemas. However, the landing craft carrying the
Renault tanks hit a shoal far from the beach, and they could not land on the
first day as had been planned. They landed the next day.[12]

Lack of funding, not doctrinal conservatism, was the major problem with
the development of Spanish armor; indeed, these issues more generally drove
the system. Funding was the crucial issue with the proposed Trubia Serie A,
which included two independently operating machine guns, a new caterpillar
system, and a speed of 18.6 miles per hour thanks to a four-cylinder Daimler
engine. Four prototypes were ordered in 1934.

In imperial warfare, France itself used its surplus World War I tanks in
Morocco in 1925–26. It also did so in Syria in establishing its occupation in
1920 in the face of Arab opposition and against the Druze revolt of 1925–26. In
the first case, tanks were used at the battle of Maysalun on July 24, and, under
fire, they had a role in storming the center of the Syrian defensive line.[13] In
1925–26, tanks were thought to have acquitted themselves well, including in
overawing opposition.

In 1919 the Italians sent a prototype Fiat 2000, as well as two FT 17s, to Libya.
The Fiat 2000 took part in a fight against local rebels around Misurata. Later,
the FT 17s were brought back to Italy, but the Fiat 2000 remained in Libya,
although it was not used. The other Fiat 2000 never left Italy and was not used.
With an average speed of 4.3 miles per hour on-road and 1.8 off-road, it was
too slow and was, in effect, abandoned that year. The lighter, more mobile Fiat
3000 was sent to Libya in 1926.

The emphasis on imperial conflict encouraged the preference for lighter
tanks, such as the British Vickers Medium Mark I. At the same time, there was
a more general concern with speed. Thus, the World War I tanks were replaced
with quicker ones. Whereas the British World War I tanks had weighed 28
tons, the Vickers weighed 11.7. Moreover, its speed across country was fifteen
miles per hour, compared to the four miles per hour of its predecessors.[14]

On the whole, the focus in imperial warfare was on armored cars, not tanks,
as, for example, used by Britain in Ireland. No Medium Cs, the most modern
tank, were sent to Ireland. Instead, Mark As (Whippets) and Mark Bs were
employed there. Alongside light tanks, which were employed, for example,
in 1926, Italy used columns of armored cars and motorized infantry to help
subdue opposition in Libya in 1928–32. The commitments of empire certainly
affected ideas of mechanized warfare.[15] Fuller, however, criticized the British
Indian Army for not being keen on mechanization. He had argued in 1920
that the large army there should be replaced by a far smaller mechanized

force, a view that ignored the value of mass itself, as well as issues of terrain and distance.

TANKS AND OTHER ARMS

At the same time, growing interest in tanks was affecting the perception of other arms. This was particularly so at the expense of cavalry, although World War I had shown its more general vulnerability to firepower and thus its obsolescence. In 1926, Colonel George Lindsay, the inspector of the British Royal Tank Corps who had commanded an armored car unit in Iraq in the early 1920s in cooperation with aircraft, was in no doubt that cavalry was too vulnerable, and he linked this to wider questions of the role of technology: "All civil evolution is towards the elimination of manpower and animal power, and the substitution of mechanical power. . . . In the army we must substitute machine and weapon power for man and animal power in every possible way."

Lindsay was certain that this capacity was linked to industrial capability: "We are the nation above all others who can develop the mobile, mechanical and weapon-power army, for we have long service soldiers and a vast industrial organisation."[16] Lindsay cited Liddell Hart and Fuller in his report to the 1926 committee on the reorganization of the cavalry.[17] They saw tanks as the modern form of cavalry. Lindsay later worked on the Experimental Mechanized Force and, in 1934, commanded the first experimental armored division.

Other military commentators, however, were less happy about the wisdom of dispensing with cavalry, which had been very useful at times in World War I, and, instead, urged its combination with mechanized forces. What that would mean was unclear. It was not until March 1942 that the Office of the Chief of Cavalry was abolished in the United States. In 1942, the last Italian cavalry charges occurred.

It was also unclear what vehicles, and, in addition, what capabilities, would be most appropriate. Thus, in 1927, Field-Marshal Sir George Milne, the chief of the British Imperial General Staff, told the officers of the Experimental Mechanized Force that it was necessary to have vehicles that would be immune to poison gas, a view advanced by Fuller, as in his 1920 book when he presented gas-proof tanks as operating like submarines.[18] This assumption looked toward post-1949 North Atlantic Treaty Organization (NATO) concerns about tanks that would be resistant to radioactivity from the use of Soviet nuclear weaponry. With a clear sense of transience, Milne also claimed: "In a very few years the petrol engine itself will have to give way to something else."[19] Sweden acquired its first tanks in 1921—wartime German light tanks in a preproduction stage—and, from 1925, acquired armored cars.

FUNDS AND DOCTRINE

In 1928, General Sir Archibald Montgomery-Massingberd, then head of Britain's Southern Command and like Milne a former gunner, wrote of developments with tanks: "The whole question is one of money." He also emphasized the problems of choice, not least in terms of the diversity of developing possibilities in mechanized warfare, and the sense of new potential:

> What we want most at present undoubtedly is light tanks or machine gun carriers, people are not however clear which will be best.... It looks to me as if the cavalry will want the light tanks and the infantry the machine gun carriers. I don't think there is really very much difference between the two, except that the tanks will have more armour and normally machine guns will fire from them, while it will be the exception to fire from the machine gun carriers, and they will normally be taken out and used on the tripod.... The latest Carden Loyd tanks ... a great advance.... One trial machine did 49 miles an hour, which for a track machine seems almost undreamable.[20]

The Light Tank Mark I was a development of the two-man Carden Loyd tankettes that were tried out on maneuvers by an Experimental Mechanized Force in 1927 and 1928.[21] The two-man version was regarded as preferable to one-man tankettes, which were also tested then, as it would be difficult for one individual both to drive and fire. Carden-Loyd was part of Vickers Armstrong, the leading British military manufacturer.

British commentators found the apparent potential of tanks valuable because it drew on their sense of the legacy of World War I. In the winter of 1921–22, under the influence of Fuller, Liddell Hart had become revolutionary as far as tanks were concerned, despite the significant deficiencies of their capability at that time. Liddell Hart, who retired from the army in 1924 after active service in World War I, albeit less than he implied,[22] became a military correspondent, first of the *Daily Telegraph* (1929–35) and then of the *Times* (1935–39), and was particularly keen to advocate advances that did not entail frontal attacks: what he termed the "indirect approach" that emphasized maneuver and not attrition. Mechanization became a key theme for him as the way to ensure mobility.[23] In his *The Decisive Wars of History* (1929), Liddell Hart pressed the case for attacking the enemy where they were not expecting it and for mechanized forces bypassing the flanks of enemy armies in order to hit their communications and bases. This was a theme to which he returned in *The British Way in Warfare* (1932) and one that earned him fame and fortune, interacting with his commitment to armor and leading the two concepts—outflanking opponents and armor—to be seen as important to what became operational thought and the maneuverist approach.[24]

Fuller was less of a publicist but was more influential in military circles in the 1920s and from Germany to Spain, where some of his works were translated. Having worked as chief general staff officer of the Tank Corps from 1916 to 1918, and at the War Office from 1918 to 1922, Fuller lectured at the Staff College in Camberley from 1923 to 1926. In 1926, he returned to the War Office as military assistant to Milne only to find their relationship deteriorate. Milne, who, in 1926, referred to World War I as "abnormal," and thus not a guide to the future, was not keen on original ideas. Fuller himself lacked Liddell Hart's commitment to the indirect approach, writing to the latter in 1929: "The object is to defeat the enemy and if this can be done by a direct approach so much the better."[25]

There has been valuable work on Fuller's ideas, and a major biography is anticipated from Alaric Searle, but the sources are limited—certainly as compared to those for Liddell Hart. As Fuller later noted, "The only time I kept a real diary was when at the War Office at the end of and after World War One. It ran to some 6 or 7 foolscap volumes and was destroyed in the Blitz [bombing of London, 1940–41]."[26]

Funds were far from the sole issue in Britain, the United States, or elsewhere. The idea of machines as a way to deliver increased capability at lower cost clashed with institutional preferences for continuity and size and with careers bound up in traditional military structures. In 1930, Milne told a staff conference that "the infantry soldier will be required in the wars of the future just as much as in the wars of the past. Of course the more armoured formations we can have the better it will be, but we always get back to the infantry soldier."[27]

Milne's approach clashed with the direction of Fuller's arguments, for the latter was a believer in the juxtaposition of revolutionary innovation with inevitable obsolescence. Thus, in the introduction, dated November 20, 1919, to his account of tanks in World War I, Fuller offered a determined, indeed stark, prospectus for change: "The history itself is purposely uncritical because any criticism which might have been included is so similar to that directed against the introducers of the locomotive and the motor-car that it would be but a repetition, tedious enough to the reader, were it here repeated."

Having also drawn attention to the role of conservatism in opposing the introduction of gunpowder (which was a travesty of the continued relative merits of archery for a while), Fuller pressed on: "The tank . . . has come not only to stay but to revolutionise, and I for one, enthusiastic as I am, do not for a minute doubt that my wildest dreams about its future will not only be realised but surpassed, and that from its clumsy endeavours in the Great War

will arise a completely new direction in the art of warfare itself ... still has ...
many open critics ... a compliment, for the masses of mankind are myopic."[28]

He also foretold a different type of soldier, one focused on machinery and
brainpower, such that there was no need for mass conscript armies. Fuller
and Liddell Hart failed to appreciate, sufficiently and consistently, what was
to become readily apparent in World War II: the dependence of success for
tanks on being part of combined arms formations.

THE UNITED STATES

A lack of funds was also a major problem for the interwar US armed forces
and led to deficiencies in equipment. Yet there were also limitations in doctrine linked to those of organization. In accordance with advice from General
Pershing, tank warfare was given little role and no independence under the
National Defense Act of 1920. Instead, the Tank Corps was abolished, all but
six battalions were demobilized, and tanks were allocated to the infantry,
leading George Patton to transfer to the cavalry in 1920.[29] Tank strength was
then reduced, although the Liberty heavy tank, of which one hundred were
available, was used to equip some units until it was phased out in 1932–34. The
infantry, however, was focused on light tanks, which hindered the development of heavier ones. Five tanks were sent with a Marine Expeditionary Force
to Tientsin in China in 1927–28, but interest in tanks was limited.

There were differences of opinion over the value and use of tanks. Proponents of infantry support disagreed with those, such as Patton, Severo Brett,
and Dwight Eisenhower, who were in favor of maneuver warfare by faster
tanks. Patton and Brett had each commanded the First Tank Brigade in 1918,
and Brett commanded the Expeditionary Tank Force in 1923–24 in Panama.
Eisenhower, who had trained tank crews in 1918, commanded a tank unit in
1921–22. In 1928, after observing maneuvers in England, the secretary of war
from 1925 to 1929, Dwight Davis, a veteran of World War I, ordered the development of a tank force. This encouraged mechanization. The allocation of
tanks, however, was only challenged in 1931 when light tanks were allocated to
the cavalry.[30] The cavalry had circumvented the earlier structure by purchasing tanks and calling them "combat cars."[31] Despite important changes in the
1930s, it took the fall of France in 1940 to inspire the creation of the United
States Armored Force.

ITALY AND JAPAN

Factors that played a major role in the response to tanks included not only
the real and apparent need for numbers but also the political and military

preference for the very idea of a large army, which was widely equated with the impression, at least, of national strength. The clash became apparent in Italy. General Antonino Di Giorgio, a veteran and the minister of war (1924–25), favored a small army, with modern weapons providing firepower, mobility, and offensive capability, but the military leadership argued that this choice would weaken Italy. The cost was also a major problem. Unable to prevail with Benito Mussolini, Italy's Fascist dictator from 1922 to 1943, Di Giorgio resigned.[32]

The Fiat 3000, the first tank produced in quantity in Italy, was based on the French FT and entered service in 1921. It was equipped with two 6.5 mm machine guns. However, there was a reluctance within the Italian military to deal with tanks. On the grounds that they were mobile artillery, they were offered first to the artillery, which did not want them as it preferred to deal with fixed positions rather than shooting during movement. The cavalry, realizing the tanks were the quickest way to lose their horses, also said no. Both branches were very influential in the army leadership. After the tanks were turned down by the Engineers, they were put under the infantry. This ensured that tanks were studied and used by officers who considered them essentially as infantry support.

In Japan, the Imperial Way faction in the army pressed for "flesh before steel": a focus on manpower and the military spirit rather than on machines, which were seen as less manly. In 1928, the army's strategic manual was rewritten accordingly. In the context of a serious fiscal situation after the devastating Tokyo earthquake of 1923, General Kazushige Ugaki, the minister of war from 1924 to 1927 and 1929 to 1931, cut numbers in the mid-1920s in order to focus on equipment. The Japanese army, which had imported some Whippets from Britain, began designing a tank in 1925 and completed its first one in 1927. Because the weight increased from the fifteen tons of the design to nineteen tons, the target speed of 15.5 miles per hour could not be realized. It had a maximum speed of 12.5 miles per hour and carried a 57 mm gun as well as two light machine guns.

FRANCE, GERMANY, AND THE SOVIET UNION

In France, there was an attempt to understand the potential role of tanks as well as their use, notably in Syria and Morocco. Interest in tanks led to special commissions in 1921 and 1925 and to two new manuals on tank units appearing in 1929. However, there was less emphasis on tanks than there would be in the 1930s. There did not appear to be a great need for tanks in the 1920s.

In Germany, there was interest in new ideas, not least with the emphasis on maneuver war and an effective combined arms doctrine developed under

Hans von Seeckt, commander of the Reichswehr in 1920–26.[33] From 1929 to 1933, under an agreement signed in December 1926, the Germans operated a training school for tank commanders at Kazan in the Soviet Union in order to circumvent the restrictions in the Treaty of Versailles on operating any tank or air force. The school was also used to develop new tank designs. There was also the testing of German tanks in Sweden.

The Germans no longer had colonies to worry about, and so they could focus more on a future European theater. Moreover, to employ a concept from comparative economics, they had the advantages of being behind. They had lagged behind the British significantly in both the production of tanks and their offensive usage, but, while the British had generated an impressive body of tank experience, they could not forge ahead as much as the Germans were later able to in the theory and practice of tank usage in warfare on Continental Europe.

At the same time, defensive planning remained important in Germany, and much doctrine focused on the infantry,[34] although traditional operational concepts continued to play a central role in the thinking and practice of the German army. Ironically, given the emphasis on the novelty of blitzkrieg, this conservatism and continuity can be seen as a source of success in 1939–40. Seeckt's ideas were focused not so much on the potential offered by armor as on the exigencies arising from having to adopt a doctrine appropriate for a small regular force rather than a mass conscript army. This posed challenges on how best to use the established concept, advanced notably in Moltke's *Instruction for Large Unit Commands* (1869), of the *kesselschlacht* (battle of encirclement and annihilation). Movement in smaller numbers, but helped by mechanization, was a solution.

In the Soviet Union, there was a move toward the use of large numbers of tanks. Whereas, in the early 1920s, there had been emphasis on the role of cavalry in breakthrough operations, as employed recently in the Russian Civil War, by the late 1920s, the Soviets were building large numbers of tanks to serve that purpose as well. These tanks were small and lightly armored and carried machine guns. In 1928, the military's procurement plan was that just under half the tanks it would receive over the next five years would be of this type. The Soviet army's massive 1932 tank program of ten thousand tanks included five thousand T-27s of this type, and in 1941 there were still three thousand of these light tanks of various models. These light tanks were intended to take cavalry roles of screening, reconnaissance, raiding, and the exploitation of breakthroughs.

Meanwhile, other states acquired small numbers of tanks in order to evaluate their potential. Thus, Denmark purchased one.

WAR USE

World War I had been followed by conflicts in which maneuver played a key role, notably the Russian Civil War, the Polish-Soviet war, the Greek-Turkish war, and civil wars in China.[35] These did not see much use of tanks. Instead, cavalry played a major role in the Russian Civil War. In October 1919, the White army of Nikolai Yudenich, advancing from Estonia on nearby Petrograd (St. Petersburg), included six tanks supplied by Britain together with their volunteer crews. These tanks were unable to overcome defending Soviet infantry once the latter had mastered their initial panic. However, the key reason for the failure of the offensive was not this failure but rather large numbers of Soviet reinforcements arriving at Petrograd by rail.

As part of the wide-ranging, but unsuccessful, intervention in the Russian Civil War, British and French tanks were also used elsewhere in Russia. Thus, France sent five FT tanks to Odessa in 1919, although they were of no importance in the conflict. Britain sent a tank detachment to South Russia the same year to help the White army of Anton Denikin, providing seventy-four tanks in all. A single British tank helped storm the fortified city of Tsaritsyn (later Stalingrad) on June 17, 1919, but the city was retaken by the Communists the following January. The North Russian Tank Detachment deployed two Mark Cs, both of which were lost, as well as Mark Vs, a captured one of which survives as a war memorial in Archangel. From 1920, the Communists made use of captured tanks as well as manufactured their own, a copy of the French FT, from 1920. These tanks were employed in the Communist capture of Tbilisi in February 1921.

In 1920, the Poles made good use of motorized infantry and armored cars against the Soviets. These provided firepower to supplement the cavalry. Although French-supplied FT tanks helped in the defense of Warsaw, they were not crucial in that conflict: the realities of conflict did not match some of the hopes for tanks that were entertained elsewhere. Later prominent as an exponent of French armor, Charles de Gaulle, on the staff of the French Military Mission to Poland, acted as an instructor of Polish infantry.

The French sent tanks to other allies and would-be allies. Their assistance ensured that the First Armored Battalion was established in Romania in 1919. Seventy-six FTs were provided. Tanks were available in China after being introduced by Zhang Zuolin, the warlord of Manchuria who obtained French

FT tanks. However, although the tanks were used in conflict in China in 1926, they did not play a significant role there. The light FTs were readily transportable and were a key tank of the 1920s as part of the major continuation from World War I.[36]

Tanks were also used in civil conflict and confrontation. In 1919, German Freikorps, in resisting revolutionary Communist activism, notably in Berlin, used A7Vs and captured British tanks as well as constructed armored cars. The tanks were frequently photographed. In Britain, six Medium Mark C tanks were deployed against strikers in Glasgow on February 3, 1919. Sent from Bovington, Dorset, after rioting on January 31, they arrived after the rioting was over. The *Glasgow Herald* of February 4, 1919, commented that "the presence of this latest arm of warfare has an entirely new and awe-inspiring aspect." There were no fatalities.[37]

CONTEXTS

Alongside the uncertainty about potential usage came the pressing nature of cost. Compared to the 1930s, the fiscal issues of the 1920s do not appear overly serious. That was not, however, how they struck the governments of the period. World War I had led to unprecedented debt, which acted as a major postwar overhang, most notably so in Britain. Fiscal conservatism—not printing money to get out of problems in a superficial manner—was also significant, not least as governments sought to remain on the gold standard.

Cost was not the sole issue, but it also interacted with the question of what type of tank should be developed. Heavy tanks were more expensive. They had thicker armor and required more engine horsepower. Their more powerful guns also required a larger turret and, therefore, again more armor.

Aside from cost, there was the problem, as so often with weapons both established and new, with reconciling the varied tasks the tank could be called upon to undertake with its apparent multipurpose capability. A temptation was to go for a multipurpose tank, which, then as now, poses serious problems of the trade-offs of armor, firepower, and speed and in terms of design and engineering feasibility, as well as spare parts and maintenance requirements.

Compromise in design was one solution, but it did not work well. Similar issues were to recur throughout the history of the tank. So also with other aspects of the tank, notably its role in encouraging morale. Indeed, that had been a key reason for the idea of infantry support. Tanks were seen as a key way to maintain morale, not so much on the defense but, crucially, on the offensive in the face of defensive firepower. As a result, it was assumed that British tanks supporting infantry would fire smoke shells.

A lack of experience with the range of armored warfare that appeared possible posed a major problem when considering doctrine. The problem for tank enthusiasts in the 1920s and 1930s was an inability to see what the tank needed to become in order for it to fulfill their dreams. No tank in this era could achieve anything like what they wanted, and a lot of what was suggested, including by Fuller, was fantasy.

NOTES

1. Wilson to Marshal Foch, July 20, 1918, in *The Military Papers and Correspondence of Major-General J. F. C. Fuller*, ed. A. Searle (Stroud, 2017), 128.

2. T. Travers, *How the War Was Won: Command and Technology in the British Army on the Western Front, 1917–1918* (London, 1992).

3. E. C. Kiesling, *Arming Against Hitler: France and the Limits of Military Planning* (Lawrence, KS, 1996).

4. R. Bacon, J. F. C. Fuller, and P. Playfair, *Warfare Today* (London, 1944), 18.

5. T. Gale, *The French Army's Tank Force in the Great War: The "Artillerie Spéciale"* (Farnham, UK, 2014).

6. B. H. Reid, "'Young Turks, or Not So Young?': The Frustrated Quest of Major General J. F. C. Fuller and Captain B. H. Liddell Hart," *JMH* 73 (2009): 147–75; L. C. Jackson, "Possibilities of the Next War," *RUSI* 65, no. 457 (1920): 84.

7. J. Stone, "The British Army and the Tank," in *The Sources of Military Change: Culture, Politics, Technology*, ed. T. Farrell and T. Terriff (Boulder, CO, 2002), 193.

8. Chetwode to Montgomery-Massingberd, September 6, 1921, LH. MM. 8/22.

9. Chetwode to Montgomery-Massingberd, July 21, 1921, LH. MM. 8/22.

10. G. Phillips, "Douglas Haig and the Development of Twentieth-Century Cavalry," *Archives* 28 (2003): 160.

11. J. E. Alvarez, "Tank Warfare during the Rif Rebellion," *Armor* 106 (1997): 26–28.

12. J. E. Alvarez, "Between Gallipoli and D-Day: Alhucemas, 1925," and J. Pérez, "The Spanish Military and the Tank, 1909–1939," *JMH* 63 (1999): 75–78, 80 (2016): 762.

13. M. P. M. Finch, "Outre-mer and Metropole: French Officers' Reflections on the Use of the Tank in the 1920s," *War in History* 15 (2008): 294–313.

14. D. Fletcher, *Mechanised Force: British Tanks between the Wars* (London, 1991).

15. W. Ryan, "The Influence of the Imperial Frontier on British Doctrines of Mechanised Warfare," *Albion* 15 (1983): 123–42.

16. LH. MM. 9/5/7, quotes pp. 9–10, 21.

17. LH. MM. 9/5/7, p. 2; J. F. C. Fuller, "Progress in the Mechanicalization of Modern Armies," *RUSI* (February 1925): 25.

18. J. F. C. Fuller, *Tanks in the Great War* (London, 1920), 310.

19. LH. Milne papers, Box 3, quote p. 3.

20. Montgomery-Massingberd to Chetwode, 3 December 1928, LH.MM. 10/1.

21. H. R. Winton, *To Change an Army: General Sir John Burnett-Stuart and British Armoured Doctrine, 1927–1938* (London, 1988).

22. B. Bond, ed., *Liddell Hart's Western Front* (London, 2010).

23. B. Bond, *Liddell Hart: A Study of His Military Thought* (London, 1988); A. Danchev, *Alchemist of War: The Life of Basil Liddell Hart* (London, 1998), 117, 122–23.

24. A. Danchev, "Liddell Hart and the Indirect Approach," *JMH* 63 (1999): 313–37; J. Kiszely, "The British Army and Approaches to Manoeuvre Warfare," *Journal of Strategic Studies* 19 (1996): 179–206.

25. A. Gat, *A History of Military Thought: From the Enlightenment to the Cold War* (Oxford, 2001), 682.

26. Fuller to Liddell Hart, August 22, 1963, LH. Liddell Hart papers 4/27.

27. LH. Adam 2/1, p. 111.

28. Fuller, *Tanks in the Great War*, xvii–xviii.

29. G. F. Hofmann, "The Demise of the U.S. Tank Corps and Medium Tank Development Program," *Military Affairs* 37 (February 1973): 20–25.

30. D. E. Johnson, *Fast Tanks and Heavy Bombers: Innovation in the US Army, 1917–1945* (Ithaca, NY, 1998); R. S. Cameron, *Mobility, Shock, and Firepower: The Emergence of the U.S. Army's Armor Branch, 1917–1945* (Washington, DC, 2008); T. K. Nenninger, "The Development of American Armor 1917–1940," *Armor and Cavalry Journal* 3 (March–May 2010): 10–21.

31. G. F. Hofmann, *Through Mobility We Conquer: The Mechanisation of U.S. Cavalry* (Lexington, KY, 2006).

32. J. Sweet, *Iron Arm: The Mechanisation of Mussolini's Army, 1920–1940* (Westport, CT, 1980).

33. J. S. Corum, *The Roots of Blitzkrieg: Hans von Seeckt and German Military Reform* (Lawrence, KS, 1992); R. M. Citino, *The Path to Blitzkrieg: Doctrine and Training in the German Army, 1920–1939* (Boulder, CO, 1999); W. Mulligan, *The Creation of the Modern German Army: General Walther Reinhardt and the Weimar Republic, 1914–1930* (New York, 2005).

34. M. Strohn, *The German Army and the Defence of the Reich: Military Doctrine and the Conduct of the Defensive Battle, 1918–1939* (Cambridge, UK, 2010).

35. Major-General Sir Percy Rawcliffe, Director of Military Operations, Report on the Franco-British Mission to Poland, 1920, NA. WO. 106/6238, p. 19.

36. S. J. Zaloga, *The Renault FT Light Tank* (London, 1988).

37. I. McLean, *The Legend of Red Clydeside* (Edinburgh, 1983).

THREE

THE 1930s

When you get inside a tank before an attack, you feel you are in
a battle cruiser about to demolish a wooden frigate. But when
the enemy opens fire at you ... you feel like a hare ... trying to
hit a hidden hunter who is equally or better armed than you.

Spanish Republican tank crewman of the unsuccessful
attack near Madrid on October 29, 1936[1]

ARCHIBALD WAVELL, A BRITISH BRIGADIER AT THE TIME AND
commander-in-chief Middle East in 1939–41, argued in 1930 that the focus
on the tank as the principal fighting arm, a focus he associated with Fuller,
Liddell Hart, and Seeckt, was a revival of the previous confidence in cavalry.
Perceptively, Wavell noted the developing capabilities of tanks, especially in
speed, but also the problems posed by antitank weaponry and the difficulties
that greater armor protection would bring in terms of the burdens of size and
weight, which, respectively, made tanks more conspicuous targets and slower.
As a result, Wavell emphasized speed and firepower for tanks, with the former
a key means of protection. Wavell also pointed out that the skill set required
to man tanks would be provided best by professional soldiers, and not by conscripts, and drew attention to the constraints of terrain. At the same time, he
concluded that frontline troops intended for the attack must be mechanized
and armored. Four years earlier, the piece had been turned down, as overly
visionary, for an essay competition set by the *Army Quarterly*.[2]

The issues in the 1920s about the need for particular characteristics and
models of tanks thus continued during the 1930s. However, the shadow of a
forthcoming war made these considerations more urgent. It was not known
when the next war would occur or in what circumstances. Thus, the respective

combatants and field of combat were unclear and had very different requirements for tanks accordingly, both in terms of specifications and with reference
to doctrine and strategy. The United States versus Japan would not mean the
same as Germany versus the Soviet Union. Britain versus Germany would not
mean the same as Britain versus Italy.

Moreover, whenever war did break out, it would not be possible to manufacture, in large numbers and immediately, the most advanced tank available.
Instead, in the meantime it was necessary, as Oliver Lyttelton, the British minister for production, pointed out in the House of Commons on July 1, 1942,[3] to
provide large numbers of tanks for which production facilities were available
and crew had been trained. Yet doing so risked ensuring obsolescence for the
tank force if there was no immediate need for them, as, in effect, happened with
the Soviet T-26s. To determine the numbers required was also impossible.[4]

Meanwhile, there was a wider cultural resonance of tanks. Not only were
they brought to the attention of civilians, but this awareness was internalized
indirectly because the memory and cultural awareness of tanks, like trucks
and cars, became part of the automotive culture. This was the case with the
drive for exquisitely technical specialization, with the experiential and formal
education to instill this at the individual level and with the desire for movement, speed, and control this culture represented and encouraged.

Less positively, the time frames involved expressed the collective memory
of tanks in World War I, as well as contemporary views and futuristic visual-
izations of tanks. Novels of World War I mentioned tanks as dehumanized,
pitiless, monstrous devices that devoured humans. Indeed, the conjunction
of horror and this epitome of insensate, industrialized warfare was the tank,
which was expressed vividly in the widely read novel *All Quiet on the Western
Front* (1928) by Erich Maria Remarque, which was translated into English.
Tanks "that'll go over anything" are mentioned in the 1930 film of the novel,
as are aircraft.

WEAPONS

Discussions during the 1920s and 1930s in Britain and the United States
about the role of tanks in any future war led to the development of the so-
called "infantry" or "infantry support" tank. The emphasis was on support
for advancing infantry. Although slow and thickly armored, the armament
of this type of tank was frequently inadequate. Thus, the British Matilda I
had only a single heavy machine gun, and the Matilda II had nothing bigger
than a 2-pounder gun and nothing that could fire high-explosive rounds.

The more powerfully armed battle tank was neglected in favor of these tanks and the faster, underarmored, more maneuverable "cruiser" tanks that, in World War II, proved vulnerable in combat with other tanks.[5] Thus, in Britain in 1932, what was seen as a battle tank, the proposed "Sixteen Tonner" medium tank, the Medium Mark III, was cancelled due to the costs entailed. Ordered in 1928 to replace, with improved armor and a new turret, the abortive A6 that had been proposed in 1926, only three were built. It carried a 3-pounder gun and three machine guns and had a crew of seven and a speed of thirty miles per hour. Instead, "infantry tanks" were popular in Britain.

Similarly, Germany did not possess well-armed tanks until the arrival of the up-gunned Mark IVs in 1942. Thus, if it is assumed that battle tanks were, and are, required to overcome opposing tanks, the role of the tank was not clearly assessed in the interwar period. The French had already developed the Char B, which was impressive in infantry-support roles and outgunned and especially outarmored the German tanks of 1940, although it was not well suited to fighting other tanks. However, more generally, the role of tanks only changed from infantry support to tank-versus-tank encounters during World War II.

The significant developments in the interwar years included the Christie suspension, a system that enabled tanks to have a significantly lower profile as well as excellent cross-performance and was used on the T-34 series and some British tanks. Sloped armor was also significant, as were bigger-caliber guns, although none was bigger than about 76 mm. A great deal of research and development went into armor (the nature of the steel and its construction and thickness), gasoline and later diesel engines, transmissions, broad tracks, and suspension. The last two had a huge impact on cross-country ability. At the same time, many states did not use tanks. Denmark was typical of many in focusing on armored cars.

ANTITANK WEAPONRY

While they dominated the imagination of many as far as ground warfare was concerned, tanks were affected, as a key limitation, by the development of what can be termed antiweaponry. This is an aspect of the "interadoption" more generally seen with military change,[6] although, to an extent, all weapons are antiweapons. Antiweaponry moves in concert with weaponry, and the tank was no exception. Antiweaponry tends to receive insufficient attention, which is a mistake, as antiweaponry helps define the possibilities presented by existing new weapons and leads to pressure for their development and use to confront particular challenges.

During World War I, although mines were employed against tanks, armor-piercing bullets fired by machine guns and low-velocity shells from artillery were each of particular significance. These guns could be mounted in tanks but more commonly were in carriages that were towed in the field. As a major challenge, antitank gun technology far exceeded tank technology in the 1920s and 1930s, partly because a gun had only to fire a high-velocity projectile on a flat trajectory whereas a tank had to do a great more besides. In 1930, George Patton, then a US army major, argued that the effectiveness of tanks had been reduced because "now every arm has its quota of antitank weapons which are quite effective."[7] In 1934, the British Committee of Imperial Defence pressed for antitank guns for the artillery.

At the same time, British antitank weaponry and doctrine were inadequate to match German developments, not least because the British failed to grasp German doctrine with its emphasis on low-level combined arms co-ordination and integration.[8] There was a lack of German-language knowledge among British officers, as well as access issues relating to German military literature and, perhaps, a shortage of military intellectual curiosity.

So also with the inadequacies in the United States, where, in the late 1930s, artillery officers saw their role as supporting attacks and not as opposing tank advances.[9] In the late 1930s, many states—for example, Hungary—had no antitank guns, but others introduced them; Belgium put a 47 mm antitank gun into service from 1934. However, the big guns (the 75 mms, 88 mms, and 17-pounders) that became necessary as antitank guns in World War II generally were not produced or even considered in the 1930s.

THE GRAN CHACO WAR, 1932–35

In Asunción, the sunny capital of Paraguay, a rather small tank played a prominent role on the War Memorial in Constitution Square until 1990. Visitors were not supposed to go close, and crawling underneath awakened the understandably hostile attention of the forces of order, but the information there proclaimed the place and year of manufacture and the identity of the manufacturer: Newcastle, 1929, Vickers.

Paraguay had no tanks at that stage, but its rival in the Gran Chaco War, wealthier Bolivia, had purchased three Vickers Mark E six-ton tanks, which were armed with machine guns, as well as two Carden Loyd Mark VI tankettes, or poorly armored machine-gun carriers able to act as mobile firing platforms, all from Vickers in Britain in 1932. One of the Vickers tanks proved resistant to small-arms fire and effective against defensive positions at the second battle of Nanawa in July 1933. However, all three were lost: a Type B was knocked out in July 1933 by a 75 mm artillery piece and then blown up by Bolivian sappers, and the turret was on display in the army museum in Asunción until it was returned to Bolivia in 1990 as a goodwill gesture. The other two, one Type A and a Type B, were captured in December 1933 in an ambush by Paraguayan forces. One was sold to Spanish Republicans in 1937, and the other was on display until returned in 1990.

The Carden Loyd Mark VIs were used at the battle of Boquerón in 1932, but one was lost during the second battle of Nanawa in July 1933. They were then withdrawn. Bolivia purchased 15 mm antitank rifles in 1934 due to the threat that the captured Vickers tanks would be used against them. Bolivia also bought twelve Italian Ansaldo L3/35 tankettes at the close of the war.

As an indication of the relative importance attached to different arms, the contract with Vickers was also for 196 pieces of artillery, 750 machine guns, and twelve aircraft. The initial contract signed in 1926 had been for twelve tanks, but this number was reduced due to the Great Crash.[10] The allocation for particular weapons within general orders is always instructive.

The tanks had been of tactical significance in 1933, but their overall importance was limited. In part this was due to a lack of numbers, experience, and doctrine, as well as to logistical issues in the harsh environment. There was no understanding of combined operations, and this led to the successful ambush of the two tanks in December 1933. The tank use in that war was against infantry and artillery. There was no tank-versus-tank conflict. Foreign commentators took little from the war and nothing really about tanks.[11]

THE SPANISH CIVIL WAR

World War II repeatedly cast a harsh light on earlier tank models of all countries. However, there had been earlier comments on them based on certain experiences and perceptions of conflicts in the 1930s. This was not the case with the Gran Chaco War, but the Spanish Civil War (1936–39), which was far easier to cover and of a much greater scale, enabled powers to test out weapons and led others to observe.[12] Lieutenant-General Walter von Reichenau, formerly a member of Seeckt's staff and head of the German Wehrmachtamt (Armed Forces Office), in 1938 commander of the Fourth Army Group, and later a commander in World War II (where he was very impressed by the Soviet T-34), told a meeting of German leaders, in a lecture circulated in July 1938 to the Cabinet by the British foreign secretary: "The experience of the Spanish war has made it easier for us to abandon the wrong path we were treading as regards tanks. The war in Abyssinia, where the Abyssinians lacked all means of countering tanks, had established the reputation of the light tank. This led us to launch ourselves upon the wholesale construction of these light and fast machines. We neglected the building of heavy armoured tanks. On the Spanish battlefields it turned out that it was precisely the heavy tanks with their steel armour plates that proved far away the more efficient."[13]

This argument represented a turning away from the colonial experience in the case of the recent example offered by the Italian conquest of Abyssinia (Ethiopia) in 1935–36. The Italians presented themselves as using tanks in a modern fashion. Thus, on the cover of the February 1, 1936, issue of *Illustrazione del Popolo,* a supplement of the *Gazzetta del Popolo,* two tanks are shown advancing alongside infantry and two aircraft in a victorious overcoming of the Ethiopians. In practice, large numbers of Italian troops, air support, and the weaknesses of the Abyssinian forces were each more significant to the conquest than the availability of tanks, and the conquest itself proved difficult to achieve. The use of tanks was affected by the roughness of the ground. About two hundred tanks and armored cars were deployed from Eritrea and far fewer from Italian Somaliland. The latter was more distant from Italy, ensuring a greater shipping distance, while the route from Mogadishu, the capital of Italian Somaliland, to the Abyssinian capital, Addis Ababa, was longer than that from Eritrea.

The Spanish Civil War was the largest conflict in Europe in the 1930s until the outbreak of World War II, and it attracted much attention. Fuller, then a retired major-general and a newspaper correspondent covering the Spanish Civil War, sent a report to British Military Intelligence in March 1937 that drew attention to the deficiencies of the rebel Nationalist (anti-Republican) army under Francisco Franco, with whose politics he strongly sympathized:

> Of tanks I saw few: on Franco's side the Italian light tank is an indifferent and blind machine.... Tank tactics is conspicuous only through their absence. Machines are generally used singly, or, if in numbers, they split up over a wide front. The result is that they are met by concentrated fire.... In fact, there are no tactics, no proper training or maintenance. One of Franco's officers told me that the largest number so far used in an attack was 15! I do not think we have to learn from either tanks or antitank weapons in this war, because the basis of tactics in training, and this is mainly a war of untrained men with a sprinkling of foreign mercenaries.[14]

Fuller's view was overly critical, not least because there were many experienced men in the armies. Indeed, French observers stressed the effectiveness of the use of antitank weapons against tanks. Fuller, however, was correct about the emphasis on infantry in the Civil War and the difficulties posed by insufficient resources. The Spanish army had only around twenty tanks on the eve of the conflict, but only three or four were operational. Indeed, in April 1938, the British assistant military attaché in Paris commented, after visiting Nationalist Spain, that it was "a war in which modern weapons are used but not in the modern scale."[15] There were also many problems posed by stony terrain, inadequate roads, and poor logistics, notably of fuel.

During the conflict, the Republicans were provided with 535 armored vehicles, including 281 T-26s, 80 BA-3/6s, 60 FA-1s, and 64 FTs, the last French tanks supplied by Poland. The Nationalists received 284 tanks and other armored vehicles, including 155 tanks from Italy and 121 from Germany—the last Panzerkampfwagen light tanks that had many limitations. The Italian tanks, which landed on September 29, 1936, were first used on October 21. Three days later, Italian and Soviet-made tanks clashed for the first time.

When tanks were available, they could also be used inadequately, as with the poorly commanded Italian Guadalajara offensive in March 1937, and those of the Republicans in the battle of Brunete that July (sixty T-26s and twenty BA-10s were deployed), and against Saragossa in August–September 1937. The following July, the Republicans deployed twenty-two Soviet-supplied T-26s for their unsuccessful attack in the battle of the Ebro. The Nationalists, with their superior artillery and air power, defeated them.

Franco tried and failed to defeat the Republicans with a knockout advance on Madrid in November 1936 that was supported by only one company of tanks. Subsequently, Franco, focusing, as he had to, given his circumstances, on long-term destruction of the Republicans and a war of attrition, rejected the Italian concept of *Guerra celere* (lightning war) or *Guerra di rapido corso* and the ambitious plans involved. However, there was also a process of learning lessons. In March 1938, the Nationalists used tanks as part of a motorized force that exploited a breakthrough on the Aragonese front. Truck-borne infantry, and similarly mobile artillery, combined well with the tanks. Nevertheless, the resources for such operations were limited: the Nationalist armor was equipped only with machine guns, and there were no modern self-propelled artillery or armored personnel carriers.

The use of armor by both sides suffered from the limited numbers available; the deficiencies of the tank, notably thin armor (for example, the T-26); limited firepower and poor communications; and, least predictably, the difficulties of securing infantry support. As a result of the last, the pace of advance was slow, and the tanks often found themselves without any, or adequate, support, as with Italian attacks breaking through near Madrid on October 21 and November 15, 1936, and with Soviet T-26s on October 24, 1936, near Madrid and the Soviet BT-5s at Brunete. The Republicans generally backed infantry advances with tanks advancing from behind while the Nationalist tanks screened their infantry. Yet, in August 1937, the Italian tanks played a key role in breaking through the defensive system for Santander and going on to seize the city.

The war showed that tanks that were equipped only with machine guns were of limited value. The war thus encouraged the Germans, Soviets, and Italians to improve their armor. The Soviets replaced the slow T-26 with the BT-7 and moved toward the T-34. The Germans moved from the Panzer Mark 1 to the Mark 3, and the Italians, with greater difficulties due to financial issues, moved from the L3/35, which were inferior to the T-26s, to the M15/40.

However, as a whole, the war suggested that artillery would be more significant than armor and that the ability of tanks to provide mobile artillery was limited. Much of Spain is excellent tank country, albeit not the flat, stoneless open plains of much of Poland and the western Soviet Union. Parts of Spain (and, indeed, Poland and the western Soviet Union) were not excellent tank country, but it was the deficiencies and poor use of the tanks that were crucial. Tanks failed to create breakthroughs; when breakthroughs were achieved, tanks were not important to their exploitation. Frequently, their operations were unsuccessful.[16] Nevertheless, victory parades at the end of the war, for example, on May 11, 1939, at Valencia, showed a plentiful use of tanks, albeit light tanks.

PLANNING RESPONSES

The question of most appropriate armor types and doctrine was made more urgent from the mid-1930s by the increasing prospect of a major war. The World Disarmament Conference of 1932–34 proved a total failure, and tensions increased with the Japanese invasion of Manchuria in 1931 and Hitler gaining power in Germany in 1933. World War I, then the Great War, served as an increasingly apparent warning about the future.

The search for a doctrine of rapid victory focused on utilizing the operational possibilities of the new weaponry of tanks and aircraft, as this seemed at once the best way to respond to the apparent possibilities of this weaponry and also to avoid a recurrence of the devastation and prolonged struggle of World War I. It was a search for short-term warfare that could be effective.

There was a tendency to focus on key sectors, which encouraged debate about their identity. These key sectors were regarded as crucial force multipliers. This was seen in the French army, where the development of mechanized and motorized divisions was intended to provide a mobility capable of countering any German advance via Belgium, as in 1914, as a prelude to an engagement by the slower-moving mass French army with its infantry and artillery.

Similarly, the Germans emphasized elite units as a force multiplier ahead of the mass army. To that end, the Germans created their first three panzer (armored) divisions in 1935. While the Germans drew on Britain's use of tanks in World War I, and on subsequent British thought, notably that of Fuller, who was regarded as more important than Liddell Hart,[17] they developed their own distinctive ideas. Notably, these ideas involved using panzer divisions as combined arms units able to achieve a deep breakthrough. There was not Fuller's confidence in tanks alone as proclaimed by him in 1920.

The experience of World War II lay ahead, but later judgment of the 1930s too readily assumes otherwise. Instead, it is necessary to note the lack of clarity about what constituted military progress, the variety of possible responses, and the role of political suppositions and institutional structures and values. The processes of learning lessons and doctrinal innovation sound easier and far more clear-cut than they are in actuality. The same is also true of the contemporary and subsequent valuation of these processes.

One particular problem for all powers concerns the assessment of "anti-" strategies and tactics. If, for example, the doctrine and technology of a period favor the offensive, then investing in the defensive can be seen as anachronistic or, more favorably, as a way to try to lessen the impact of the offensive. In the latter view, such investment can be regarded as prescient or even forward looking.

FRANCE

Thus, French investment in the defenses of the Maginot Line, the expensive defenses against German attack across their common frontier, is often treated as both failure and anachronism—indeed, as made both redundant and foolish by the development of the tank—and demonstrably so with the total French defeat by Germany in 1940. However, French strategy was more nuanced and flexible than this criticism might suggest. The fortifications were regarded not as a definition of a defensive stance but, instead, as an aspect of a force structure that could support an offensive and/or a defensive strategy. The intention was to constrain German options (as indeed happened), to channel the Germans into Belgium, and to advance to fight them there. This approach, however, was seriously hindered by Belgium's unwillingness to commit itself to joint preparations. Indeed, the neutrality of some of Hitler's victims gave his strategy of aggression a major advantage over that of his opponents.

Key British commentator General Sir Archibald Montgomery-Massingberd, chief of the Imperial General Staff from 1933 to 1936, observed of the Maginot Line in 1935: "My recollections of our attacks against strong lines during the war, even with masses of heavy guns and tanks, is that this frontier, in three or four years will be practically impregnable, always provided of course that the French keep up their present garrison and maintain everything at the standard they are doing at present. Here again the underlying idea of economy in men so as to set free as many troops as possible for the mobile army."[18]

French tank strength was built up in the 1930s with new tanks and manuals, and the best French tank, the Char B, had far thicker armor than its German counterpart. The French, however, failed to develop an effective doctrine for their armor. Tanks were seen, like artillery, as best integrated with infantry they were to support as if mobile artillery and not as a separate arm capable of shock action.[19] There was a concern that the latter would not be able to cooperate with infantry and artillery. The first French tank division was not formed until January 1940, although the first light mechanized division had already been formed using light S-35 tanks that entered service from January 1936, with about 288 in frontline service by the spring of 1940. They fought well against the advancing Germans in Belgium from May 13 to 15.

A critical view of the French situation was taken by Charles de Gaulle, an ambitious armor officer, especially in his *Vers l'armée de métier* (1934), which, with interest rising due to the onset of war, was translated as *The Army of the Future* (1940). De Gaulle pressed for the deployment of tanks in an autonomous fashion, rather than accompanying the infantry, and, to that end, for the establishment of six divisions of heavy tanks organized into a single corps and manned by highly trained professional soldiers.[20] This work was much touted later, notably by himself, as prescient for his recognition of the need for a professional army of movement, relying on a large and mobile armored corps. De Gaulle was presented as a prophet in the wilderness, with his stance prefiguring his later rejection of the Vichy government of Marshal Pétain, a more conventional military figure.[21]

Typically, Liddell Hart, who also saw himself in such a light, was critical—correctly so—of de Gaulle for claiming credit for French armor developments.[22] Very much separate to Liddell Hart's view, it is unclear how far France was deficient in armor, how far more tanks would have been a good use of resources, and how far tanks could yet fulfill the tasks required. The French also had major colonial commitments for which their existing light tanks were well suited. Separately, to exert power in the Mediterranean, where Italy was a threat, France put strenuous effort into developing their navy. In 1940, if the Germans had not advanced through the Ardennes and fought their way across the Meuse, and if the French army had been better trained, the French defensive doctrine might have succeeded.

Vers l'armée de métier had a print run of 1,500 but was greeted with scant favor by a political establishment committed to conscription, and thus massive numbers of infantry, and by an army that was used to that system, which, indeed, provided the necessary numbers of infantry. Separately, Marshal Pétain regarded tanks as vulnerable to antitank weapons, and the two men disliked each other. De Gaulle exaggerated the influence of the book abroad. Nevertheless, it was read by Tukhachevsky (who had been imprisoned by the Germans alongside de Gaulle at Ingolstadt during World War I) and was translated into Russian. The book was also read by Guderian. A copy with comments by Hitler was found at Berchtesgaden in 1945.

In 1937, appointed to command a tank regiment, de Gaulle used field maneuvers to press for a major role for the armor, including bypassing well-defended villages. The commander-in-chief, Maurice Gamelin, criticized this stance and argued that tanks would only play a more modest role. De Gaulle himself was angry that France did not fight Germany in 1938, instead helping negotiate the Munich agreement. He claimed that tanks would be able to break through the German Siegfried Line, their defenses on the western frontier. Thus, the armor, he argued, provided a major strategic option.

BRITAIN

Britain also faced the need to assess many different defense requirements, and calls to build up a tank force had to sit alongside pressure for greater air force and naval strength, as well as for support of policing operations in the colonies. The last was advocated in Major-General Sir Charles Gwyn's *Imperial Policing* (1934), a key work on low-intensity conflict and small wars, in which he had been engaged as a lieutenant in West Africa in 1893–94. Many individual careers reflected a colonial commitment. Trained in the Royal Engineers, Gwyn had served as chief of staff of the II Anzac Corps during World War I and was commandant of the Staff College, Camberley, from 1926 until 1931. Similarly, General John Burnett-Stuart, who had served on the North-West Frontier of India (1897–98) and in the Boer War in South Africa (1899–1902), became a staff officer in World War I before becoming a commander in India and then director of military operations and intelligence at the War Office (1923–26). While a divisional commander (1926–30), he directed exercises of the Mechanized Force in 1927 before commanding in Egypt (1931–34) and with the Southern Command in England (1934–38).

For Britain, the world's largest empire, there was no clear mission, with the exception of the somewhat diffuse one of protecting the empire, and this situation affected the response to the potential of armor. In 1934, a report

from the Defence Requirements Sub-Committee of the Committee of Imperial Defence noted: "The complete mechanisation of the army is not today, or
in the near future, a possible or desirable measure. It would demand a highly
specialised army trained and equipped for one contingency only, vis. war in a
European theatre and on ground suitable for its employment . . . it would not
be possible to organise a larger mechanised force than the one we recommend
below without upsetting the whole system by which our forces overseas are
maintained by the Home Army."

The committee proposed a tank brigade as part of the expeditionary force
but argued that imperial commitments could not "be met by the creation of a
highly specialised 'robot' army at home, even if that were the best system for
a continental war, itself a matter far from certain."[23] The "robot" army was a
reference to an infantry-light army.

The British had successfully tested light tanks on India's North-West Frontier in 1930. Moreover, operating against the Faqir of Ipi (an Islamic funda-
mentalist leader) in Wasiristan on the North-West Frontier in the late 1930s,
the British deployed over sixty thousand troops, as well as about fifty to sixty
armored cars, which were used mainly to escort road convoys and proved
quite effective in that limited role. A handful of light tanks also went for an
occasional trundle on open ground but could not approach the mountainous
terrain on which the principal engagements took place. The five-ton Light
Tank Mark VI produced from 1936 was designed for such operations. It carried
machine guns but no other gun. Similarly to Britain, when France deployed
forces to Corsica in 1931 to challenge control by bandits, they used armored
cars, and not tanks, for the mobile columns sent into the mountains.

At the same time, alongside tactical constraints and financial exigencies was
a clear appreciation in Britain of the operational possibilities created by the
tank. This appreciation was the case in the army with practical modernizers;
but they had to be more aware of financial restrictions than the publicists
criticizing from the outside, even more so due to the greater favor shown to
both the air force and the navy. Montgomery-Massingberd, chief of the Imperial General Staff from 1933 to 1936 and a key practical modernizer, favored
the mobilization and reweaponing of infantry and cavalry alongside armor,
which was at variance with the emphasis by Fuller and Liddell Hart on tanks
alone. Montgomery-Massingberd made the Experimental Tank Brigade per-
manent and gave its command to Percy Hobart, a keen enthusiast for armor.
Montgomery-Massingberd became colonel commandant of the Royal Tank
Corps in 1934, an honorary but indicative position. Later in 1934, he decided

to form a mobile division, which, when established later in the decade, was Britain's first armored division.[24]

Debate itself interacted with improvements in the capabilities of tanks in service, with a degree of causal relationship but also with separate trajectories. For example, the light tanks produced by Vickers became more powerful with the design of the Light Tank Mark VII (A17), also known as the Tetrarch, which carried a 2-pounder (40 mm) gun as well as a machine gun. Designed in 1938 and produced from 1939 to 1941 as part of an (understandably) overhasty period of expansion for the army, it could go on-road at forty miles per hour and off-road at twenty-eight miles per hour and had an operational range of 140 miles, but its design flaws, and the weakness and vulnerability of light tanks, meant it was not used in North Africa in World War II.

With the Tetrarch, as so often, investment in the 1930s meant the procurement of weapons that proved inadequate in the first stages of World War II, let alone later. Research and development were insufficient. There was no advances for tanks comparable to those in aircraft, which included the Hurricane, the Spitfire, and radar. Indeed, talk about the superiority of the tank continued to face the limitations of availability as well as armor, firepower, speed, and range. Oliver Lyttelton, the minister of production, was to tell the House of Commons on July 1, 1942, that until the end of 1938: "Our armoured forces consisted of eight battalions of the Royal Tank Regiment equipped with light tanks, which were armed only with machine guns, obsolescent medium tanks, also armed with machine guns, and two cavalry armoured car regiments."[25]

Aside from the tanks being undergunned and underarmored to take on other tanks, British infantry was not adequately trained to cooperate with tanks, a situation that continued into World War II.

Of the publicists, Liddell Hart was later to claim part of the credit for German success in 1939–40. It has been argued also that his ideas, along with those espoused by other British exponents of tank operations and reports of British maneuvers, did not influence German blitzkrieg tactics to the extent once proclaimed,[26] although this, in turn, has been challenged. At any rate, the theme of a prophet ignored in his own country, but heeded elsewhere, proved attractive to commentators and appeared to add a military counterpart to the idea that Britain had been betrayed politically by Appeasement. Certainly this was a theme of Liddell Hart's *Memoirs* (1965). In reality, and to a degree he never accepted, Liddell Hart had only scant influence in Germany, unlike Fuller.

Liddell Hart was definitely unpopular in the British army. In 1939, Sir John Dill, commander of the First British Corps in France, complained about the "incalculable" harm he had done, adding: "Thanks largely to Liddell Hart's advice, battalions were cut down. The argument was that it is fire power, not man power, that is wanted on the battlefield. That may be true up to a point, but at night, in fog, and when the enemy uses smoke, one must have men on the ground."[27]

The following year, Liddell Hart was accused by Montgomery-Massingberd of "misstatements, perversions of fact, half-truths, and quotations taken out of their context."[28] As an instance of the need to put this in context, Montgomery-Massingberd had also claimed that he had to "fight" those he termed "the air mad."[29]

Liddell Hart had been close to Leslie Hore-Belisha, who became secretary of state for war in 1937 and was keen on reform. This drive angered many in the army, and neither man was able to push through change to the degree they thought necessary. The two men parted company in early 1938. Hore-Belisha himself was dismissed in January 1940.

In practice, by the 1930s, both Fuller and Liddell Hart, who fell out over the former's support for Fascism, had come to appreciate that tank offensives could be blunted by an effective defense, as was to be the case, eventually, with the German invasion of the Soviet Union in 1941.

GERMANY

Other powers were improving their armor. The partition of Czechoslovakia, in October 1938 and March 1939, provided Germany with Czech tanks and with the military-industrial capacity in the shape of BMM and Škoda, both tank manufacturers, to increase tank production. At this stage, however, there was an emphasis on light and medium tanks, but not heavy ones. As with aircraft, this matched the concern of the Nazi regime with the appearance and presence of many tanks, as well as the question of manufacturing capability and engineering convenience. The Panzer Mark I, which had entered service in 1934, was a light tank at 5.4 tons and was only armed with machine guns. The Panzer Mark II, which followed in 1937, was 8.9 tons and carried a 20 mm gun as well as a machine gun. It could go 24.5 miles per hour and was Germany's most numerous tank at the start of World War II. Heinz Guderian, the commander of a panzer division, was clear that the Mark 1s and 2s were not what the Germans wanted, but what they had to order, as German industry could not deliver larger tanks, which disappointed him.[30]

In contrast, the Mark III, which entered service from 1937 (mass production following in 1939), was twenty-three tons and carried a 37 mm gun. A medium tank designed for combat with other tanks, its off-road speed was only 7.5 miles per hour. The Mark IV, another medium tank, was designed originally for combat against infantry and artillery, with a heavier gun than the Mark III. Production began in 1936. It had a 75 mm gun as well as two machine guns and an operational range of 120 miles.

The fit between tanks and the mobile warfare envisaged by the Reichswehr in the 1920s and expressed in General Ludwig Beck's *Die Truppenführung* (United Command, 1933–34)[31] might appear both clear and obvious. Tanks represented and guaranteed mobility, although there was not yet a commitment to large tank units. The potential of tanks was taken further in a range of works—for example, *Der Kampfwagenkrieg* (1934) by General Ludwig von Eimannsberger, a leading figure in the Austrian army. He saw armor as a key means to attack the flanks and rear of opposing forces. This book also appeared in French, Polish, Romanian, and Russian editions.

Yet aside from the practical problems of tanks, including speed, reliability, firepower, and vulnerability, mass mobility in the context of Germany in the 1920s and 1930s could only be provided by rail, horses, and marching. Alongside concepts of tanks as a transforming force, giving teeth to older ideas of envelopment,[32] most generals thought they would have to be an adjunct force. The forms in which tanks might provide this were unclear in terms of roles, capabilities (both desired and actual), organizations, and interaction with other arms. Initially, the German tanks were regarded as part of a defensive maneuverability set by challenges, real or potential, from the west—France—and the east—France's allies (Czechoslovakia and Poland) and/or the Soviet Union. Thus, the panzer divisions, established in 1935 after a staff exercise involving three notional divisions, at first served as a mobile means to counter strategic vulnerability, only changing into consideration as an offensive capability as German aspirations altered. The alteration was the crucial element, not the specifications of the tanks themselves.

Major-General Oswald Lutz, the inspector of motor transport troops from April 1931 to 1935, had Guderian, a protégé, as his chief of staff. In 1935, Lutz was made commander of the new Armored Troops Command while Guderian was put in command of one of the three panzer divisions established that year. Walter Nehring, another member of Lutz's staff, became a major commander of panzer units during World War II. However, many officers were opposed to the panzer divisions; they saw tanks, instead, as a support for infantry.

It was certainly difficult to fulfill potential. Half the German tanks entering Czechoslovakia after the 1938 Munich Conference broke down. Fine-tuning traction and mechanical issues was an arduous process that was necessary in advancing operational usage and theory. Despite the considerable progress made since 1918, the mechanical reliability of tanks was a major problem.

SOVIET UNION

Soviet tanks had been influenced by British Vickers designs. Based on the British Mark E and built under license from Vickers, the T-26B, which entered service in 1931, was 9.4 tons and had a 45 mm gun, making it a powerful threat at the time, while the fast BT-2, also from 1931, was 10.2 tons and had a 37 mm gun. However, there was also an interest in heavier tanks. Entering service in 1935, the T-35 had much thicker armor (30 mm), was heavier (45 tons), and carried a 76.2 mm gun. Yet it required a crew of ten, which was not the way ahead. Also in that year came a light tank, the BT-7, with a speed of thirty-three miles per hour, a weight of 13.8 tons, and a 45 mm gun.

In the Soviet Union, politics played a major role in doctrine to a degree not seen in the United States. The cavalry was built up in the 1920s and early 1930s by Semyon Budënny, a protégé of Stalin, but was in the process of being phased out in the late 1930s, although the Soviets still had cavalry in World War II. Talented cavalry officers, such as Semyon Krivoshein (1899–1978), were transferred to the armor. Marshal Mikhail Tukhachevsky, the key figure in military reform, was committed to large-scale mechanized warfare and seizing the offensive and was responsible for the creation of an armored division in 1931 and a mechanized corps the following year. In the 1935 *Instructions on Deep Battle* and the *Provisional Field Regulations* of 1936, Tukhachevsky built on the ideas of Vladimir Triandafillov (1894–1931), the chief of the operations department of the General Staff from 1923, who had published works on army operations in 1926 and 1929 that developed the idea of "deep operations."[33] The Communists rejected much of the czarist past and felt no need to be burdened by the older military establishment. As both technological visionaries and pragmatists, at least some Soviet commanders eagerly adopted outside innovations.

However, feeling it necessary to terrorize the armed forces, and fed information of a conspiracy between the Soviet and German armies, Stalin had Tukhachevsky shot in June 1937 at the start of a wide-ranging and lengthy purge of the military leadership and officer corps. Not only commanders were disgraced. Others included I. A. Khalepskii of the Mechanisation and Motorisation Administration who had worked with the Germans in Kazan and was a key figure in improving production.[34] This purge led to a major change in Soviet doctrine. The emphasis shifted from the large armored formations advocated by Tukhachevsky, and his commitment to a "deep" attack based on the rapid and far-flung operational exploitation of tactical successes, to smaller units integrated with the infantry.

In part it was the use of the "experience" of the Spanish Civil War as a tool in the purges, specifically the recommendation of General Dmitri Pavlov, a Soviet adviser to the Spanish Republic who had commanded Soviet tanks in that war, that tanks were better suited as infantry support, that led to the disbanding of the mechanized corps in 1939. This advice may have reflected a wish to escape Tukhachevsky's fate. Pavlov became head of the Directorate of Tank and Armoured Car Troops of the Red Army only to be executed for failure in July 1941.[35] In turn, this disbanding was to be reversed in 1940. Even so, G. S. Isserson, who developed Tukhachevsky's ideas, publishing part of *The New Forms of Combat* in 1940, was arrested in June 1941, just before the German attack, and imprisoned for criticizing Soviet command in the Finnish Winter War.[36] Pavlov's predecessor as commander of the Soviet tanks in the civil war, Semyon Krivoshein, who had played a valuable role in the battle of Madrid in late 1936, met Guderian in 1939 when both, separately, were invading Poland, and he became head of the Department of Training in the Main Directorate of the Red Army Tank Forces from 1941 to 1943 before playing a major role in armor conflict with Germany in 1943–45.

Tukhachevsky's interests in "deep battle" and mechanization are usually praised and are generally linked to Soviet successes in 1944–45.[37] This praise and linkage are aspects both of the developmental nature of history that is so attractive in narrative and analysis alike and of modern concerns with doctrine. Nevertheless, aside from the problematic nature of this linkage, which was at the very least far from direct, this interest can be criticized for exaggerating, as did most of Tukhachevsky's calls for military development, the economic potential of the Soviet Union, for failing to pay due attention to the actual state and capability of the Soviet army in the late 1930s, and for underestimating the importance of the defensive.[38] The Soviet Union had as many as seven thousand tanks in 1935. The quality of Russian tanks impressed a large number of military attachés who attended a maneuver in 1936, notably because the tanks did not break down, although see the comments on those maneuvers in the following. The T3E2 tank, equipped with the Christie suspension, readily crossed obstacles during tests that year. The BT2-2 tank of 1932 and the T-34 used the Christie system.

Nevertheless, the 1936 maneuvers revealed design problems in the models available, as well as serious tactical and operational flaws in their use. Thus, before the purges, there were already major issues with the Soviet army, as well as with the rapidly expanding economy. The purges did not help, but it is mistaken to put all the weight on them for the Soviet failures in the initial stages of the war—failures, moreover, than can be exaggerated. Rather than points specific to armor, the Red Army (its title until 1946) was affected in the late 1930s and early 1940s by more systemic issues including the problem of matching improved effectiveness to increased size. In this, a lack of secondary and technical education for so many of its officers, inadequate training systems, and organizational weaknesses all played a role, as did a terrible transport system.[39] The emphasis on the purges replicates that on Stalin's refusal to accept clear warnings in 1941 of an imminent German attack. Both were important, but not the only factors.

At the same time as its weaknesses, however, the army retained, as the US military attaché noted, an important defensive capability.[40] In August 1939, the Soviets decided to build two new powerful tanks, the T-34/76A and the KV-1/A, which entered service in 1941 and 1940 respectively.

Although the theme of the loss of talented officers in the purges affects the perception of the Soviet army and, in particular, the use of armor, the Soviet army made effective use of its tanks to defeat Japan in fighting on the Manchurian/Mongolian border at Khalkin-Gol (also known as the battle of Nomonhan) in August 1939. This followed Soviet failure in the battle of Lake Khasan (July 29–August 11, 1938). In the latter border clash, a surprise Japanese attack, in which seventeen Soviet tanks were destroyed, was followed by the Soviets using their rail system to assemble their forces. These included 354 tanks and self-propelled guns: 257 T-26s (10 of them KhT-26 flamethrower tanks), 3 ST-26 bridge-laying tanks, 81 BT-7 light tanks, and 13 SU-5-2 self-propelled guns. The poorly commanded Soviets attacked from August 2 to 9, but the Japanese antitank defense proved effective as part of a successful overall defense in terrain less than suited for the deployment of tanks and against uninspired Soviet tactics.[41] Forty-six Soviet tanks were destroyed and another thirty-nine damaged. The Japanese, however, pulled out on August 11 in order to stop the conflict from broadening.[42]

In contrast, in 1939, at Khalkin-Gol, over one thousand Soviet tanks and armored vehicles, including large armored cars, were used to envelop Japanese forces. The Soviets were able to transport their tanks thousands of miles east to points not so distant from the Khalkin-Gol area. Tanks in their own way are fragile and benefit from being transported by other means as much as possible prior to arriving on the battlefield. The Japanese only had two tank brigades in Manchuria and initially deployed 73 tanks and in total about 135. Against the Soviet tanks, the Japanese employed 37 mm antitank guns, antitank mines, and Molotov cocktails. The Japanese suffered from the able Soviet use of combined arms, which added tactical and operational skill to superior firepower. Soviet tanks, with only very limited radio communication both within and between units, could be deployed within a limited area, which meant Soviet weaknesses in command and control could be partially mitigated.[43] The Japanese failed to adopt combined arms tactics and the necessary defensive skills. Their essentially infantry force, employing tactics used more successfully against the Chinese, was heavily defeated.[44] The battle saw the emergence of General Zhukov, and his ruthless, but effective, leadership style presaged his later important role in some of the key battles of World War II.

Defeat led Japan to prefer peace with the Soviet Union, which was important to the negotiation of a nonaggression pact between the two powers in May 1941. This enabled the Soviet Union to focus its military resources on Germany during the conflict between the two powers that broke out in June.

In attacking Finland on November 30, 1939, the Soviet Army had planned a bold war of maneuver in which it would overrun southern Finland and also cut through mid-Finland to the Gulf of Bothnia at Oulu. The T-34/76A and KV-VA were not yet available. Instead, large numbers of T-26s and BTs were used.[45] This plan fell victim to an impressive resistance as well as to the weather. Soviet training and leadership in the "Winter War" proved poor. The T-26s proved vulnerable to the British-supplied Boys antitank rifle. The Soviet attack relied heavily on tanks and artillery, which consigned its columns to a limited number of forest roads and tracks, especially in the southern sector. They failed to appreciate the ability of the Finns to operate on skis away from the roads, and they found their columns being isolated and destroyed piecemeal by relatively small Finnish forces using "motti" tactics. Many Soviet troops simply froze to death as they guarded their immobilized tank columns.

In 1940 the new Soviet commander, Marshal Semyon Timoshenkoq, focused not on maneuver but on an attritional attack, which brought the war to a successful close on March 12, 1940. Massed artillery and tanks had been successfully used to support infantry in breaking through the Mannerheim Line in February.[46] The Soviets were able to fight a conventional war involving armor, although they were not ready, as was certainly both a planned option and mentioned at the time, to launch an offensive against Germany in 1940–41.

JAPAN

In 1928, the Japanese army had decided to develop a tank of about ten tons, referring to the Vickers Mark C tank. This became the Type 89A tank, which entered service in 1929 and was Japan's first main tank. It weighed 11.5 tons, had a maximum speed of 15.5 miles per hour, and was equipped with a 57 mm gun. Equipped with a water-cooled gas engine, the tank faced fire risks. As a result, the Type 95 Kyugo of 1935 built by Mitsubishi Heavy Industries was equipped with an air-cooled diesel engine and had a 37 mm gun and two machine guns. It was followed by the T97 Chi Ha (1937, 15.8 tons, 57 mm) and Type 97 Chi-Nu (1944, 15.8 tons, 75 mm). The tanks were first used in Manchuria in 1931 and at Shanghai in 1932. In contrast to Kazushige Ugaki, the minister of war from 1924 to 1927 and 1929 to 1931, General Sadao Arkadi, the minister of war from 1931 to 1934, at a time when Japan's economy was reeling from the Great Depression, was a keen supporter of the Imperial Way with its emphasis on manpower.[47]

Japan's tanks, which drew on British Vickers designs, were not particularly effective and were used largely for infantry support. None was a heavy tank. Production of motor vehicles of any and all kinds was very limited in Japan, and tanks were very hard to build, maintain, and, most importantly, fuel. The severe shortage of trained mechanics was a major limitation on the integration of armored vehicles into the army, as it was in other countries with few cars or trucks. There was a broader problem of developing a mass automobile culture in which people, usually the younger ones, become hard-wired to anything connected with automotive mechanics and tools, and this new cultural encounter becomes part of the air breathed.

Sensha (tanks), nevertheless, were considered highly impressive and were worked into every possible army propaganda shot. There were tank scenes in the documentary *Soldiers at the Front* (*Tataku Heita*) and in a noted film, *The Legend of Tank Commander Nishizumi* (*Nishizumi Senshachō Den*), made in 1940 and featuring a heroic tank commander. The film's promotional trailer included a song that presented the tanks "biting into the dust of the infinite plains" as a dramatic sign of Japanese technological mastery. The infantry are shown advancing behind the cover of the tank.

Defeat by the Soviet Union in 1939 encouraged the Japanese to rethink their use of armor, but the first armored division was not prepared for service until 1943. In total over one thousand Type 95s were built between 1935 and 1945. Two Panzer Mark IIIs were purchased from Germany to see if they could be reverse engineered, but that difficult route was not pursued.

UNITED STATES

US military innovation in the 1920s and 1930s was hit not only by limited military budgets but also by institutional rigidity and the failure to develop adequate doctrine, including for combined arms tactics and maneuver warfare. All these issues were significant.[48] In addition, the US military was not paying attention to German-language articles and books on tank warfare. At that time the United States military regarded the tank as an infantry-support weapon.

Rapidly building up their army from a size of 187,893 active-duty soldiers on June 30, 1939, the Americans used large-scale maneuvers in 1941 prior to their entry into the war in December to test not only weapons and tactics but also mobility. However, these maneuvers were very much in open country—in Louisiana, Arkansas, and the Carolinas—and not the closed-in circumstances found on Pacific islands and in much of Western Europe during World War II. Nor was there adequate combined arms training,[49] which was a significant requirement when the Americans were attacked by the Germans in Tunisia in 1943. Phase One of the Louisiana maneuvers saw the use of two armor divisions, but antitank guns blocked their advance. As commander of an armor division, Patton, now a major-general, proved a bold success in Phase Two. Dwight Eisenhower, as Blue Force's chief of staff, was also responsible for the wide sweep of Patton's division. As a major, Eisenhower had commanded a tank unit in 1921–22.

That is a relatively positive account of the US response both to the deteriorating international situation and to the unexpected and rapid success of German armor-led offensives in 1939–41. In practice, the rapid establishment and expansion of the Armored Force faced many difficulties, including administrative turf wars and issues of doctrine and equipment. As of the start of August 1941, there were four armored divisions and some independent tank battalions, the latter very much intended for infantry support. However, two of the divisions, although trained and equipped, were under strength, while the other two were not in a state to begin training, which, in addition, was a seriously underresourced process. There was also a tension between cavalry and infantry officers, one that hindered not only the development of doctrine but also the very working of the Armored Force. Major-General Jacob Devers, who became chief of the Armored Force on August 1, 1941, was unimpressed with the views of both groups of officers. To him, tanks were neither cavalry nor only for infantry support. To build cohesion, Devers established an Officer Candidate School at the Armored Force's headquarters, which had been established at Fort Knox, Kentucky, in July 1940. The Armored Force School and the Armored Force Replacement Center both followed that October.

Devers also set out to improve both weaponry and organizational structure. The M3, the Grant, was an inadequate medium tank—indeed, it was a quickly developed stopgap. Devers pressed forward the production of its replacement, the Sherman, an outgrowth of the M2A2 series, and argued for its improvement. He also thought the projected heavy tank, the T6, was undergunned with a 3-inch main gun and underpowered; instead, he called for what would finally lead to the M26 Pershing. To increase the strength of the armored divisions, Devers advocated a self-propelled gun, which led to the M7, a 105 mm howitzer on a medium tank chassis. In organizational terms, Devers changed the regimental ratio of a division from two of light, fast tanks to one of medium to one and two respectively. He also increased the armored infantry component and replaced the artillery with self-propelled guns.[50] These changes, in substance, reflected a rejection of the two earlier traditions of armor doctrine and use. The changes, however, were still a matter of potential rather than combat-tested success.

ITALY

With a relatively poor manufacturing infrastructure and a commitment to existing models, Italy continued to focus on light tanks[51] within a context affected by a conservative military leadership and an inadequate industrial response.[52] When Italy invaded Albania in April 1939, 125 tanks were part of the landing force of thirteen thousand troops. However, the motorized column that advanced from the port of Durazzo to the inland capital, Tirana, was delayed because, in the darkness of nighttime preparations, the vehicles had been provided with diesel instead of gasoline.

Entering service in 1933, the thinly armored CV-33 tankette, which only carried two machine guns, was found seriously wanting when Italy fought the Allies in 1940–43. At the same time, based on the British Carden Loyd, this model represented a definite strand of what was judged significant in the 1930s. There were export orders to Brazil, China, and Hungary. The Germans shared the Italian emphasis on numbers of tanks, which encouraged a focus on lighter tanks than was found appropriate by the middle stages of World War II.

At the same time, Italy was developing tanks. Influenced by the British Vickers Mark I and built in 1939, the M11/39, the first Italian medium tank, was designed as an infantry-support tank for warfare in the Alps, essentially against France. Because of that, the main gun was placed in the hull, not the turret. That was not considered a weakness as the tanks were not designed for operating in the North African desert. This underlines the difficulty of anticipating the next conflict and designing weapon systems accordingly. Its successor, the M13/40, which entered service in 1940, had significant limitations in armor, firepower, and speed but was not that bad a tank compared to British tanks employed in North Africa.

POLAND

Nowhere else in Eastern Europe matched the Czech tank industry in large part because metallurgy and machine tools were most developed there. The Poles did not emulate the mechanization of the German and Soviet armies in the 1930s due to a lack of financial resources. General Wladyslaw Sikorski, the author of a text on modern warfare, pressed the value of mechanized warfare and the tank, but he was out of favor with Marshal Josef Pilsundski, the dictator from 1926 until 1935. In the late 1930s, the Polish military came to understand the value of tanks, but they were too far behind their rivals.[53] By 1939, the Polish cavalry, about a tenth of the men under arms, was armed with antitank weapons and heavy machine guns and was trained to fight dismounted, and the horses were employed to change positions after an action: in short, for mobility, not shock action.[54] Nevertheless, with modern tanks few in number or still in prototype form,[55] the Polish army was weak in tanks and antitank guns and training. This considerably affected its ability to resist German attack in 1939.

OTHER STATES

Other states also had to respond to a number of challenges and a range of options, all within resource constraints and concerns about the multiple uncertainties of requirements and the actions of others. At the time of the Gran Chaco War, Bolivia had also had a demonstration FT tank from France, although it was not used. This tank, like Bolivia's Vickers and Italian tanks, reflected the extent to which only certain powers were then exporting tanks. Their preference for tank types, therefore, was more immediately significant and was enhanced by the degree to which much of the world was under the control of Western imperial powers. Thus, the Nationalist government of China gained control of many of Manchuria's French FTs and also bought twenty-four British Carden Loyd Mark VI tankettes, soon followed with twenty Vickers Mark E tanks and twenty-nine Vickers amphibious Carden Loyd tanks. War with Japan and turning to German military advisors led China to purchase twenty Italian L3/33 tankettes as well as fifteen Panzer Mark Is. Many of these were destroyed or captured by Japan when it launched a full-scale attack on China in 1937.

The withdrawal of German advisers in 1938 at Japan's behest was linked to China turning to the Soviet Union for assistance, which the Soviets provided because they wished to keep Japan busy against China. Soviet tanks—eighty-two T-26s—arrived in China from March 1938. The Soviets trained the Chinese tank crews. In 1938, the tanks were used against the Japanese in the battle of Lanfeng and then in that of Kunlun Pass in late 1939. The latter was a victory, albeit with heavy costs.

The British sold Vickers tanks to Argentina, Belgium, China, Finland, Latvia, Lithuania, and Switzerland. Although there were no tanks in the army in the Netherlands in 1940 because, after trials, it was concluded that they were unsuitable for deployment in Dutch polder land and flooded terrain, the Dutch ordered two Vickers light amphibious tanks and two Vickers light tanks in 1937 for service in the Dutch East Indies (now Indonesia). All four were delivered. The Dutch then ordered seventy-three of the latter in 1938. Twenty were delivered, but the others were confiscated by the British government after the outbreak of World War II. Subsequently, US Marmon-Herrington tanks were ordered, and some were delivered in time to take part in the unsuccessful resistance to Japanese invasion in 1942. In 1936, Romania decided to create an armored division comprised of two regiments. They drew on Czech and French tanks, and, in 1939, thirty-four French-made Polish tanks that had fled to Romania after the German-Soviet conquest of Poland were added.

ATTITUDES

The use of tanks did not mean they were necessarily the focus of developments. Nevertheless, attitudes to tanks reflected in part the "mechanization" of the imagination—both public and military—about war. More particularly, this "mechanization" was prominent in a motorized fashion, one that became more significant from the 1920s. There was also a degree of transferring cavalry values to a new context. This was the case in Britain where there was an important attempt at modernization. Thus, the British army committee that, in 1938, recommended the merger of the Royal Tank Corps and the newly mechanized cavalry commented that, in the past, troops had been trained within their own regiments but that "this system is impracticable for a corps equipped with armoured fighting vehicles, and it is clear that in future training will be necessary at a depot equipped with suitable vehicles and staffed by technically qualified instructors."[56]

The report also noted resistance to the merger from the officers of the now-mechanized cavalry regiments who complained about a different ethos in the Royal Tank Corps, one of nonaristocratic officers who could not afford the expensive clubbability of the cavalry regiments, where the officers were presented as having a hereditary military role. Wealth was required for uniforms and socializing and was measured by the ownership of civilian horses, notably for hunting.

In part, this resistance to the merger reflected a cultural issue about command and control that was to affect British armored performance in World War II. This context for evaluation is at least as pertinent as that of equipment. Indeed, contrary to frequent remarks, the British Expeditionary Force that was sent to France in September 1939 was well equipped in some respects.[57] However, as Lyttelton was to point out in 1942:

> In October, 1939, we had, as so-called armoured units, three regular cavalry regiments, and three battalions of the Royal Tank Regiment. They had 200 light tanks of the Mark VI series, that is, a 5 1/2 ton tank, very lightly armoured and mounting two machine guns.... Apart from light tanks armed with machine guns, there were only 117 Cruisers of Marks I and III and 90 infantry tanks.... The only British tanks mounting more than a machine gun which fought in France in those battles, in which the Germans deployed between four and five thousand tanks, were 23 Mark II infantry tanks and 158 Cruisers.[58]

POTENTIAL

Predictions of war ahead and the resulting role for armor varied considerably in the 1930s, although the threat of war centering on German aggression became more prominent from the mid-1930s. The prospect that Germany would rely on armored and mechanized forces in conjunction with air power was increasingly understood. Indeed, in September 1935, the Imperial General Staff predicted that Germany would outflank France's defenses by advancing through Belgium and that Britain would need armor to help resist this.[59]

In contrast, in the "Note on the Development of the 'Army Rearmament Programme,'" drawn up in May 1939, General Sir Ronald Adam, deputy chief of the Imperial General Staff, recorded that under the plan approved in April 1938, the Field Force, the British army force available for overseas commitment, was "to be organised primarily with a view to reinforcing the Middle East.... The crisis in September 1938 emphasised the danger in the assumption that a Continental commitment was to be given a low order of priority. It also focused sharply the fact that, even when the programme was complete, our forces would be inadequate for a major Continental war."[60]

Yet that was far from Britain's sole military commitment. Indeed, for Britain and other powers, tasking repeatedly was a key element in the development of capability and in related doctrinal issues. The failure, despite high hopes after the Munich Agreement on September 29, 1938, to restrain German aggression (which was apparent from mid-March 1939) and to avoid war in Europe, dramatically changed the tasking, as did the German-Soviet agreement, the Molotov-Ribbentrop Pact, of August 23, 1939. Neither was predictable, but their consequences pushed armor to the fore in the war with Germany that began soon after.

A sense of military potential continued to focus on machines, as can be seen in George Patton's writings, notably "The Effect of Weapons on War," published in the *Cavalry Journal*, which discussed armored vehicles, his 1932 War College thesis, and a 1933 piece titled "Mechanised Forces: A Lecture."[61] Major J. Halpin Connolly wrote in the *Infantry Journal* of July 1939: "The mechanistic . . . runs along engulfing the professional soldier under a cataract of machines that he strives to convert to war."[62] Industrial capacity meant that the possibility of doing so would be possible, albeit to a varying extent. In 1927, writing in *RUSI*, Major McLeod argued for the dominance of the machine in the shape of the tank in attack. The May 1936 issue of the US magazine *Science and Mechanics* depicted on its cover "The Mechanized Army in the Next War." This showed tanks, some three stories and others with four tracks, with multiple firing positions, advancing over barbed wire toward a trench defended by infantry who are clearly going to be crushed. The apparent lessons of World War I were still being assessed, by planners and commentators alike, in terms of new weapon systems and new doctrines.[63] Such weaponry was rarely as fanciful as the idea of glue guns for blinding tanks.

New doctrines included developing interest in the operational level of war, not least by armies, such as the Americans, that did not use the relevant term.[64] The operational level was that between tactics and strategy. As such, a new conceptual and doctrinal space was up for grabs, and discussion of the respective capabilities of weapon systems played a role in this context. Organizational procurement and training issues all followed. Tanks were seen as the way to be successful at this level and at the tactical one. The need was for a knockout blow, apparently, and, drawing on the term *lightning*, strategy accordingly was described in terms of blitzkrieg prior to the outbreak of World War II, both by military figures, such as Tukhachevsky in 1937, and by journalists from 1938.[65]

The Germans displayed another use of tanks with tanks as propaganda and to demonstrate power. This was for domestic as much as international purposes. Tanks were similarly used in the drills of the Soviet paramilitary youth sports organization DOSAAF, which operated in close contact with the Red Army. In a very different context, tanks were also used in democracies in order to exert power. Thus, in July 1932, six M1917 tanks under Patton were deployed in Washington, DC, including on Pennsylvania Avenue, in the crisis caused by the "Bonus Army" and their demand for payment of their service certificates. Six years earlier, in Britain, armored cars were used to escort food convoys during the General Strike, and tanks were also deployed.

CONCLUSIONS

The wars of the 1930s did nothing to show up and overcome the deficiencies of how tanks were being used. Moreover, many tanks of this period were only slight advances over earlier models and contained little that was new, so that the fundamental problems were not addressed for the most part. There was a widespread focus on speed and numbers making up for armor and armament for the same reasons the British navy had earlier turned to battlecruisers. Thus, the Red Army had huge numbers of BT tanks and T-26s and did not develop the T-34 until 1939. Everything was to change in World War II.

NOTES

1. I would like to thank Charles Esdaile for letting me use this item.

2. A. P. Wavell, "The Army and the Prophets," *RUSI* 35 (1930), reproduced in *RUSI* 155, no. 6 (2010): 86–93; A. Fort, *Archibald Wavell: The Life and Times of an Imperial Servant* (London, 2009), 76–77.

3. *HC*, July 1, 1942, vol. 381, cols. 253–57.

4. J. Maiolo, *Cry Havoc: How the Arms Race Drove the World to War, 1931–1941* (New York, 2010).

5. D. Fletcher, *British Light Tanks, 1927–45: Marks I–VI* (Oxford, 2014).

6. T. Andrade, *Lost Colony: The Untold Story of China's First Great Victory over the West* (Princeton, NJ, 2011), 326.

7. G. Patton, "The Effect of Weapons on War," *Cavalry Journal* 37, no. 5 (November 1930): 483–88.

8. D. P. O'Connor, "The Twenty Year Armistice: RUSI Between the Wars," *RUSI* 154, no. 1 (2009): 87–88.

9. B. L. Dastrup, "Travails of Peace and War: Field Artillery in the 1930s and Early 1940s," *Army History* 25 (winter 1993): 35.

10. M. Hughes, "Logistics and Chaco War: Bolivia versus Paraguay, 1932–35," *JMH* 69 (2005): 411–37; A. de Quesada and P. Jowett, *The Chaco War 1932–35: South America's Greatest Modern Conflict* (Oxford, 2011).

11. W. Brandt, "The Tank Experience in the Chaco War," *Royal Tank Corps Journal* 1 (January 1937): 41–43.

12. E. De Lia, "The Role of Italian Armor in the Spanish Civil War," *Armor* 95 (May/June 1986): 40–44; G. F. Hofmann, "The Tactical and Strategic Use of Attaché Intelligence: The Spanish Civil War and the U.S. Army's Misguided Quest for a Modern Tank Doctrine," *JMH* 62 (1998): 101–33; J. L. S. Daley, "Soviet and German Advisors Put Doctrine to the Test: Tanks in the Siege of Madrid," *Armor* 108, no. 3 (1999): 33–37; A. Candil, "Soviet Armor in Spain: Aid Mission to Republicans Testing Doctrine and Equipment," *Armor* 108, no. 2 (1999): 31–38; S. J. Zaloga and K. W. Estes, "Armor: Was the Spanish Civil War a Testing Ground for the Military Use of Tanks?," in *History in Dispute*, vol. 18, *The Spanish Civil War*, ed. K. W. Estes and D. Kowalsky (Detroit, MI, 2005), 33–40; S. J. Zaloga, *Spanish Civil War Tanks: The Proving Ground for Blitzkrieg* (Oxford, 2010).

13. Reichenau lecture, NA. CAB. 24/277 fol. 281.

14. NA. WO. 106/1576, pp. 1–7.

15. NA. WO. 106/1580.

16. C. J. Esdaile, *The Spanish Civil War: A Military History* (London, 2019).

17. A. Gat, *British Armour Theory and the Rise of the Panzer Arm: Revising the Revisionists* (London, 2000).

18. Montgomery-Massingberd to Viscount Halifax, Secretary of State for War, August 17, 1935, LH. MM. 10/4/1.

19. R. A. Doughty, *The Seeds of Disaster: The Development of French Army Doctrine, 1919–1939* (Hamden, CT, 1985); E. Kiesling, *Arming against Hitler: France and the Limits of Military Planning* (Lawrence, KS, 1996).

20. J. Jackson, *A Certain Idea of France: The Life of Charles de Gaulle* (London, 2018), 73–74.

21. B. Bond and M. Alexander, "Liddell Hart and de Gaulle: The Doctrines of Limited Liability and Mobile Defence," in *Makers of Modern Strategy*, ed. P. Paret (Princeton, NJ, 1986), 598–623.

22. A. Danchev, *Alchemist of War: The Life of Basil Liddell Hart* (London, 1998), 121.

23. Committee of Imperial Defence, Defence Requirements Sub-Committee, Report, February 28, 1934, NA. CAB. 16/109, fol. 15.

24. H. Winston, *To Change an Army: General Sir John Burnett-Stuart and British Armoured Doctrine, 1927–1938* (London, 1988); J. P. Harris, *Men, Ideas, and Tanks: British Military Thought and Armoured Forces, 1903–1939* (Manchester, UK, 1995).

25. *HC*, July 1, 1942, vol. 381, col. 250.

26. Gat, *British Armour Theory*.

27. Dill to Montgomery-Massingberd, September 25, November 18, 1939, LH. MM. 10/14.

28. Montgomery-Massingberd to Lincolnshire branches of the British Legion, June 15, 1940, LH. MM. 10/10.

29. LH. MM. 10/6.

30. H. Guderian, *Panzer Leader* (New York, 1972), 17–18.

31. B. Condell and D. T. Zabecki, eds., *On the German Art of War: Truppenführung* (Boulder, CO, 2001).

32. T. M. Holmes, "Classical Blitzkrieg: The Untimely Modernity of Schlieffen's Cannae Programme," *JMH* 67 (2003): 745–71.

33. V. Triandaffilov, *The Nature of the Operations of Modern Armies* (1929; repr. Abingdon, 1994).

34. G. F. Hofmann, "Doctrine, Tank Technology, and Execution: I.A. Khalepskii and the Red Army's Fulfilment of Deep Offensive Operations, "*Journal of Slavic Military Studies 9* (1996): 283–334.

35. S. Bialer, *Stalin and His Generals: Soviet Military Memoirs of World War II* (New York, 1969).

36. R. W. Harrison, *Architect of Soviet Victory in World War II: The Life and Theories of G.S. Isserson* (Jefferson, NC, 2010).

37. S. W. Stoecker, *Forging Stalin's Army: Marshal Tukhachevsky and the Politics of Military Innovation* (Boulder, CO, 1998).

38. A. Hill, *The Red Army and the Second World War* (New York, 2017), 562.

39. D. M. Glantz, *Stumbling Colossus: The Red Army on the Eve of World War* (Lawrence, KS, 1998).

40. M. Glantz, "An Officer and a Diplomat? The Ambiguous Position of Philip R. Faymonville and United States–Soviet Relations, 1941–1943," *JMH* 72 (2008): 141–77.

41. Hill, *The Red Army*, 88.

42. A. D. Cox, *The Anatomy of a Small War: The Soviet-Japanese Struggle for Changkufeng/Khasan, 1938* (Westport, CT, 1977).

43. Hill, *The Red Army*, 108, 563.

44. E. J. Drea, *Nomonhan: Japanese-Soviet Tactical Combat, 1939* (Fort Leavenworth, KS, 1981); A. D. Cox, *Nomonhan: Japan against Russia 1939* (Stanford, CA, 1985).

45. M. R. Habeck, *Storm of Steel: The Development of Armor Doctrine in Germany and the Soviet Union, 1919–1939* (Ithaca, NY, 2003), 113–15.

46. R. R. Reese, "Lessons of the Winter War: A Study in the Military Effectiveness of the Red Army, 1939–1940," *JMH* 72 (2008): 830.

47. L. A. Humphreys, *The Way of the Heavenly Sword: The Japanese Army in the 1920s* (Stanford, CA, 1995).

48. W. O. Odom, *After the Trenches: The Transformation of U.S. Army Doctrine, 1918–1939* (College Station, TX, 1999); K. Finlayson, *An Uncertain Triumph: The Evolution of U.S. Army Infantry Doctrine, 1919–1941* (Westport, CT, 2001).

49. R. W. Stewart, "The 'Red Bull' Division: The Training and Initial Engagements of the 34th Infantry Division, 1941–43," *Army History* 25 (winter 1993): 3.

50. J. R. Lankford, "Jacob L. Devers and the American Thunderbolt," *On Point* 16, no. 3 (winter 2011): 34–41.

51. F. Cappellano and P. P. Battistelli, *Italian Light Tanks, 1919–45* (Oxford, 2014).

52. J. J. T. Sweet, *Iron Arm: The Mechanisation of Mussolini's Army, 1920–1940* (Westport, CT, 1980); M. Knox, *Hitler's Italian Allies: Royal Armed Forces, Fascist Regime, and the War of 1940–1943* (Cambridge, UK, 2000).

53. P. D. Strachura, "The Battle of Warsaw, August 1920, and the Development of the Second Polish Republic," in *Poland Between the Wars, 1918–1939*, ed. P. D. Stachura (Basingstoke, UK, 1998), 54–55.

54. A. Suchcitz, "Poland's Defence Preparations in 1939," in *Poland Between the Wars, 1918–1939*, ed. P. D. Stachura (Basingstoke, UK, 1998), 109–10.

55. J. Czarnecki, "The Rebirth and Progress of the Polish Military During the Interwar Years," *JMH* 83 (2019): 755.

56. NA. WO. 33/1512, p. 3.

57. D. Edgerton, *Britain's War Machine: Weapons, Resources and Experts in the Second World War* (London, 2011), 62–64.

58. *HC*, July 1, 1942, vol. 381, col. 251.

59. General Staff, "The Future Reorganisation of the British Army," September 9, 1935, NA. WO. 32/4612.

60. LH. Adam 2/3, pp. 2–3.

61. J. F. Daniel, *21st Century Patton: Strategic Insights for the Modern Era* (Annapolis, MD, 2016).

62. J. Halpin Connolly, "War in a Mechanistic Civilisation," *Infantry Journal*, July-August 1939, 306–13.

63. M. Calhoun, *General Lesley J. McNair: Unsung Architect of the U.S. Army* (Lexington, KS, 2015).

64. Habeck, *Storm of Steel*; M. R. Matheny, *Carrying the War to the Enemy: American Operational Art to 1945* (Norman, OK, 2011).

65. W. J. Fanning, "The Origin of the Term 'Blitzkrieg': Another View," *JMH* 61 (1997): 283–302.

FOUR

WORLD WAR II: THE AXIS ADVANCES, 1939–41

MOST OF THE HISTORY OF THE TANK FOCUSES ON WORLD WAR II (1939–45). This is also true for the potent public histories represented by film, monuments, museums, and, very differently, scale models. The case for the war's demonstration of the value of the tank has centered throughout on the German blitzkrieg successes of 1939–41. However, these successes are apt to be too prominent in the discussion of the war and, moreover, are frequently misrepresented in public history. Each contributes to problems with the overall understanding of tank warfare and capability.

To take the discussion first, tanks certainly played a very diverse role in the war, much more so than in World War I. The tanks of World War II, of course, were scarcely the same weapons as their predecessors of 1916–18. This was just as well as they were expected to engage in a very different war characterized by greater mobility, both tactically and operationally. Moreover, unlike in World War I, tanks were also used across the range of land operations, from the deserts of North Africa to the islands of the Pacific, as well as in amphibious assaults. In particular, there was a large-scale use of tanks in conflict between Germany and the Soviet Union on the Eastern Front from 1941 to 1945 whereas, in World War I, tank use had essentially focused on the Western Front and excluded the Eastern Front.

Planning and policy helped frame key responses to the new challenges requiring and facing tanks during World War II, but there also was a considerable degree of improvisation, as with the German need on the Eastern Front to adapt to poor roads and the dust that hit tank engines and clogged filters.[1] Sand also had a serious impact on the operations of tanks in North Africa and was still significant in the two wars in the Persian Gulf (in 1991 and 2003).

During World War II, as before and after, there were difficult trade-offs in tank warfare among speed, armor, armament, and durability, as well as in design and procurement between these factors and ease of production. Moreover, these trade-offs occurred in a context made more dynamic and difficult by the need to shape change effectively and, in particular, respond to the action-reaction cycle posed by developments, actual and potential, in opponents' weaponry, including tanks and other antitank weapons.

There was also the need to plan for the environments, military and physical, that would be faced. This need related, for example, to the balance between what the British presented as "cruiser" and "infantry-support" tasks. Linked to that balance was the question of how far the same tank could do both or whether separate tanks were required and the consequences of particular tank types for doctrine and vice versa. The role of German armor and antitank guns made these questions even more unsettled, but also urgent, for Germany's opponents.

In this and other respects, tanks drew together, or at least focused, a number of technologies, capabilities, doctrines, and tasks. The tank certainly became more a part of an integrated system in World War II than in World War I, when it had been used for a shorter period, by fewer powers, in far smaller numbers. Armor and firepower became crucial to success in battle and to dealing with both opposing tanks and artillery/infantry defenses. In contrast, questions of reliability, range, refueling, and mechanical support were all important to breakthrough operations. Engineering was also significant. Moreover, the ability to negotiate difficult terrain depended on the suspension system of tanks, as well as on the type of tracks.

These factors, which became readily apparent under the strain of operations, were, as with air power, more disruptive and disturbing because of a combination of initial uncertainty and the unrealistic high expectations of effectiveness. These expectations were further excited by the rapidity of German success in 1939 and, even more, 1940. In particular, much intellectual and emotional effort was put into explaining this success in terms of the use of armor. US major Paul Raborg's account of sixty-ton German tanks equipped with flamethrowers and communicating by radio directly with Stuka dive-bombers was inaccurate for 1940.[2] The heaviest German tank, in fact, weighed nineteen tons; there were no flamethrower tanks and, as yet, no such communications. Nevertheless, his *Mechanized Might: The Story of Mechanized Warfare* (1942) proved popular in the United States and was a call to armor as well as arms for the Americans. In practice, the Germans in 1940 had fewer heavy battle tanks suited to fight other tanks than the Allies did. However, such reports heightened expectations.

THE GERMANS ATTACK POLAND, 1939

The explanation of German success in 1939–41 as due to the use of armor certainly represented a limited and flawed interpretation. Most notably, the Germans were not really preparing for blitzkrieg, as it was enacted only in 1940; instead, they learned what could be achieved from their successful war of maneuver in Poland in September 1939. The Germans also were helped in that war by a range of other factors, including the greater vulnerability of Poland following the German takeover of Czechoslovakia to its south in 1938–39; the Polish deployment, notably defending the full extent of their lengthy borders and lacking defense in depth; complete German air superiority; and eventual Soviet intervention on the German side, which further denied the Poles defense in depth.[3]

The nature of German armored practice was significant. Attacking Poland on September 1, 1939, German armored forces broke through, and isolated and enveloped the dispersed Polish military formations. In order to signal their determination not to match the fate of the Czech Republic in 1938, which had lost frontier regions to external intimidation, the Poles had defended the full extent of their borders, rather than concentrating in the heart of Poland to conserve reserves, provide defense in depth, and respond to German thrusts. Their deployment, however, greatly facilitated the German operational method of penetration and encirclement. Moreover, the Germans were helped by taking the initiative and by the flat terrain of most of Poland, as well as by the dryness of the soil and roads following the summer. It proved good tank weather. Hitler had explained in August 1939 to Count Ciano, the Italian foreign minister, that Germany could not long delay as otherwise rain would make the ground unsuitable for operations. In addition, the Polish army was weak in tanks, in both quantity and quality, as well as in antitank guns and training.

In contrast, the German army had five panzer divisions, each with about three hundred tanks, as well as four light divisions that were destined to be panzer divisions, although they had far fewer tanks. Most of the panzer and light divisions were in Army Group South in Silesia. It was entrusted with taking Warsaw. In contrast, Army Group North had only one panzer division. It cut off the Polish Corridor, but it was in the south that the key early breakthroughs were made. The location of the panzer divisions had become an important indication of operational planning and prioritization, and this remained the case subsequently in the Cold War, the Arab-Israeli and India-Pakistan wars, and the wars in the Persian Gulf.

The Germans put the Poles at a tremendous disadvantage by forcing them into a very one-sided war of maneuver, and Polish positions were successively encircled. Inner and outer pincers created by German armored columns closed, isolating Polish armies and making it difficult for them to maintain supplies or launch counterattacks. Confidence in the latter enabled the German armor to advance ahead of the marching infantry and with exposed flanks. This, however, was a risky technique, especially when the Poles were able to counteract the disorganization and fear that came from German attack. The Germans also faced problems with supplies, especially that of fuel, for which the panzer divisions had substantial requirements. Nevertheless, the Germans advanced too fast for the Poles to organize effective resistance and were able to cope with the problems that occurred and regain momentum. Thus, a temporarily successful Polish counterattack on the Bzura River launched on September 9 was quashed by German tank reinforcements and air and artillery superiority.

Yet, as an important indication of the limitations of armor, a German tank advance into Warsaw on September 9 was stopped due to street fighting by Polish antitank guns and artillery. In the end, Warsaw was not captured by land assault. In contrast, under heavy artillery and air attack, and short of food and ammunition, its garrison surrendered on September 27. The check at Warsaw on September 9 contributed to the heavy German losses of about seven hundred tanks in the campaign, although part was through wear and tear, which was exacerbated by poor maintenance. In the event, about 180 were eventually repaired.[4] These losses led a number of German generals to oppose follow-up attacks on France that year.

During the supporting 1939 Soviet invasion of Poland launched on September 17, the Fifteenth Tank Corps, which had about 460 BT-7 light tanks, was resupplied with fuel by parachute. When they attacked Grodno on September 20, however, the Soviet forces were weakened by a lack of experience in urban warfare and insufficient infantry support. The defenders had no antitank guns but used Molotov cocktails. The initial Soviet attacks were repelled, with the loss of nineteen tanks, but the destructiveness of Soviet artillery led the Poles to abandon Grodno on September 22. The commander of the Soviet corps, Mikhail Petrov, a graduate of the armored commanders' refresher courses, had served as a tank battalion commander in Spain in 1936–37, moving on to command the Fifth Mechanized Corps in 1937. Formed in 1934, that corps was converted into the Fifteenth Tank Corps in 1938. The 1939 campaign revealed deficiencies in the Soviet armor.[5]

DEVELOPING BLITZKRIEG

The ad hoc and opportunistic nature of blitzkrieg helps put supposed German operational brilliance in its proper context. Moreover, much of the German army in 1939 was heavily reliant on railways and draft animals for transport, which was still true in 1945. In practice, moving toward blitzkrieg was linked to active retraining after the Poland campaign; the Germans, who were preparing to attack, made much more profitable use than their opponents of the "Phony War," or lull on the Western Front, in the very cold winter of 1939–40.

Furthermore, the changing politics of command preference within the German army proved significant for the development of blitzkrieg, as Hitler felt emboldened to advance particular generals. Thus, in practice, the Germans were developing an operational level doctrine in an ad hoc fashion. Alongside a seriously misplaced self-confidence, this ad hoc character helped set them up for greater problems when they invaded the Soviet Union in 1941 and faced sustained opposition in depth.

In contrast, the Anglo-French forces failed to respond to German success in Poland with an appropriate training regime. The French took a deliberative approach in the planned operations of their new armored divisions. Mobility was not to the fore. Instead, they emphasized sealing the advance of opponents. De Gaulle complained about this situation, not least in his pamphlet *L'avènement de la force mécanique* (*The Advent of Mechanised Forces*), published in January 1940,[6] although his focus was operational and doctrinal, rather than based on a grasp of strategic issues.

THE CONQUEST OF FRANCE

The rapid defeat of France and its allies in 1940, a marked contrast to the situation in 1914, reflected German military strengths at the tactical and operational levels—strengths that helped overcome the superior numbers of well-equipped opponents.[7] The Germans launched their offensive on the Netherlands, Belgium, and France on May 10; advanced through the wooded and hilly region of the Ardennes in southern Belgium and into France; pushed across the Meuse River on May 13 with Guderian's Nineteenth Panzer Corps; reached the English Channel near Abbeville on May 21, cutting off large British and French forces to the north; took the surrender of the Dutch on May 14 and of Belgium on May 27; entered Paris on June 14; and dictated terms to the French on June 22. For fewer than twenty thousand of their own troops killed (and that in a campaign in which their sole ally, Italy, joined late, on June 10, and did not play an effective role), Germany had transformed the situation in Western Europe. Cutting off the British and French in Operation Sichelschnitt (Sickle Cut) was suggested by General Gerd von Rundstedt, commander of Army Group A; his chief of staff, Eric von Manstein, had pressed for this advance, rather than attacking France via Belgium and its rivers as in 1914.

In this offensive, German panzer divisions again proved operationally effective as formations, maximizing the weapon characteristics of tanks. The Germans were able to make the offensive work in both operational and tactical terms, amply displaying the tactical potential of an offensive spearheaded by armored forces. Having taken the risk of advancing through the hilly Ardennes, with too many tanks advancing on too few roads, before fighting their way across the Meuse and its few pinch points, the Germans entered more open terrain in France where tanks could move across country, limiting the need to tie forward units to roads.[8]

The French had more tanks than the Germans; and these French tanks were, for the most part, more heavily gunned; and had more effective protection. German tanks were vulnerable to both tank fire and antitank guns. However, French tanks were also somewhat slower, and many had to turn in order to fire. Tanks with one-man turrets left the commander to be the gunner and the communicator, which lessened their effectiveness.[9] This was an issue for the Fourth Armored Division under de Gaulle when it attacked at Montcornet on May 17. Their lack of radios also created problems for French tanks: communication was by signal flag, which made unit coordination harder. This indeed happened when de Gaulle's tanks attacked at Abbeville on May 28 and 29. Tank commanders had to stick their heads and shoulders out of the tank hatch, and look away from the oncoming danger, to try to find their superior officer and read the signal flags. This procedure was very hazardous.

Aside from a poor overall strategy for the army as a whole, the French failed to develop an effective doctrine for their armor. They persisted in seeing tanks, like artillery, as a support for infantry. Most French tanks, accordingly, were split up into small groups for use as mobile artillery, rather than employed as armored divisions for their value. Tactics, and operational control and coordination, were more important for German mobility and success in 1940 than the actual technological capabilities of the tanks.[10] The lack of adequate signals equipment and training made it difficult for the French to respond to developments. Furthermore, French generals had only a limited understanding of mechanized warfare and certainly had not conducted any worthwhile training for it. Due to poor doctrine for armor operations, their tanks did not attack in a coordinated strike.[11]

When German and French tank forces first clashed—in Belgium on May 13—the Germans were successful thanks to their offensive tactics. In the Montcornet attack on May 17, the French ran out of fuel, suffered from a lack of supporting infantry, and were thwarted by German antitank guns, dive-bombers, and reinforcements: twenty-three French tanks were destroyed. Another attack by de Gaulle's unit, on May 19, again suffered from a lack of fuel and supporting infantry, as well as from the German air attack. German antitank guns were effective then and later in the campaign. The fuel problem reflected the frequent need for refueling of the French heavy tanks, which had small fuel tanks. Fuel supply was a varied problem during the war that had tactical, operational, and strategic dimensions.

Allied tanks could be effective when handled well, as by the British in their counterattack near Arras on May 21. The counterattack by the Matilda I and II tanks had some initial success, and the armor of the Matilda II was effective against the German 37 mm antitank guns. A number of German infantry units broke under the attack, and it took Erwin Rommel, showing great leadership, to gather his artillery, including 88 mm antiaircraft guns, into a gun line to stop the British attack. The Germans anticipated using their 88 mm guns in a dual role, and they were supplied with antitank ammunition as well as their antiaircraft rounds. The British counterattack was eventually stopped, in part due to a lack of coordination and to the German artillery screen, but it led to concern on the part of German commanders.[12]

In the French counterattack by the Twenty-First Corps on Guderian's bridgehead over the River Meuse, the French tanks fought hard at the village of Stonne south of Sedan. Nevertheless, on the whole, the Germans controlled the pace of the armored conflict, not least because, aside from forcing luck to their side in part through improvisation, their tank doctrine was more successful.

Allied defensive successes also indicated the significance of artillery. At Gembloux in Belgium on May 14–15, "the French artillery-infantry team imposed itself handily on the German tank-plane team, despite the fact that the defense was much more improvised on open terrain than French doctrine intended." The "weaknesses of the 'Blitzkrieg' tactical system" were demonstrated in the face of French artillery, but "the German command refused to recognize the lesson of the limitations of mechanical attack against a conventional defense."[13] This failure was also seen by most subsequent commentators. More generally, however, neither the British nor French proved effective at defensive maneuver, for which they had not been trained, while reliance on artillery to stop a tank campaign had been found wanting in the speed and surprise of the German advance.

Subsequently, in Fall Rot (Operation Case Red), launched on June 5, the Germans pressed south into France. The French army by this stage was heavily outnumbered, especially in armor: much of its equipment, including over half the tanks, had already been lost. Despite a French armored counterattack on

June 10, the Germans crossed the River Marne, where they had been stopped in 1914. More generally, after an initial struggle, French resistance rapidly collapsed, and the swiftly advancing Germans, fanning out on a number of axes, entered Dijon on June 16, Brest on June 19, and Lyons and Vichy on June 20.

The blitzkrieg operations appear as a consequence of the new availability of tanks and aircraft in interpretations predicated on technology and novelty. Whereas, in 1914, a German advance that unfolded at walking pace and on exterior lines was thwarted by a French redeployment by rail (and motor vehicle) on interior lines, in 1940 the equations proved different. Yet the effectiveness of the blitzkrieg was exaggerated, then and subsequently,[14] by commentators under the spell cast by the sheer shock and drama of the German offensives, and they have overrated the impact of military methods that, in practice, represented more of an improvisation than the fruition of a coherent doctrine. Blitzkrieg never existed as a unified concept, and it is possibly better to employ phrases such as "the effective use of air and mechanized forces."

The potential, let alone reality, of weaponry and logistics based on the internal combustion engine was less fully grasped than talk of blitzkrieg might suggest, not least because much of the German army was unmechanized and, indeed, walked into battle. In particular, despite an emphasis in propaganda on *panzergrenadiers*, there was a shortage of motorized infantry. *Panzergrenadiers*, in many ways the descendants of the *Sturmtroopers* of World War I, were specialists, and the majority of infantry was conventional. More generally, alongside the effective tactical and operational use of the armored tip of the army, the contribution and quality of the unmotorized German infantry and artillery were significant. As a consequence, so were the constraints under which they operated.[15]

There was a parallel in the air. Blitzkrieg relied not only on tanks but also on Ju-88 Stuka dive-bombers, and as long as no fighters opposed them, they achieved much, a point relevant for tanks versus antitank guns. But Stukas were effectively sitting ducks for fighters; hence their decline after the fall of France and the Battle of Britain in 1940, although they still played roles in North Africa, Yugoslavia, Greece, and the Soviet Union. Following the battle of Kursk in 1943, the Stuka was used much less but was not completely withdrawn as there was no substitute. By 1944, however, its role had been largely superseded by ground-attack variants of the Focke Wulf 190. The same can be said of the dive-bombers operated by other belligerents: they were highly effective as long as there was no hostile fighter intervention. The Soviets used the Pe-2 as a dive-bomber but concentrated more on ground attack with the Il-2. Analogies between land and air conflicts have to be handled with care, but they can, nevertheless, prove instructive.

Moreover, the success of the risky German strategy and operational plan in 1940 owed much to the serious deficiencies of French strategy and planning, particularly the deployment of mechanized reserves on the advancing left flank so they were not available in a reserve capacity and, linked to this deployment, the absence of French defense in depth. Helped by this, the German tank units were able to operate with open flanks and, in general, unconstrained by the need to wait for support. The experience of the Polish campaign was also significant for the Germans, who would probably have been less successful had they attacked the French in 1938. In 1940, as with the Allies in 1918 (but not, earlier in 1918, the Germans), the attacking side won. The ability to take the initiative was a key point, as was the opponents' response.

In 1918, the Allies had responded more effectively to German attacks than they did in 1940. German mobility was an important factor in 1940, not least the triumph of an operational war of movement over position warfare, but it was not the only factor. Indeed, French strategic and operational inadequacies, rather than deficiencies in weaponry, ensured that interwar German efforts at innovation, which had aimed at incremental improvement, produced, instead, a "striking and temporarily asymmetrical operational revolution."[16] The French were outmaneuvered in part because their attempt to take the initiative in Belgium contributed to a disastrous position.

There was also the greater strategic context set by the German-Soviet system, created in August 1939. This system allowed Germany to fight a one-front war in 1940 and again helped when Germany attacked in the Balkans in April 1941. It collapsed that June when the Germans attacked the Soviet Union.

At the same time, strategic culture was a key element. Prussia, and then Germany, had been trying to keep their wars short since the days of Frederick, the Great Elector (r. 1640–88), and Frederick the Great (r. 1740–86) in part because they believed, rightly or wrongly, that a short war was the only kind they could win due to respective resources. This tradition was carried on into the nineteenth century, and Moltke the Elder, the chief of staff in the German wars of unification in 1864–71, proved the short-war commander par excellence. Nevertheless, the attempt to achieve a repeat in 1914 came to naught. In 1939–41, there was an attempt to return to this earlier tradition of strategy and operations.[17] However improvised the campaign planning, the Germans had a doctrine that called for the strongest and most mobile force of the army, now the armor, to be used where the enemy was weakest in order to encircle and destroy them in a *kesselschlacht*, or encirclement battle. The "Sickle Cut" of 1940 was based on this doctrine, as were most of the opening battles in the invasion of the Soviet Union in 1941. This doctrine made use of the mobility of the tank and so made more effective use of the capabilities of the weapon than French doctrine, which employed it for infantry support.

In practice, however, the presence of armor did not change the fundamental strategic situation. Repeatedly, both in 1914–18 and 1941–45, German tactical skill and operational proficiency did not translate into strategic success. This owed much to the limited political grasp the Germans showed and its serious impact on their strategy. Moreover, the key element in weaponry, both technology and doctrine, that advances, in turn, were matched and/or countered, with a closure of the capability gap, was to be repeated.

BRITAIN VERSUS ITALY, 1940–41

The possibilities for armor operations increased from June 1940 as Italy entered the war on the side of Germany. This created new zones of conflict centered on the Italian colonies in Albania, East Africa, and Libya and on neighboring targets: Greece and the British colonies of Kenya, Sudan (modern Sudan and South Sudan), British Somaliland (northern modern Somalia), and Egypt. The Italians invaded Egypt from Libya with a large but slow-moving force only to be successfully counterattacked in December 1940, after which the British went on to conquer Cyrenaica (eastern Libya). Winston Churchill's decision to send tanks, an important part of Britain's strategic reserve, to Egypt, in the face of military warnings about the risk of an invasion of Britain by German forces, including panzer divisions, was significant to the success of the fast-moving British offensive. At Sidi Barrani on December 9–11, 1940, a far larger Italian army was defeated in large part because the British took the initiative and deployed the Matilda tanks that had been sent. The Italians had no reliable defense against them. These tanks were heavily armored, and although they only had a 2-pounder main armament, this high-velocity weapon was effective against Italian armor. However, it did not have an ability to fire high-explosive rounds. Subsequently advancing westward, the British used the Matildas to break into Italian defended positions, notably at Bardia on January 3, 1941, and Tobruk on January 20–21. At Beda Fomm on February 6, 1941, British tanks inflicted heavy casualties on a far larger Italian armor column, with the British employing hull-down firing positions against the Italian medium tanks.

In 1941, the British invaded Italian East Africa, showing an appreciation of the strategic imperative of securing the region in order to maintain the Indian Ocean sea lines of communication. The Italians there had 141 armored vehicles but only 63 tanks. The Italians had already used tanks in their conquest of British Somaliland in August 1940, although their tanks suffered from the mountainous terrain and rocky cover, as did the British. The Italians also lost tanks to British antitank rifles, which were effective against light tanks.

The British invasion of Italian East Africa required seizing and using the initiative against larger forces. Italian Somaliland was conquered in February by troops advancing from Kenya, with the Italians proving psychologically, as well as operationally, immobile. Their units were instructed to focus on static defense and lacked the quantity of vehicles to do much else. Indeed, Italian vehicles were cannibalized to provide spare parts for others.

The British showed the ability of boldly advancing forces to disorientate and defeat a larger static opposition to be the key to success. This element proved more significant than the presence of tanks, although the Italians suffered from a lack of good equipment, in part due to the limitations of their industrial base. For example, the Italian M13/40 tank, which had entered service in 1940, was slow (maximum speed nineteen miles per hour), its 47 mm gun was inadequate, and its 40 mm armor was thin. There were also no large-caliber Italian antitank guns. Effective doctrine, well implemented by able commanders and impressive troops, brought Britain victory and could do so with few casualties for the attacker. This depended, however, on a capability gap: opponents had to fight less well and, crucially, lack a well-deployed and capably directed mobile reserve.

In Eritrea in 1941, the Italians put up a firmer defense in the difficult terrain near Keren. The British successfully used tanks in the valley bottoms, but, in the mountains, progress was slower and largely dependent on artillery.[18] The battle for Keren proved to be tough and hard-fought, but, after the town had been taken, a small number of British tanks led a breakthrough to the Red Sea ports of Asmara and Massawa. The retreating Italians tried to stop the mobile columns with roadblocks backed up with artillery, and the tanks proved useful in forcing through these. After the ports had been liberated, President Roosevelt declared the Red Sea no longer a war zone, and this allowed US shipping to use it, which improved the resupply position for the British forces in the Middle East.

GERMANY INTO THE BALKANS, 1941

German intervention in North Africa and the Balkans, meanwhile, had transformed the situation in the Mediterranean. The key sphere was the Balkans, where, against Yugoslavia from April 9, 1941, German tank advances proved particularly effective in the general absence of antitank guns. Thus, armored forces captured Zagreb on April 10 and crossed the Drava River en route for Belgrade. The Fortieth German Panzer Corps captured Skopje and Bitolj, cutting Yugoslavia off from Greece. The rapidly moving German forces overthrew resistance.

The campaign was also a success for the Italian armor. The armored division Littorio advanced southward in Dalmatia from Trieste to Zara. On Albania's northern frontier, the Centauro tank division, which had one tank regiment and, due to losses when fighting the Greeks, only fifty light tanks and fifteen medium M13/40s, was able to resist attacks from larger Yugoslav forces, albeit, when it successfully switched over to the attack, losing tanks to Yugoslav antitank guns.

German armor also proved effective in the invasion of Greece launched on April 9, which the Fortieth Panzer Corps joined after overrunning Macedonia. The invasion was typical of German successes in 1939–41 and in the analysis of them. It is possible to put an emphasis on the tempo of advance, especially the use of airborne troops, ground-support aircraft, and tanks, which were supplemented by armored assault guns, and to note the British failure to understand the capabilities of armor, especially on difficult terrain.[19] Yet poor weather and roads did affect the impact of German aircraft and tanks. Moreover, in practice, the weakness of the Greek army, particularly in command, equipment, and logistics; the lack of coordinated Anglo-Greek command; and the readiness of the hesitant commanders of the British forces to withdraw in the face of fear of being outflanked were all significant.[20]

GERMANY INTO NORTH AFRICA

German forces sent to Libya in response to Italy's defeat proved better than the British at mobile warfare and rapidly drove the British back into Egypt in early April. Erwin Rommel, a talented commander who was a favorite of Hitler's, was a bold and effective commander of the German forces, while British tank-infantry-artillery cooperation was inadequate, and, in tank-on-tank combat, the outgunned British tanks were poor.[21] Using the British technique, as applied against the Italians, of outflanking their less mobile opponent with their tank units through the desert, the Germans proved more successful in combined arms capability and tactics and benefited from the intelligence gained by radio intercepts. Moreover, air support for the British also was not well organized in this period of the war. German successes challenged Allied morale, which helped focus the wider significance of tank combat in

North Africa. In the *Sunday Pictorial*, a British newspaper, of April 27, 1941, Fuller commented on the Germans driving back the British forces in North Africa: "Like a ladder in a girl's stocking, our splendid desert campaign is running backwards up our strategical leg from its ankle to its knee." The British forces in North Africa had been seriously depleted by the requirement to send troops to Greece and Syria.

British weaknesses made Rommel's task a lot easier without detracting from his bold and imaginative tactical use of his armor. Several logistical innovations made the use of German tanks more effective. They employed tank transporters to take their vehicles to the battle area, which made their maintenance a lot easier, and they also had a highly effective tank recovery and repair organization that ensured many tanks that had been disabled were quickly returned to frontline service. The British lagged behind in both of these areas, and the majority of British tanks were notoriously unreliable, which compounded the situation.

Tobruk, a Libyan port, was besieged by the Germans from April 10, 1941. In June, Robert Menzies, the Australian prime minister, wrote to Thomas Blamey, the commander of the Australian forces in the Middle East: "A disaster at Tobruk coming on top of those in Greece and Crete might have far reaching effects on public opinion in Australia and a reverse in Egypt itself would, I think, produce incalculable difficulties in Australia."[22] The British lacked an effective antitank gun, while the Crusader tank, which entered service in 1941, was mechanically poor. British tanks were outgunned. The Select Committee on National Expenditure uncovered serious problems in tank production. Operation Battleaxe, launched on June 15 in order to relieve Tobruk, was stopped by German 88 mm guns—antiaircraft guns used against tanks to deadly effect. However, the siege of Tobruk was lifted after Operation Crusader was launched on November 18. Two days later, Churchill claimed in the House of Commons: "This offensive has been long and elaborately prepared, and we have waited for nearly five months in order that our Army shall be well equipped with all these weapons which have made their mark in this new war. . . . This is the first time we have met the Germans at least equally well-armed and equipped."[23] British armor took heavy losses, notably at the Sidi Rezegh ridge, but also inflicted serious ones, and Rommel withdrew from December 8.

In response to German successes, British doctrine had changed. General Claude Auchinleck, Wavell's successor and the perceptive commander in chief in the Middle East in 1941–42, drew up instructions in October 1941 in which he stressed the value of engaging the Germans in maneuver warfare and also offered "general principles governing all the strategy of the defense" that reflected the challenge posed by the greater mobility of contemporary warfare:

> All main communications, road or rail, will be denied to the enemy by a series of defensive areas sited astride of them, and arranged in depth. These defensive areas will be made tank proof, and capable of all round defence, and stocked so as to make them self-supporting for at least 60 days . . . mobile reserves operating between the defensive areas. It is essential that all idea of maintaining a linear defence in the face of superior enemy armoured forces be abandoned. Penetration between the defensive areas . . . must be expected and accepted . . . so long as these areas hold firm and thus deny to the enemy the use of the main arteries of communication, he can not continue for long to press forward with large forces.
>
> The garrison of each defended areas . . . should, if possible, include infantry tanks for counter attacking purposes, but the bulk of such armoured and motorised forces . . . will be held . . . to bring the enemy to battle on ground of our choosing and to make the fullest possible use of the defensive areas as pivots of manoeuvre.[24]

OPERATION BARBAROSSA

The largest tank conflict up to then was launched on June 22, 1941, when German and Romanian forces (Finnish, Hungarian, and Italian forces joined in subsequently), including 3,350 tanks, invaded the Soviet Union, the biggest target yet for a mechanized assault. The German plan reflected bold and untested assumptions about mobility, but necessarily so. The attack was to be concentrated between the Pripet Marshes and the Baltic, with much of the armor (two of the four Panzer Groups) under Army Group Centre, whose commander was Field Marshal von Bock. This unit was ordered to destroy opposing Soviet forces and then move from Smolensk to help Army Group North under Field Marshal von Leeb capture Leningrad (now St. Petersburg). This success was seen as a prelude to the advance on Moscow, which reflected Hitler's priorities, rather than military advice, which had pressed for a concentration on Moscow. Meanwhile, Army Group South, under Field Marshal von Rundstedt, was to capture Kiev and then encircle Soviet forces in Ukraine, preventing these forces from falling back to defend the interior. In the next phase, forces from Leningrad and Smolensk were to drive on Moscow while Army Group South advanced to Rostov in order to open the way to the Caucasus, both to seize the oilfields there and to threaten an advance into the Middle East.

The German plan reflected an overbold prospectus that drew heavily on assumptions about German armored capability and likely Soviet responses.

The Germans attempted to seize all objectives simultaneously, a source of potential weakness that arose from the failure both to settle the core target of the operation and to devise a time sequence of even limited plausibility. It was also assumed that the defeat of the Soviet forces near the frontier would lead to the Soviet collapse. On July 31, 1940, Hitler indicated to senior commanders that he was determined to shatter the Soviet Union with one blow.

Soviet forces were numerous, including 10,400 tanks (albeit of very mixed quality) in the western Soviet Union, but poorly prepared and deployed for the German attack. The extent to which the Germans would be able to advance had been underestimated. Stalin's instructions that units hold their positions and not retreat, and his encouragement of counterattacks, ensured that the Soviets proved vulnerable to German breakthrough and encirclement tactics, losing heavily as a result, including many tanks.

Aside from his complete and direct responsibility for the unprepared condition of the Soviet military at the outset of the war and, particularly, for the dire state of the command structure, Stalin had not appreciated that the Soviet army would suffer from blitzkrieg, and certainly not the degree to which it would suffer. The Winter War with Finland in 1939–40 had revealed Soviet deficiencies, but these were only on the attack.[25] A full-scale assault by Germany was far more serious. Soviet preparations, strategy, and doctrine were all inadequate. For example, the Soviet Union had relatively few mines in store in 1941 because an interest in mines was seen as a defeatist focus on the defense.

The Germans were dazzled by the success of the frontier battles, their deep advances into the Soviet Union, and the large number of prisoners; and these victories spurred Nazi euphoria and planning, including that of the Holocaust. The speed of the German advance also impressed foreign observers. These successes in part drew on German capabilities and in part arose from Soviet deficiencies. The Germans were more successful than the Soviets at the tactical level in linking firepower and mobility while, operationally, they outmaneuvered Soviet defenders and were able to impose their tempo on the flow of conflict.

The Soviets suffered from a general lack of relevant command and fighting experience, certainly in comparison with the Germans; the absence of supply and maintenance systems to match the impressive quantity of weapons they had, including poor logistics and inadequate transport; and a general staff that did not match that of the Germans. Thus, the Soviets did not understand, as well as the Germans, the operational implications of mechanized warfare. In the first part of *The New Forms of Combat* (1940), G. S. Isserson analyzed the German invasion of Poland, underlining the potential that mechanization gave the offensive, but he was affected by the wide-ranging purges and was arrested in June 1941.

Although mechanized corps had been established, there had been no time to implement and assess these changes before the Germans attacked. Decreeing improvement—for example, the better all-arms coordination called for in Order No. 120 issued in May 1940—was not the same as implementing it. Aside from the degree to which their armor was still being reorganized, the Soviets were also adjusting to the introduction of new tank models. Moreover, their mechanized corps were still underequipped. Thus, the Ninth Mechanized Corps had only 30 percent of its allocated fighting vehicles and a maximum of 50 percent of its supposed manpower.[26]

Yet, recovering rapidly from initial confusion, many of the Soviets, as noted by the head of the British Military Mission in Moscow, fought hard and effectively from the outset, as in the defense of Brest-Litovsk, consistently inflicting greater losses than the Germans had anticipated. This was especially true of the Southwestern Front, which was strong in armor. Most Soviet tanks were in this area, and, despite confusion and frequent German air attacks, attempts were made from the outset to launch counterattacks. These were handicapped by poor doctrine and a sense of chaos, but a series of attacks proved difficult for the Germans and, though failing, indicated that the Soviet forces would not be easily overcome.[27]

In addition, the subsequent battle of Smolensk from July 8 to July 31 (Soviet dating is different) saw the Western Front—in its counterattacks, notably from July 21 to 30—inflict heavy casualties on the German Army Group Centre, including the destruction of 214 tanks. Indeed, these casualties were such that, by mid-August, much of the German army was in grave difficulty, compromising chances of victory. The experience of the assault in Western Europe in May 1940 had been totally different. Although benefiting from a highly flexible command practice within panzer divisions, one that aided both combined arms tactics and adaptation to circumstances,[28] and defeating Soviet counterattacks, notably on July 6 near Lepiel thanks to the use of antitank guns, the Germans were also seriously affected by wear and tear on their tanks and other vehicles. The Germans were also faced with growing logistical problems far greater in scale than any they had faced so far.[29] Moreover, their panzer divisions were short of drivers, radio operators, and winter equipment.

While Soviet resistance could not wrest the initiative from the Germans, it affected German tactics, operations, and strategy and accentuated the consequences of a prior failure to settle grand strategic choices. The apparent effectiveness of the German armor had accentuated this problem, notably the tension among desires to seize particular areas, dissent over what these should be, and, alternatively, the intention to provoke a key battle that would wreck Soviet opposition. Hitler, on July 14, diverted the panzer divisions of Army Group Centre to affect an encirclement of Soviet forces in Ukraine, which would thus crush completely the Soviet Southwestern Front, as well as seize the important economic resources of the region. This diversion led to a major victory after the panzer pincers met on September 15, closing the Soviet pocket east of Kiev but seriously delayed the advance on Moscow.

Traditionally castigated as a diversion from the necessity to drive on Moscow, this Ukraine operation was opportunistic not only in the sense of the target but also as a response to the serious problems posed by the concentration of Soviet troops blocking the route to Moscow. Conversely, while fragmenting the effort of Army Group Centre, the Ukraine operation provided a degree of the concentration of force and effort that had been so conspicuously lacking hitherto in the operations of the three separate army groups with their different goals and diverging advances.

At the same time, the attritional factors affecting Germany were not only manpower and tanks, neither of which could be speedily replaced, but also time, notably prewinter time, and some of that was consumed by the Ukraine operation. The factor of time had moved against Germany, unlike in its earlier campaigns, because of the strength of the defensive. The latter strength was in part disguised due to Stalin's serious and repeated command errors, but, while these could help provide Germany with successes, they could not bring victory. In particular, while defense in depth was forced on the Soviet leadership, the German leadership was totally unwilling to consider a compromise peace. The depth, moreover, was enhanced by being members of an alliance able to provide assistance. On September 3, 1941, Stalin asked Churchill for a minimum monthly delivery of five hundred tanks, and, two days later, Churchill promised to provide that.[30]

A tension in German planning (an oxymoron at the strategic level) between overcoming space and defeating troops was in part linked to the very different capacity for rapid advance of armor and the unmechanized infantry. This tension became more serious because German war making, with its emphasis on surprise, speed, and overwhelming and dynamic force at the chosen point of contact, was designed for an offensive strategy that was most effective against linear defenses. This war-making proved less successful against a defense in depth that retained the capacity to use reserves and that did not weaken with further German advances. The Soviet ability to create defense in depth proved effective once the initial shock and surprise of the German attack had been

absorbed. Indeed, after the psychological shock of the initial German successes had been overcome and effective antitank weapons had reached the
battlefield, the defense could begin to cope well with the German attack.

This was a multifaceted defense in depth as it included military reorganization and rebuilding, movement eastward beyond the limit of German attack
of manufacturing plant (factories), and an eventual political resilience that
owed much to the lack of any viable prospect for a compromise peace. Initially in Leningrad, production of the KV-1 was moved east to Chelyabinsk,
which became known as Tankograd. It was there that the IS-3 was developed. The Kharkov tank factory moved to Nizhi Tagil, that from Kolomna
to Kirov, and that from Moscow to Sverdlovsk. Because some tanks were
already partially completed, production began even before the new factories
were complete.

The Germans also suffered from a lack of investment in tank production;
they certainly had nothing to match the purposeful intensity of their Soviet
counterpart. German armor was insufficient in number, and increasingly
so, not least because the front of its advance was unprecedentedly wide, and
the armor was affected by serious fuel shortages and maintenance problems,
including a shortage of spare parts and ammunition. Taking up a theme he had
advanced in 1920 in his study of tanks in World War I, Fuller had speculated, in
the *Evening Standard* of July 19, 1941, that "if tanks can be supplied by air, then
the whole organisation of the mechanised forces will have to be modified,"
but no such development was possible. Because the infantry could not keep
up with the armor, it not only was difficult to seal pockets, but also a problem
when the tanks encountered antitank guns. Fuller, indeed, had claimed, in
the *War Weekly* of November 10, 1939, that "because of the enormous numbers
of anti-tank weapons which today will be met with in attacks on narrow and
strongly fortified fronts, the tank, originally designed to storm parapets and
trenches, had ceased to be an effective siege warfare weapon."

While operations in the Soviet Union offered weak resistance, even open
flanks, Fuller's judgment was inappropriate, but that did not remain the case in
1941. Moreover, the vastness of the Soviet Union drained the invader of energy,
as had happened to the Germans in World War I. In contrast to the relatively
small size of the crucial field of operations in Poland and northern France, the
Germans were handicapped by the length of the front and the area they had
to advance across, ensuring they had fewer reserves and, therefore, were less
able to maintain the tempo of advance.

Distances were exacerbated by the primitive nature of the road network. The
overwhelming majority of the roads were unpaved. The weather was a major

issue. Even in normal times, movements in eastern Poland and the western part of the Soviet Union prior to German gains in Poland in 1939 were greatly affected prior to mid-May by widespread flooding and boggy terrain. Spring thaw brought thick, glutinous mud that clogged resupply to a halt.

The winter of 1941 was bad and lasted longer than normal. As late as the beginning of June, the River Bug was over its banks for miles. Similar conditions prevailed further north. There was heavy rain in East Prussia in late May and early June. If the invasion had been launched earlier, the prospect would have been poor. The weather of 1940 had been all too favorable to the invasion of the West, but the weather of 1941 was very different. As early as the first week of July, heavy rain affected the movements of Army Group Centre. On August 2, 1941, Fuller pointed out in the *Evening Standard*, "Mud is Stalin's ally." This repeatedly proved the case—for example, as a result of rain near Moscow from October 10. Moreover, summer dust and autumn mud were succeeded by winter freezing. Each posed serious difficulties, notably so to tank movements.

More generally, the serious deficiencies in the German army, and their improvised solutions in combat conditions, had not been exposed by earlier opponents but became clear in late 1941. For example, not helped by the problems in regauging Soviet railways, by the destruction caused by their advance, and by a lack of trucks, logistical support could not keep up with the advancing German forces, while the German High Command had failed to make the necessary logistical arrangements to support an extended campaign. For armor, there were particular problems with the supply of fuel and with tank numbers. These had risen prior to the resumed German drive on Moscow launched in October thanks to the arrival of new tanks from the factories and two divisions that had been refitted after their success in the Balkans earlier in the year. By November 1941, however, too many tanks were destroyed, damaged, or no longer fit for service.

This situation affected the renewed German offensive, launched in mid-November, that sought to benefit from the valuable firmness frost brought to the ground. In practice, however, German tank divisions could not act then as the intended operational center of gravity. The High Command had not placed sufficient weight on the problems affecting the armor and its impact, as, even more, had not Hitler. The weather hit both combat operations and the crucial element of logistical support. The cold froze oil and lubricants and killed many of the horses on which the army relied for resupply. More significant was the failure to outline coherent and winnable strategic goals. The offensive ground to a halt in early December 1941 in the face of strong and effective Soviet resistance.[31]

This was not the last of the German armor offensives on the Eastern Front. Indeed, the following May, a poorly planned and executed Soviet attempt to make a breakthrough near Kharkov instead led to a successful German encirclement of the attacking forces. Although the Soviets now had impressive tanks in the T-34/76A and KV-1A, the Germans proved more effective in mobile warfare and were greatly helped by air support.[32] The Soviets were also developing armored units at the level of tank corps (the first of which was formed in May 1942), having effectively gone back to the battalion and brigade as the basic armored units at the end of 1941, both in order to throw tanks into battle as quickly as possible and because command and control was too weak for the coordination of larger armored units. Forming tank corps put more tanks into a concentrated area. However, as yet, Soviet tank tactics did not match those of the Germans.

Nevertheless, the shock of confronting the Soviet tanks[33] pushed the Germans to improve their tanks. The forty-seven-ton Soviet KV-1A, with its 90 mm armor, was followed by the KV-1B with 110 mm. Moreover, its 76.2 mm gun was a challenge. The same gun was carried by the T-34/76A, a medium tank (26.3 tons) with 45 mm armor and a top speed of thirty-two miles per hour. These were formidable tanks. The introduction of sloping armor, especially the glacis plate first seen in the T-34, effectively increased the thickness of the armor and, because of the slope, made solid shot glance off.

The Soviet tanks led the Germans to upgrade their medium tanks, as well as to press forward with the development of heavy tanks. The first of the latter, the Tiger I, was not ready until 1942, but an upgrade in 1941, the Mark III J, had, at 50 mm, thicker armor than its predecessor. The same was true of the Mark IV G, which entered service in 1942.

BRITAIN

Meanwhile, rapidly attempting to replace losses in the Battle of France in 1940, and to prepare for a possible German invasion, the British had upgraded their tanks in response to the deficiencies revealed in France: the Valentine, for example, was in some respects the equal of the panzers, but it was undergunned. The Churchill I, which entered service in 1941, had 102 mm armor and a 76 mm gun while the Crusader I, also that year, had 40 mm armor and a 40 mm gun, although it was mechanically poor. Manufactured by the London, Midland and Scottish Railway Company, the lightly armored Covenanter was so mechanically unreliable that it was not accepted for active service. It was also undergunned with a 2-pounder gun. Thicker armor led all powers to a concern for larger, high-velocity guns, whether these guns were provided by other tanks, tank destroyers, self-propelled guns, or antitank guns.

The British had also responded to defeat in 1940 by greatly increasing their tank force. However, the resulting six new armored divisions were overly dominated by tanks, rather than matching the German attempt to provide sufficient mechanized infantry and mobile artillery. This proved a problem in North Africa, where the Germans heavily relied on antitank guns for defense. The British tanks were not helped by their 2-pounder tank guns and the difficulty of delivering accurate tank fire while on the move. Moreover, although the US Stuart tank, which began to arrive to equip British units in 1941, suffered from inadequate armor and armament, its reliability compensated for these deficiencies in the eyes of the British tank crews who received the vehicles. They had suffered from a series of chronically unreliable British tanks in part due to the almost "cottage industry" nature of British tank production. The Stuart benefited from production line techniques still to be introduced into British factories. This made it a real "honey" to operate, and the nickname stuck. In addition, US machine tools were very good, indeed better than those of Britain, which was linked to US tanks having higher standards of reliability.

For the British, the failure to coordinate with the infantry and artillery was the key problem, but the latter were insufficiently mobile. Doctrine and tactics that had worked in 1940 when employed against the limited antitank guns available to the Italians, notably for strongly armored "infantry-support tanks," particularly Matilda IIs, to lead attacks on enemy positions, did not work the following year against German armor. British "infantry-support" tanks, in practice, could achieve relatively little and required infantry protection. In North Africa in 1941, the Germans proved more skilled in tank warfare than the British, not least at coordination between armor and artillery cover. British armored units lacked the tactical acumen of their German opponents and tended to attack head-on without adequate infantry and antitank support. The British also failed to use their 3.7-inch antiaircraft gun in an antitank role, as the Germans did with the 88 mm gun.

JAPAN

The new Japanese war of expansion launched in December 1941 made use of tanks—for example, in Malaya in the battle of Slim River on January 7, 1942.[34] However, they played a far smaller role than for the Germans. This reflected the prior commitments of the Japanese army to conflict in China and to confrontation with the Soviet Union, the exigencies of amphibious operations, and the serious limitations of the Japanese tank force.

The first US tanks to clash with opposing tanks during the war did so during the Japanese invasion of the Philippines. 108 new M3 Stuart light tanks had been sent there alongside 46 half-tracks. The 192nd and 194th Tank

Battalions—Army National Guard units combined as the Provisional Tank Group—were ordered on December 21 to counterattack the Japanese landing forces. However, they faced fuel shortages, and only five tanks could be sent into conflict the next day. The Japanese Type 95s they engaged were able to hit all five of the US tanks. One was destroyed then, and the other four fell victim to Japanese aircraft soon after. Subsequently, the US tanks retreated toward Bataan and played a role in its subsequent defense. The tanks were destroyed when the garrison surrendered.[35]

CONCLUSIONS

The focus in contemporary discussion was on Germany and its use of tanks and not on Japan. Separately, in contrast, armored cars played a far smaller role in consideration due to their lack of protection and vulnerability to tank fire. The experience of the use of armor led to a rapid response process. Thus, looking to the later stages of the war, the experience of combating German tanks led the British to decide to upgrade theirs while combating Soviet tanks led the Germans to do likewise. Meanwhile, the United States was producing many tanks and activating armored divisions—the Eighth, for example, was activated on April 1, 1942. The Tenth followed on July 15 and the Fourteenth on August 15. The same occurred with maneuvers. Those for the Second began on July 13, for the Sixth on August 3, for the Third and Fifth on August 31, for the Fourth on September 20, and for the Seventh a day later.

The greater significance of armor, as well as of aircraft and warships, increased the prominence of oil supplies in strategic planning. Whereas fuel supplies had not been to the fore in the German planning for the invasion of the Soviet Union in 1941, the situation was different in 1942.[36] The Middle East was also of importance for this reason and attracted attention, including from the German navy. Moreover, it was argued that seizing oil-producing areas would deprive opponents of oil sources.[37] The latter was the logic behind subsequent Allied air attacks on Germany and Romania. This focus on oil supplies reflected the move toward a more attritional war as well as the role of armor.

Traditional German operational planning focused on a *Schwerpunkt*, or point of main effort. In World War I, the limited mobility of the combat arms, interacting with the strength of defensive firepower—notably if benefiting from field fortifications—and the consequence for stasis of very large conscript armies, helped create a crisis for mobility at the tactical, operational, and strategic levels. The tank appeared to be an answer, but, in practice, it was only an answer as a means,[38] and, in wider terms, the tank was to be proved an expedient and not an answer. Blitzkrieg worked very well against inferior armies but was dependent on these inferiorities, whether in weaponry, force structure, command, strategy, or doctrine.

A key inferiority was that in antitank weaponry and the relevant doctrine. In 1940-41, the British were using trifling numbers of (French) 25-mm guns as well as two-pounders and Boys antitank rifles, with minimal training and scant doctrinal awareness of their importance. The Germans were always stronger in antitank design and use, irrespective of the 88 mm, which proved a game-changer, mostly due to its longer range and penetrating power. German guns also benefited from finely ground sights, which were consistently better than whatever the Allies could employ and ensured greater accuracy. Indeed, what both sides needed was not so many more or better tanks but more good antitank guns.

NOTES

1. S. H. Newton, ed., *Panzer Operations: The Eastern Front Memoir of General Raus, 1941–1945* (Cambridge, MA, 2003).

2. P. Raborg, *Mechanized Might: The Story of Mechanized Warfare* (New York, 1942), 255.

3. S. J. Zaloga and V. Madej, *The Polish Campaign, 1939* (New York, 1985); A. B. Rossino, *Hitler Strikes Poland: Blitzkrieg, Ideology, and Atrocity* (Lawrence, KS, 2003).

4. R. Forczyk, *Case White: The Invasion of Poland, 1939* (Oxford, 2019), 326.

5. A. Hill, "Voroshilov's 'Lightning' War—The Soviet Invasion of Poland, September 1939," *Journal of Slavic Military Studies* 27 (2014): 404–19.

6. N. Smart, *British Strategy and Politics During the Phony War* (Westport, CT, 2003).

7. R. H. S. Stolfi, "Equipment for Victory in France," *History* 55 (1970): 1–20.

8. F. Bartelmann, "Besieged Outside Stalingrad," *MHQ: The Quarterly Journal of Military History* 15, no. 2 (winter 2003): 30.

9. S. J. Zaloga, *French Tanks of World War II*, 2 vols. (Oxford, 2014).

10. J. A. Gunsburg, "The Battle of the Belgian Plain, 12–14 May 1940: The First Great Tank Battle," *JMH* 56 (1992): 243.

11. M. S. Alexander, *The Republic in Danger: General Maurice Gamelin and the Politics of French Defence* (Cambridge, UK, 1992).

12. J. Murland, *Frankforce and the Defence of Arras 1940* (Barnsley, UK, 2017).

13. J. A. Gunsburg, "The Battle of Gembloux, 14–15 May 1940: The 'Blitzkrieg' Checked," *JMH* 64 (2000): 138–40.

14. W. J. Astore, "Loving the German War Machine: America's Infatuation with *Blitzkrieg*, Warfighters and Militarism," in *Arms and the Man: Military History Essays in Honor of Dennis Showalter*, ed. M. S. Neiberg (Leiden, Netherlands, 2011), 5–30; re: tanks, 9.

15. K. Frieser, *The Blitzkrieg Legend: The 1940 Campaign in the West* (Annapolis, MD, 1995).

16. W. Murray, "May 1940: Contingency and Fragility of the German RMA," in *The Dynamics of Military Revolution 1300–2050*, ed. M. Knox and W. Murray (Cambridge, UK, 2001), 173; E. O. Goldman and L. C. Eliason, eds., *The Diffusion of Military Technology and Ideas* (Stanford, CA, 2003), 349.

17. R. Citino, *The German Way of War: From the Thirty Years War to the Third Reich* (Lawrence, KS, 2005).

18. H. E. Raugh, *Wavell in the Middle East, 1939–1941: A Study in Generalship* (Norman, OK, 2013).

19. P. Ewer, "The British Campaign in Greece 1941: Assumptions about the Operational Art and Their Influence on Strategy," *JMH* 76 (2012): 733–45.

20. C. Stockings and E. Hancock, *Swastika over the Acropolis: Re-interpreting the Nazi Invasion of Greece in World War II* (Leiden, Netherlands, 2013); D. Horner, "Britain and the Campaigns in Greece and Crete in 1941," *Proceedings of the NIDS International Forum on War History* (2014): 40–41.

21. C. Robins, "Orders of Battle of British Tank Forces, and Tank Types at Key Dates in the Western Desert, 1940–42," *Journal of the Society for Army Historical Research* 93, no. 373 (spring 2015): 48–59.

22. Menzies to Blamey, June 21, 1941, AWM. 3 DRL/6643, 1/1; M. Kitchen, *Rommel's Desert War: Waging World War II in North Africa, 1941–1943* (Cambridge, UK, 2009).

23. *HC*, November 20, 1941, vol. 376, cols. 467–68.

24. Auchinleck, memorandum, October 18, 1941, AWM. 3 DRL/6643, 1/27.

25. R. Edwards, *White Death: Russia's War on Finland, 1939–40* (London, 2006).

26. C. Van Dyke, "The Timoshenko Reforms, March–July 1940," *Journal of Slavic Military Studies* 9 (1996): 69–96; C. Bellamy, *Absolute War: Soviet Russia in the Second World War* (London, 2007), 484.

27. V. J. Kamenir, *The Bloody Triangle: The Defeat of Soviet Armor in the Ukraine, June 1941* (Minneapolis, MN, 2009).

28. R.H.S. Stolfi, *German Panzers on the Offensive: Russian Front. North Africa, 1941–1942* (Atglen, PA, 2003).

29. D. M. Glantz, ed., *The Initial Phase of the War on the Eastern Front, 22 June–August 1941* (London, 1997) and *Barbarossa Derailed: The Battle for Smolensk, 10 July–10 September 1941*, vols. 1–3 (Solihull, UK, 2010–14).

30. D. Reynolds and V. Pechatnov, *The Kremlin Letters: Stalin's Wartime Correspondence with Churchill and Roosevelt* (New Haven, CT, 2018), 41, 44.

31. C. W. H. Luther, *Barbarossa Unleashed: The German Blitzkrieg through Central Russia to the Gates of Moscow, June–December 1941* (Atglen, PA, 2013); D. Stahel, *Operation Barbarossa and Germany's Defeat in the East* (Cambridge, UK, 2009) and *Operation Typhoon: Hitler's March on Moscow, October 1941* (Cambridge, UK, 2013); N. Zetterling and A. Frankson, *The Drive on Moscow 1941: Operation Taifun and Germany's First Great Crisis in World War II* (Havertown, PA, 2012).

32. D. M. Glantz, *Kharkov 1942: Anatomy of a Military Disaster through Soviet Eyes* (Rockville, NY, 1998).

33. S. J. Zaloga, "Technological Surprise and the Initial Period of War: The Case of the T-34 Tank in 1941," *Journal of Slavic Military Studies* 6 (1993): 634–46.

34. M. N. Stanton, "A Study in Armored Exploitation: The Battle of the Slim River, Malaya, 7 January 1942," *Armor* 105 (May/June 1996): 26–31.

35. B. Anderson, "Company C, 194th Tank Bn. in the Philippines, 1941–42," *Armor* 105 (May/June 1996): 32–36.

36. J. Hayward, "Hitler's Quest for Oil: The Impact of Economic Considerations on Military Strategy, 1941–42," *Journal of Strategic Studies* 18 (1995): 94–135; A. Toprani, "The First War for Oil: The Caucasus, German Strategy, and the Turning Point of the War on the Eastern Front, 1942," *JMH* 80 (2016): 815–54.

37. P. Hoffmann, "The Gulf Region in German Strategic Projections, 1940–1942," *Militärgeschichtliche Mitteilungen* 44 (1988): 67–68.

38. R. M. Citino, *Quest for Decisive Victory: From Stalemate to Blitzkrieg in Europe, 1899–1940* (Lawrence, KS, 2002).

FIVE

WORLD WAR II: THE ALLIES ATTACK, 1942–45

TANK CONFLICT REPEATEDLY PROVED SIGNIFICANT IN THE SEC-ond half of the war, that of Allied victory, although it often lacked the novelty and drama claimed for, and invested in, the German blitzkrieg attacks of 1939–41. Tanks also became iconic for at least some Allied successes, as with the photograph of Lieutenant-General Bernard Law Montgomery standing on a M3 Grant (the British version of the American M3 Lee) after the British victory at El Alamein in late 1942. It was also a period in which the number of tanks increased as vastly greater production outweighed losses, notably for the Americans and Soviets, while the specifications of tanks improved. Given the number of tanks required, ease of production was a key factor. So, more generally, was a problem-solving approach to capability and the linked ability to devise effective feedback mechanisms during the process of implementing the development of new weapons. The varied aspects of design and production were involved, as were related changes in tactics and doctrine, making the tank ever more part of a team with other types of tracked and/or armored vehicles.

Moreover, this process required an appreciation of the interdependencies involved in adapting to particular environments, as well as the responses of opponents.[1] The choices that were made were contextual and contingent as much as driven by any debate about doctrine. These factors, however, can be difficult to gauge and certainly require a departure from monocausal explanations. Thus, there is the view that Lieutenant-General Lesley McNair, an artillery officer who became the thoughtful head of the US Army Ground Forces from 1942 to 1944 (and was killed in a "friendly fire" incident in the Battle of Normandy by US bombers), was primarily responsible for the US army focusing on the 57 mm antitank gun and tank destroyers, rather than a stronger tank. This remains a contentious decision.

It is also a decision that relates to longstanding differences. Thus, the competition, or the challenge, between gun and armor is a key issue in the history of tanks. An instructive point is the respective cost, including of training, of a tank crew and antitank teams. Moreover, it is not clear that heavier tanks were a better answer to enemy tanks than an effective antitank arsenal. Now the infrared targeting systems directed against the tank are immediately spotted by the electronic defensive systems on the tank, which is given all the information necessary to fire, but in World War II, the situation was different. Because the targeting then was simply optical, the tank did not realize it had been spotted by an antitank gun and was destroyed before noticing what was going on.

There is also the argument that the key issue was that of producing and transporting sufficient numbers of heavy tanks to make a fundamental difference in Western Europe.[2] This was, in part, a response to the difficulties involved in transportation: more space was required in shipping, and there were more significant problems in loading and unloading. In addition, heavy tanks faced the issue of bridge capabilities, which was a particularly serious issue in northwest Europe given the number of rivers there.

Separately, in considering interdependencies and choices, there is the point that doctrine, tactics, and weaponry that worked for tanks in one area, for example, for the British in Libya, might be less appropriate in others, say Italy and, for different reasons, Normandy. Thus, the British Seventh Armoured Division did well in North Africa but not, admittedly in more difficult circumstances, as well in Normandy in 1944, notably with Operation Goodwood. The same occurs with the question of other aspects of war—for example, fire support for amphibious operations. Thus, methods employed in the Pacific proved less appropriate on Omaha Beach.[3] There was also the significance of maintenance and support doctrine and organization, which were better for the United States and Britain than for Germany, especially in Normandy in 1944.

TANK TYPES

Unlike the Germans, the Americans and Soviets concentrated on weapons that made best use of their capacity for mass production because they were simple to build, operate, and repair, such as the US Sherman M4 tank. This was the first truly universal fighting vehicle, able to fight in such different environments as Europe, the Southwest Pacific, and North Africa. The ubiquitous (in addition to the prototype, 49,234 were produced in 1942–45) and very reliable Sherman was medium weight, with moderate armor (12.7 mm) and a medium-caliber (75 mm) gun. That meant, however, that, alongside its

impressive range, the Sherman was underarmored and undergunned for much
of the war. The Americans took a very pragmatic approach to tank development. In the interest of rapid development, the Sherman used a suspension
system that was already employed on commercial tractors. Failure to rely on
a diesel engine, however, did cause an issue: due to its gasoline-fueled engine,
the Sherman burned too easily, which increased the already serious hazards
of tank conflict for the crew. The armor of Shermans, indeed, was too thin to
make them appropriate for close infantry support. The Sherman was also provided to allies, including the British, the Canadians, New Zealanders, Poles,
French, and South Africans.

The Sherman evolved into numerous versions, all intended to increase firepower against German armor as well as to enhance protection from German
guns. Thus, an up-armored version was designated the M4A3E2 Assault Tank.
One of these was the first to reach the besieged US lines around Bastogne in
December 1944 during the Battle of the Bulge. Producing some of the Shermans with the more capable 76 mm gun, refitting others with a 17-pounder,
and using a 90 mm gun on M36 tank destroyers reflected an awareness of the
need for up-gunning.

The Americans were content to ride through the war on a tank that was a
product of 1930s technology: the Sherman was not a feat of advanced technology, but it was one of production.[4] So also with the Soviet T-34. The first T-34
models were very crude inside, the turret layout was difficult for the crew, and
there was no significant upgrading until 1944, when a new model, with 85 mm
guns and a three-man turret, was deployed. The bigger Soviet KV series, which
led to the IS (Joseph Stalin; Iosif for Joseph) series, were also crude inside.
Yet the T-34 offered armor, armament, and mobility, as well as poor observation and a lack of radios. The use of a diesel engine in the T-34—originally
developed for aerial employment—reduced the risk of destructive fire and
gave the tank a good operational range. The most cost-effective tank of the
war, it was not always matched by the "human software" of command. Separately, the decision not to employ part of the production for turretless versions as armored personnel carriers, or APCs (as happened, for example, with
Shermans and other tanks to produce Canadian "Kangaroos"), is possibly
questionable.

In contrast to the Shermans and the T-34s, German tanks were complex
pieces of equipment and, partly as a result, often broke down. Much German
armor, moreover, was no better than Soviet armor or, indeed, worse. In 1941,
the Soviet KV-1 and T-34 tanks proved superior to their German opponents.[5]
In response, the Germans increased the armament of their tanks. Thus,

from 1942 until the end of the war, the Mark IV replaced the Mark III as the backbone of the panzer divisions: the Mark IV had a new version from 1942, the Mark IV G, which had a high-velocity 75 mm (just below 3-inch) anti-tank gun, as well as wider tracks for use in the snow and mud of Russia. The power-to-weight ratio and the ground pressure both affected performance on soft ground, and not only there; this issue led to an emphasis on wider tracks to spread the weight. Improvements, however, brought problems. Thus, although the 75 mm gun of the Mark IV was fitted with a muzzle brake to reduce recoil impact, the longer barrel of the gun added stress to the brake mechanism.[6] Moreover, although the Mark IV was fitted with what was effectively spaced armor in the form of side plates to the body of the tank, it was weaker than the T-34 in armor and mobility. In turn, the latter was inferior in one-to-one combat with the Panther and the Tiger.

Germany gave Italy permission to copy its tanks, but the Italians found it difficult to do so. They tried to follow German role models, especially the Panther, with their P-40 tank. Its 75 mm gun was very effective against Allied tanks, but the 50 mm armor was weak and only riveted, and the tank had a weak motor. Italian production, instead, turned to the production of assault guns (Semovente), which, despite serious weaknesses, especially in motorization, proved more effective than their tanks.

For long, the British and Americans had tanks that did not match their German rivals and were understood in that light, including by their opponents. The British Infantry Mark I, Matilda, Valentine, Crusader, Churchill, and Cromwell tanks suffered from inadequate armor, and the first four were undergunned. In the Tobruk campaign in North Africa in June 1942, the Crusader proved mechanically poor: the air cleaners and the water pump and engine lubrication systems were defective, and it was difficult to use the tank. On July 1, 1942, in the House of Commons, Sir John Wardlaw-Milne, moving a motion for a vote of no confidence in Churchill, attacked the quality of British tanks as one of his themes: "The bulk of the tanks with which we are fighting in Libya . . . were all designed before this war began. These tanks have been manufactured for the last two or three years, and they are being manufactured today. Many of them are very good tanks for their purpose, but they are quite unequal to those with which the Germans are now armed. . . . There is on the Tank Board no officer with recent experience of fighting with tanks in the desert."[7]

In the debate, Earl Winterton pointed out the large number of tanks out of service due to mechanical problems, especially Churchills.[8] The previous day, the *Times* had published a letter from Professor A. V. Hill MP in which he observed that there was no scientific control of the processes of production of military equipment.

The deficiencies of British tanks in armor, firepower, speed, horsepower, and profile, and the resulting problems against German tanks and antitank weaponry, affected not only British tactics but also morale. As a result, there was a turn to US Grant and Sherman tanks. Grants gave the British a 75 mm gun, which their own tanks lacked. However, the Grant was a compromise tank, used to supply the British with what they needed as quickly as possible, and it was withdrawn as soon as the Sherman, which also had a 75 mm gun, became available. British armored capabilities and lethality improved with the use of both Grants and Shermans.

Separately, by 1943, the concentration of British tank production on fewer designs had helped lead to improvement.[9] The original Crusader had a 40 mm/2-pounder gun. In 1942, it was redesigned to take a 57 mm/6-pounder gun. Larger caliber British guns, the 3-inch (76.2 mm), were used by the British A27M Cromwells and A22/42 Churchills as well as to produce the 17-pounder antitank gun.

When Anglo-American forces invaded France in June 1944, the best German tanks were technically better in firepower and armor. The Tiger and the (faster) Panther were superior in both to the Sherman and could readily penetrate its armor at one thousand yards. Nevertheless, the unreliability, low mobility, and high maintenance requirements of the costly Tiger tank weakened it, and there were also serious problems with the reliability of the Panther.[10] In response to the Soviet tanks, and to the degree to which they were now on the defensive, the Germans had emphasized the antitank role for their armor, which had previously been a secondary consideration.

The resulting German focus on heavy tanks, however, limited mobility and also had implications for fuel needs. As a reminder of multiple causation, this limited mobility was also very much hit by the impact of greater Allied air power on the German rail system. Bridges and marshaling yards were particular targets. Germany benefited from its central position, notably in moving armor between fronts in late 1944 in preparation for the Battle of the Bulge, using the excellent and tightly controlled German railway system. Nevertheless, the pressure on this mobility was accentuated both by the need, notably from late 1943, to disperse armor on the Eastern Front in order to counter Soviet attacks and by the extent to which, in the summer of 1944, the war in Europe had become a multifront one with the Germans on the defensive on all the fronts.

The quality gap that favored the German tanks against the Anglo-American ones was closed by late 1944 and 1945 as new Allied tanks appeared. Bigger guns came because of the need to penetrate thicker German tank armor at long ranges. The Sherman was up-gunned and up-armored to counter tanks such as the Tiger I and the Panther but was of little use against the Tiger II. Generally, the 88 mm gun of the Tiger tanks and the German antitank guns outranged the Allied tank guns. The British introduced a modified Sherman known as the Firefly, which was fitted with a 17-pounder (76.2 mm) gun firing armor-piercing capped (APC) rounds, which could penetrate German armor at longer range. For much of 1944, this was the only Allied tank that could take on the Tiger I. It was also used by the Canadians, Poles, South Africans, and New Zealanders. Up-gunning, the Americans introduced a higher-velocity 76 mm gun to some of their Shermans in mid-1944. However, the 76 mm needed new high-velocity armor-piercing (HVAP) ammunition to penetrate the front plates (100 mm thick) of Panthers and Tiger Is. This ammunition was introduced when it was found that existing ammunition would not do the job.

Guns and ammunition had to be in synergy. Armor-piercing ammunition was crucial in operating against tanks, but high-explosive ammunition was necessary for infantry support. It was, therefore, valuable to have guns that could fire both, such as the 75 mm one on the Grant.

More generally, the thickening of armor and its increased sloping, especially in German and Soviet designs (the Mark V Panther was a response to the T-34, both of which made use of glacis plates sloped at sixty degrees), led to the response of increased velocity and hitting power. As a result, discarded sabots with subcaliber rounds and armored caps were among the innovations introduced. APDS (armor-piercing discarding sabot) was a British invention for providing subcaliber projectiles (fired from the standard tank guns) with greater kinetic energy to penetrate German armor. Developed in 1941–44 at the Armaments Research Department at Fort Halstead, it was used operationally from mid-1944 with the British 6-pounder antitank gun and from September with the 17-pounder. In contrast, tungsten carbide is not only very dense but also heavy, and a conventional full-caliber shot was extremely difficult to shoot from the barrel.

A stress on effective performance in tank combat could, in part, help compensate for the earlier emphasis on tanks that were fast and maneuverable, but, in practice, there was a tendency to put aside this emphasis and to increase protection and gun power at the expense of mobility. This was very much seen with the German Tiger. Indeed, as an aspect of attritional warfare, the closing stages of the war saw the introduction of more heavily gunned tanks by all powers. However, for the Allies, these were very much tanks entering service in 1945. Major-General Jacob Devers, commander of the European Theater of Operations for the US army from May to December 1943, had pressed that November for the production of 250 M26 Pershings, with a 90 mm gun formerly only used in the open-turret M36 tank destroyers, to confront Panthers and Tigers in the battle for Normandy. However, delayed in part as a result of a lack of support in senior military circles, notably from McNair, the Pershing only entered action in February 1945, and full production did not begin until March. Only twenty saw action in Europe, but this tank would serve well in the Korean War (1950–53). Given the production of Pershings by the end of the war, as well as the Soviet progress on the IS-3, the quality gap would definitely have closed had the European war gone into the 1945 summer campaign. Soviet concern that the Germans might try to copy the IS-2 (Joseph Stalin 2) led to instructions not to let it fall into their hands.

The British finally produced well-gunned and armored tanks, the combination proving important. The Black Prince, a prototype for a heavier Churchill tank, appeared in 1945. It was armed with an effective 76.2 mm gun but did not enter service because it was underpowered, only reaching eleven miles per hour. The Black Prince was too big and not well thought out. The Comet, which had a newly designed 77 mm gun but not full sloped armor, was a better tank but did not enter service until March 1945. With its 101 mm armor, it was considered comparable to a Panther and was the first purpose-designed British tank to be capable of taking on Panthers and Tigers on equal terms. It had a speed of twenty-nine miles per hour and was "nifty" and good to drive.[11] The Centurion had full sloped armor as well as a good gun. Developed toward the end of the war, and superior to the Pershing and the T-34/85, it was too late to see service in it.[12]

Other tanks designed to cope with German heavy armor were only produced after the war when they were configured, instead, against Soviet counterparts. Thus, the Charioteer, with an 83.4 mm, 20-pounder gun, entered service in 1947 and was seen as a rival to the IS. However, it was essentially a somewhat cumbersome up-gunned, upgraded Cromwell with a three-man crew, although a fourth had to be added to act as an external observer due to the restricted view from the turret because it was too full of gun breach. The Tortoise, with a 94 mm, 32-pounder gun, never went into production. It was ill conceived and too cumbersome. Tested in 1948, it proved difficult to transport, and that was a key consideration. This difficulty was the case by both road and rail.

In contrast, in late 1942, the Germans had begun work on a super tank, the Maus, to be 188 tons and armed with a 128 mm main gun adapted from a PaK 44 antitank field artillery piece and a coaxial 75 mm gun. Hitler approved a wooden mock-up he inspected on May 1, 1943, and ordered the production of 150. Guderian was opposed as the tank design lacked a machine gun and therefore would be unsuitable for close combat. One was then added. Tests on this tank, which was intended to break through defenses, began in December 1943. However, the ill-conceived tank was too heavy to cross bridges, and there were also problems with producing an engine able to offer sufficient power and fit inside the tank. These were systemic issues with "super tanks." Work on the project, which had only led to two hulls and one turret being built, stopped in August 1944. The turret itself weighed fifty-five tons. Hitler was interested in size as an expression of effectiveness and thus in bigger tanks. In Germany, there are counterfactual books in which the Germans are able to build these land cruisers and defeat the Allies. They are absurd.

ANTITANK WEAPONRY

Meanwhile, in the more general process of competitive development, improvements in tank specifications during the war created problems for antitank weaponry. Thicker armor resulted in pressure for more powerful weapons. The 57 mm antitank gun was ineffective against front armor unless perilously close to the target. The thick armor of the heavier Soviet tanks deployed in 1941 was resistant to German antitank shells.[13] Difficulty in destroying the heavy tanks led to the use, instead, of anticoncrete shells designed to be employed against concrete bunkers and to the development of a tank destroyer fitted with a 90 mm gun. These tank destroyers were, in effect, self-propelled antitank guns.

The relationships among (main) gun, ammunition, armor, and targeting system are at the heart of the dynamic between tanks and antitank weaponry, although this dynamic was and still is set and molded by doctrine, tactics, and fighting quality. From World War II (although not generally before), tanks, to a great degree, were mobile antitank gun platforms rather than focused on infantry support or opposition. During the war, the German 88 mm, an antiaircraft gun used in an antitank role with armor-piercing ammunition, and the British 17-pounder (76.2 mm), the first really effective British antitank gun, were both fitted to tanks—the former adapted for the Panther and Tiger, the latter fitted in Sherman Fireflies. But, as the Americans also discovered with their 76 mm gun, the type of ammunition fired made all the difference to effectiveness and, indeed, lethality.

Armor during this war was essentially ever thicker steel. It was necessary also to counter shaped-charge antitank rounds typically fired by infantry, such as the US bazooka and the British PIAT (Projector, Infantry, Anti-Tank), which was designed in 1942 and entered service in 1943. The latter was, in effect, an antitank grenade launcher. It was simple and inexpensive but heavy to carry and difficult to use. To counter these weapons, add-on protection was applied, notably metal plates at the side and concrete add-on armor. Tank crews also placed replacement tracks and wheels on the front and side of their vehicles to provide additional protection against handheld weapons. This protection could help lessen the impact of these weapons.

The advantage of the antitank gun was its relative cheapness in comparison to a whole tank. The Germans produced over twenty-three thousand PaK 40 antitank guns. The problem with the infantry antitank weapons, such as the bazooka and the PIAT, was how close the operator had to get to the target before firing, which was not the case with antitank guns. Closeness meant exposure to defending fire. The maximum effective range of the PIAT was less than 100 meters. The bazooka had a maximum range of 370 meters, but an effective one of 140, and was not good against the frontal armor of German tanks and tank destroyers, which from mid-1944 were generally supplemented with a concrete add-on layer. Nevertheless, there often was close-quarter fighting, as in Normandy, where PIATs inflicted damage on Mark IVs—for example, in Operation Charnwood on July 8–9 and later in 1944 at Arnhem.[14]

One huge advantage of antitank guns over tanks was their small size, which meant they could be concealed easily to ambush tanks, as the Germans did in Normandy in 1944. In dealing with these guns, combined arms doctrine was affirmed anew. Antitank guns, smaller and not leaving tracks visible from the air, were far less vulnerable than tanks to observation and air and tank attack, although air-burst artillery shells killed the crews. Moreover, antitank guns did not break down or require gasoline, at least until they had to be moved, and not even then if there was a reliance on horses. Thus, when combined with antitank ditches, an important obstacle, as used by the Soviets against the German attack at Kursk in 1943, the antitank gun could prove highly effective.

In response to stronger tanks, antitank guns improved. This led to guns with larger calibers—for example, 105 mm German guns, instead of 88 mm ones, and Soviet 100 mm guns, instead of 76 mm ones. Developments also included longer barrels and better projectiles. The last entailed alternatives to solid armor-piercing shot, which had proved limited against hardened armor. The muzzle velocity was improved by adapting the shot. Separately, HEAT (high-explosive antitank) warheads were one response, applying the principle used for the PIAT and other light antitank weapons. HEAT is a shaped-charge munition that employs the Munroe effect to penetrate armor. The shaped charge has a metal liner that, on detonation, collapses on itself and focuses the explosive energy to form a high-velocity, very hot, superplastic jet of metal that penetrates by virtue of kinetic energy combined with the high temperature of the jet. The use of copper reflected the extent to which its fusion occurs at a relatively low temperature. After the jet entered the tank, its high temperature caused the explosion of the shells contained inside the turret and burned alive the crew so quickly and so completely that normally nothing remained of the bodies but some bones covered by the melted and burned remains of flesh.

At the same time, the circumstances of combat affected the effectiveness of antitank guns and ammunition. Thus, on the Eastern Front and in Normandy, the impact of German long-range antitank guns was lessened by the close distance of many actual engagements. Separately, HEAT warheads did not have a long range, which meant they had to be fired from near the targeted tanks.

Frequent improvement was necessary for antitank guns and infantry anti-tank weapons. The Americans first used the bazooka antitank rocket in 1942 but failed to upgrade it as German tanks got heavier. The Germans, however, having captured and reverse engineered bazookas, developed the design into the more powerful Panzerschreck ("tank terror") rocket grenade. They also developed the handheld Panzerfaust ("armor fist"), a single-shot, antitank rocket in use from 1943. These weapons were part of the upgrading of German infantry weaponry seen also with the MG-42 light machine gun. As an instance of production history, 6.7 million of the five Panzerfaust variants were built, mostly for use by Germany but also by its allies. Its explosive charge at thirty yards could penetrate 200 mm armor. Fear of Panzerfausts induced not only caution on the part of Allied tank commanders but also, sometimes, an understandable disinclination to lead the attack.[15]

Other weapons against tanks, such as guns and rockets, were mounted on aircraft. British Spitfires and Typhoons carried 20 mm machine cannon and US P-47s and P-51s .50 caliber machine guns but used salvoes of 5-inch (127 mm) unguided rockets to strike the weakly protected upper parts of tanks. Some aircraft, such as Hurricanes, were fitted with 30 mm cannon in under-wing pods. Specialized aircraft for tank busting had an offensive range that weapons on the ground lacked. The Soviet Ilyushin Il-2 Sturmovik and the British Typhoon were the most effective aircraft, although their effectiveness against individual tanks was not high. The Soviets employed a HEAT bomb-let while the British favored a sixty-pound semi-armor-piercing rocket that, however, was ballistically unstable and thus difficult to aim. But large-caliber guns were also used, such as on the British Hurricane and the German Ju-87 Stuka, while, from 1944, the Americans dropped napalm, including on tanks. In Normandy in 1944, air superiority and support helped compensate for the

Allied inferiority in tank design. Throughout, it was an important aspect of Allied combined arms operations.

The high costs of tanks encouraged some Germans to support a focus on the artillery-manned Sturmgeschütz (assault guns), notably the StuG 3, an effective tank destroyer built on the chassis of the Panzer Mark III. Its average cost was about 87,000 Reichsmark compared to 103,000 for a Mark III, 107,000 for a Mark IV, 130,000 for a Panther, and 300,000 for a Tiger. Tank destroyers were harder to destroy than tanks because they had a lower profile and in battle had a good rate of destroying enemy tanks for their own loss. The StuG 3, however, was officially under the artillery, and Guderian's attempt to bring them under his control as inspector general of armored troops failed. Nevertheless, Hitler ordered one hundred StuGs of each month's production to be turned over to the Armored Troop Command: in 1943, it received 25 percent of the production, and the Waffen-SS received 13 percent. The idea of focusing on StuGs was discussed, not least due to problems with tank production in 1942, but Guderian opposed it because, like Hitler, he preferred strong tanks. Because the panzer divisions received more and more of the total production of StuGs, the infantry formations, for which they were originally designed as antitank weapons, received fewer and were short of antitank weaponry. The StuG 3 influenced the Italian self-propelled 75/18 mm howitzer, of which 491 were manufactured.

In the United States, McNair favored turreted tank destroyers and antitank guns over heavier tanks with bigger guns, arguing that lightly armored (and thus easier to make) tank destroyers, manned by his branch, the artillery, were the best defense against German tanks and that US tanks should focus on providing armored mass for the main attack. Indeed, "the tank destroyer was the artilleryman's solution to the problem posed by a mobile, armored target."[16] Although this approach could lead to underplaying the role of the tank as, in practice, a tank destroyer, motorized tank destroyers had an impact. Effective German versions were eventually matched by US tank destroyers. The latter were also good antibunker weapons.

The initial tank destroyers used by the Americans proved ineffective. The 37 mm guns installed on the rear decks of M6 trucks were inadequate against German armor while 75 mm guns on thinly armored M3 half-tracks were both outclassed by German 88 mms and easy targets, with their slow speed and high silhouettes. Moreover, their guns could not traverse. As a consequence, there was a turn to the Sherman tank hulls and chassis used for the M10 and M36 (the M18 was based on the M3 chassis). Aside from more powerful guns, there was also more effective ammunition. The 76 mm gun on the M18 fired tungsten-carbide-cored, high-velocity, armor-piercing ammunition.[17] These tank destroyers were, in effect, lightly armored or simpler tanks fitted with powerful guns, with tank-design chassis used to this end. The M10 and M18 were fitted with antitank guns but faced problems in penetrating the armor of heavy German tanks. The M36, armed with the 90 mm antiaircraft gun later used on the Pershing (and early Patton tanks), proved more effective. The first arrived in service in France in September 1944.[18]

The Germans used a similar concept but with the cheaper turretless tanks, such as the Hetzer (Jagdpanzer 38), which was based on a light tank and built in Czechoslovakia with a Skoda A7 cannon, which provided destructive power at very long range. Produced in 1944–45, this was Germany's most common tank destroyer. It proved particularly useful as a defensive weapon against advancing Allied tanks. The low profile of the Hetzer encouraged its value for ambushes, and a version served after World War II with the Swiss army, which, fearing Soviet invasion during the Cold War, very much focused on defense against tank attacks. Tank destroyers could also serve as substitutes for tanks. Thus, on December 15, 1944, the German attack on Kesternich in the Battle of the Bulge was headed by three tank destroyers and an armored 37 mm antiaircraft half-track. Based on the chassis of the Panther tank, and therefore heavier than the Hetzer, the Jagdpanther ("Hunting Panther") entered service in 1944; only 415 were built, as opposed to the planned 150 a month. The design, which focused on a long-barreled 88 mm PaK gun, a heavy caliber gun, had been ordered in late 1942. Other forms of turretless tanks were the Soviet self-propelled antitank and direct support guns, the SU-76, SU-85, SU-100, SU-122, and SU-152, the last a self-propelled 152 mm howitzer. Turretless vehicles were less expensive to produce but, if they had open tops, made the crew vulnerable to aerial bursts.

There was an overlap of technological developments in tanks and antitank systems. In a sense, the British Firefly was a tank destroyer. In practice, there were as many variants of tank destroyers as tanks. The reason for fitting the guns to vehicles, including half-tracks and other vehicles, was mobility. The Italian self-propelled 75/18 and (later) 75/34 howitzers were a surprise to British tanks. Italy also had the 90/53 gun, which was derived from a naval gun that could penetrate tank armor. It was successfully used, especially in North Africa, on a Lancia truck. Forty-eight were converted for use on the self-propelled 90/53 heavy tank destroyer employed in Sicily against the Allies in 1943.

A very different antitank weapon was the mine, which was responsible for between 20 and 30 percent of wartime tank casualties. Given this percentage, it is surprising that they receive so little attention. Mines were used in great numbers. In late 1942, Rommel laid half a million antitank mines, and many antipersonnel mines, in order to protect his position at El Alamein in Egypt against British attack. Such mines greatly slowed attacks and could channel them toward opposing artillery.

Mine techniques and production developed rapidly during the war. Mine-clearing units became an adjunct of tank advances, as with the British at El Alamein, and also saw developments, including the use of handheld electronic detectors and flail tanks. The last, for example, were employed by the British in the Battle of Normandy in Operation Bluecoat. In turn, there were innovations with mines, notably in producing mines that were resistant to blast-clearance devices from 1941 and nonmetallic mines to defeat mine detectors from 1943. Antilifting devices were also introduced.

ARMOR CAPABILITY

The effectiveness of antitank weaponry ensured that mixed or combined arms formations were more effective than those that focused solely on tanks. It took a while for British armor units training for the Second Front, the invasion of France, to appreciate that antitank guns were a major problem requiring infantry support. There was a need for tanks capable of firing high-explosive ammunition rather than the earlier focus on armor-piercing rounds. Commanders of armored units, in response to antitank weaponry, urged their officers to wait for support rather than charging in. In particular, this tactic was a sensible response to the German skill in defensive warfare, especially the careful siting of antitank guns to destroy advancing tanks. In July 1944, Lieutenant-General Sir Richard O'Connor (brigade major of the Experimental Brigade from 1921 to 1924 and a veteran of North African operations in 1940–41), the commander of the British Eighth Corps in Normandy, instructed the commander of an armored division to "go cautiously with your armor, making sure that any areas from which you could be shot up by Panthers [tanks] and 88s [antitank guns] are engaged. Remember what you are doing is not a risk to Paris—it is the capture of a wood by combined armor and infantry."[19]

Such advice was necessary given the heavy tank casualties suffered by the British in the Battle of Normandy at the hands of German antitank guns. Neither the vegetation, notably the readily defended hedgerows of the bocage, nor the density of forces made armored advances easy in this campaign. The situation proved very different with the successful Soviet advances of 1944–45 in easier, more open terrain in Eastern Europe and, in 1945, against the Japanese in Manchuria.

Aside from the impact of defensive firepower, the question of engineering and logistical support for tanks was a serious hindrance to mobility for the Allies and, far more, the Germans in France in 1944. Yet, by 1944–45, the effectiveness of tanks in large numbers was shown in the Soviet use of mobile tank armies for deep envelopment in maneuver-style warfare.[20] This effectiveness was seen at the expense of the Germans in Eastern Europe and in the rapid defeat of the large Japanese army in Manchuria, although it was not the sole reason for these outcomes.

The US supply of tanks to the British was an aspect of a more general movement of tanks among the Allies, which had been seen, albeit at a smaller scale, in World War I. Thus, the British supplied many tanks to the Soviet Union via the Arctic convoys, although the Soviets subsequently ignored or denigrated the help. However, Alexander Hill has drawn valuable attention to the scale of the help. Thus, one-sixth of the heavy tanks in the battle of Moscow were British supplies, while 16 percent of the Soviet tanks on July 1, 1942, were foreign, mostly British, supplied.[21]

In contrast, Germany lacked the willingness or resources to provide appropriate military assistance to its allies. This was an aspect of a broader failure of the German alliance system, one also seen in the absence of any success in transferring skills and experience through training and doctrine. The net effect was to leave large numbers of Axis forces with inadequate equipment and, therefore, unable to improve.[22] For example, the Croatian army received only about sixty German tanks and eighteen self-propelled guns, although the Germans also handed over thirty-nine tanks and thirty tankettes captured from Italian forces in 1943.

A more chronological account repeatedly demonstrates the value of tanks in many combined arms operations, but this value, understandably, was dependent in part on terrain. At the same time, the effectiveness of the use of tanks was related to experience, command skills, and doctrine, as well as weaponry and the interaction with antitank techniques.

THE EASTERN FRONT, LATE 1942

Armor played a major role in the German offensive in the Soviet Union launched on June 28, 1942. The first section of the plan was achieved in July, when, in ideal tank conditions, German forces pushed into the Don bend. Poor planning, however, ensured that the armor necessary to help clear the river crossings at the eastern end of the Don bend was in the wrong location and thus unable to help the attempt to push through to Stalingrad in late July. Soviet willingness to withdraw troops ensured the Germans were deprived of the encirclement victory in the bend they had sought and required. Instead, the Wehrmacht provided *Luftstösse*—"blows into the air"—and Soviet losses were generally during fighting retreats and no longer from encirclements.

The German advance bifurcated, with one thrust into the northern Caucasus and the other from the River Don to the River Volga. This led to an overextension that ensured the two advances were unable to provide mutual support while flank positions were weakly held. There was also serious logistical strain. To the south, the Third and Fourth Panzer Corps made major gains in the northern Caucasus in early August, with Maikop falling to the Thirteenth Panzer Division on August 9. However, growing Soviet resistance then slowed their advance, and the situation was not helped by serious shortages of reinforcements and fuel.

On the Volga, the Germans focused on trying to capture the city of Stalingrad, which, in large part due to German bombing, was a wrecked urban terrain. Armor attacks could achieve little in the ruined city. Much of the fighting was at very close range, and the Germans could not utilize their skill at mobile warfare. German armored units took heavy casualties.[23] Both sides employed massive quantities of artillery in the battle.

This unsuccessful offensive used up German reserves, and, on November 19, 1942, in Operation Uranus, the Soviets launched a powerful counterattack, outmaneuvering and rapidly encircling the German Sixth Army, then Germany's leading field army, in and near Stalingrad. The Soviets benefited in this operation from their buildup of forces, including tanks. These advantages were magnified by the success of their planning and preparations; by surprise, which reflected a catastrophic failure of intelligence gathering on the part of the Germans; and thanks to the poor quality of German command decisions, including the allocation of what became key flank positions to weak Romanian forces. The Soviet Fifth Tank Army played the crucial role in overcoming Romanian defenses when the Stalingrad counteroffensive was launched. An inadequate German response to the Soviet breakthrough was also crucial.

In the face of strong Soviet forces, and having no operational reserves, the German relief attempt failed in December. Indeed, it was overshadowed by the further advance of Soviet forces protecting their encirclement. This led to heavy Axis casualties in the Don basin.[24] The Stalingrad pocket was driven in by Soviet attack, with the Sixth Army surrendering by February 2, 1943.

The campaign was a triumph for Soviet offensive art and was far more successful than the Soviet counteroffensive the previous winter, although, with its vulnerable and poorly held flanks, the German position at Stalingrad was far more exposed than it had been before Moscow, difficult as the latter was.

The Soviets also benefited greatly from the recovery and development of their munitions industry—for example, in tank production. The campaign was badly mishandled by the Germans, in large part due to poor direction from Hitler, who failed to respond with the necessary flexibility and exaggerated the potential impact of his determination to hold out in defensive positions. Operational failure was linked to one of strategy, the two being in a mutually causal relationship.

At the same time, outcomes were far from inevitable. In Operation Mars, from November 25 to December 14, 1942, the Soviet assault on the Rzhev salient near Moscow failed with heavy casualties, including numerous tanks. In part, this was due to the strength of the defenses and the lack of an opportunity to maneuver against them, as in Operation Uranus, launched six days earlier.[25]

EL ALAMEIN, 1942

At a very different scale, the Germans and Italians had been defeated in Egypt as well. On June 20–21, 1942, Rommel captured Tobruk, having failed to do so in 1941. This followed the battle of Gazala from May 26 to June 17, 1942, in which the resumed German attack proved successful, although the initial Axis attack had been stopped on May 29 after a major tank clash. The collapse of the British armored formations indicated problems with morale. On June 18, the *Times* reported that the German Mark IVs had "dominated the battlefield" and, five days later, that "the bulk of our tank force was made up of tanks with two-pounder guns which have again and again proved almost completely useless against the German tanks." The fall of Tobruk was partly due to the degree to which the considerable antitank obstacles in place the previous year during the long siege had not been maintained in the intervening period. Many of the antitank ditches had filled with sand. The defeat led the Americans to meet Churchill's request for an immediate supply of Shermans. Rommel, having again defeated the British at Mersa Matruh on June 26, moved on eastward, with the retreating British losing much material.

However, the German advance was checked at El Alamein, about sixty miles west of Alexandria, on July 1–4 and at Alam Halfa from August 30 through September 7. In part, this reflected the impact of a lack of fuel for any German deep flanking operation, which, for example, immobilized the Twenty-First Panzer Division on June 30 when Rommel had originally planned to attack. The British benefited from new 6-pounder antitank guns, notably when resisting attack at Deir el Shein on July 1. These were a major improvement on the 2-pounders.

In addition, British operational command and tactics had now improved. There was a readiness to engage in mobile warfare, making effective strikes in combination with holding defensive positions. This was an aspect of a more general qualitative transition in the British army as it became better prepared to take the offensive against the Germans. At the same time, Montgomery did not judge the British forces as ready for a successful offensive. Their tactical grasp of combined arms combat was limited. On July 15, the British armor did not act to protect the New Zealand troops that had seized Ruweisat Ridge only, with few antitank guns, to face German tank counterattacks. The commander of the Fifth New Zealand Infantry Brigade noted the disorientating impact of the German tank movements and the need, in response, to carry "Wrigley's grenades (sticky bombs). . . . Towards morning the tanks seemed to form up in lines on either side of the main axis of our advance . . . enabled them to use cross-fire."[26]

At Alam Halfa, later in the summer, Montgomery relied on antitank guns, a technique learned from Rommel, and inflicted serious losses on the attacking German armor. In contrast, the British tanks took defensive positions and were not launched in a follow-up attack. Earlier, attacking in Operation Splendour on July 22, the Twenty-Third Armoured Brigade had incurred heavy losses. Poor armor-infantry coordination and inadequate tanks were serious problems for the British. As a result, Montgomery refused, despite intense pressure from Churchill, to attack until the Eighth Army was ready and had built up the adequate reserve necessary for sustaining any attack.

The British launched a full-scale attack in the final battle of El Alamein from October 23 to November 4, 1942. They faced prepared positions defended by extensive minefields and well-located antitank guns and supported by armor. Increased British familiarity with combined arms tactics was important but only one of a range of factors that contributed to British success, including skillful generalship; the availability of deciphered intelligence on German moves; greater numbers of men, artillery, and tanks; better tanks; improved morale;[27] effective use of artillery; air superiority and support; and attacks on Rommel's vital fuel supplies from Italy. Rommel also deployed his artillery and reserves poorly and mishandled his Italian allies, as did most German commanders. Rommel, more generally, suffered from the understandable focus of German resources on the Eastern Front.

The shift in tank warfare was shown on November 2 when a German counterattack led to heavy German tank losses. These broke the German-Italian armor, destroying the majority of the German tanks and most of the Italian units. By November 3, Rommel had only 187 tanks left, and, of these, 155 were small Italian ones that were relatively ineffective. At the end of an attritional struggle, one in which superior British artillery, as in 1918, had been crucial, while British infantry and tank numbers were under increasing pressure, Rommel felt obliged to order a general withdrawal, leaving the Ariete tank division in the rearguard. This Italian force was destroyed.

Although failing to recognize limitations adequately at the outset, including in the British armor, Montgomery had read the terrain ably, and, alongside his adaptability and flexibility, his sequential blows eventually succeeded, not least by forcing Rommel to commit his forces, thus facilitating the decisive British blow. As a reminder that tactics take precedence over technology, this was the method used by John Churchill, first duke of Marlborough, at the expense of the French at Blenheim in 1704. Despite changes in technology, there were constants in battle planning. Montgomery's *corps de chasse* provided the flexibility to change the main point of attack during the battle and the strength to maintain the momentum of the attack after the break into the Axis position. However, the initial progress had been slow, and Montgomery's ability to read the battlefield should not be exaggerated. Moreover, he was focused on the immediate battle and proved poor at planning for the exploitation phase of the battle, although, in part, his target was removed by the rapid flight of the Germans, combined with the traffic congestion affecting the larger British forces.[28] This was to prefigure the situation in France in 1944 after the Battle of Normandy. The British aerial interdiction of retreating German forces was not very effective. Many of the Italian troops were lost because they were in the rearguard, were short of vehicles, and were mostly in the interior and thus at a distance from the coast route.

The campaign in North Africa again indicated the significance of antitank guns and their integration with armor. For example, Günter Halm, a gunner with an antitank platoon in a *panzergrenadier* regiment in the Twenty-First Panzer Division, won the Knights Cross on July 22 in the First Battle of El Alamein for destroying fifteen British tanks at Ruweisat Ridge. His gun was one of the two captured 76 mm Soviet antitank guns that comprised the platoon.[29] The use of captured material, very much including tanks, was particularly characteristic of the German military dating back to World War I. It now reflected the range of German conquests, the extensive fronts that thereby had to be defended, and the large forces, both German and allied, that had to be supplied. At the same time, there were serious consequences. Maintenance issues became more serious when there was a range of spare parts that had to be provided.

At El Alamein, as elsewhere in North Africa, British tank operations benefited greatly from the support of the Royal Engineers. This element tends to be ignored or underplayed in tank accounts. In practice, engineering is crucial, not least in bridge building, and sappers played a key role with mine-laying and mine-clearance activities. Tank repair was also fundamental: for the British, it was provided by the Royal Electrical and Mechanical Engineers (REME), and very necessarily so in 1942. During the month following El Alamein, REME detachments recovered and got back into action 1,200 tanks and other vehicles.

THE MANSTEIN COUNTERATTACK, 1943

In early 1943, the Germans demonstrated their continued success in mobile warfare, but this was now as part of a mobile defense, rather than an offensive that could transform the conflict. The Soviets had followed up their successes by launching new offensives in early 1943 that rapidly captured Voronezh, Kursk, and Kharkov. They were most successful against the overextended Second Hungarian Army south of Voronezh, a force that was destroyed with the loss of over one hundred thousand men. The Soviets were better equipped and, the Hungarians lacked antitank guns powerful enough to stop the Soviet tanks, despite requesting them from Germany.[30]

However, Field Marshal Erich von Manstein, the commander of the reconstituted Army Group South, proved skillful at mobile defense and thereby at stabilizing the front. The Germans counterattacked from February 21, benefiting from the extent to which the Soviet forces had been overstretched by the need to destroy the encircled Sixth Army in Stalingrad and mount an exhausting winter offensive that had caused considerable wear and tear to their tanks. The Germans were also helped by their ability to defeat their opponents in the air. The Germans, advancing on converging axes, were able to inflict heavy casualties, destroying most of the Soviet Sixth and First Guards Armies. The Soviets lacked nearby reserves to maintain the offensive, and the Germans recaptured Kharkov on March 12–14, which provided their last offensive victory on the Eastern Front.[31]

This was an operational-level victory, however, not the strategic triumph the Germans needed and had sought in 1942. While reversing some of the Soviet advance and destroying Soviet units were successes, they were compensatory ones at best, and, for the Germans, returning to the positions they had occupied at the beginning of the 1942 summer offensive was not good enough in strategic terms. Meanwhile, the Soviets had destroyed the largest German field army on the Eastern Front, the Sixth Army, while the buildup of US forces against Germany had already led to a dramatic change in North Africa and threatened to open a Second Front in Western Europe itself. As a result, Germany had to provide more troops to protect positions in both the Mediterranean and Western Europe.

The Soviet winter offensive had indicated the incremental nature of success, contrasting with the situation in 1939–40 when the Germans had knocked opponents out. It was only possible in 1942–43 for advancing forces to achieve so much before exhaustion, losses, and supply difficulties had an impact and led first to the slackening and then the stopping of the offensive. Moreover, the Soviets failed to appreciate that offensives simultaneously mounted at great distances from one another would not automatically draw off German strength from one theater to another. Until 1945, there was to be no one-campaign end to the war as a whole or to that on the Eastern Front. This gave the conflict an attritional character and, as a consequence, led to an emphasis on resources.

TUNISIA, 1943

There was also a German riposte in North Africa. With Rommel ignoring Italian advice to take a stop on the Halfaya Pass, a natural defensive position, the retreating Germans and Italians left Egypt and Libya rapidly after El Alamein. Montgomery pursued, although the communications were extended over 1,500 miles by the time they reached Tripoli, stretching all the way back to Alexandria along a single coastal road. The difficulty of supporting forces over such long lines of communication forced Montgomery to halt at Tripoli to try to open the port. It also limited the number of divisions he could effectively deploy.

Other US (mostly) and British forces had swiftly taken Morocco and Algeria from Vichy forces in November 1942. Hitler had rapidly moved German and Italian forces to Tunisia in reply. It had also been held by Vichy French forces, but there was no effective resistance there to the German advance. Very large gliders were used to transport supplies and reinforcements, and these proved easy targets for Allied fighters. As part of the response, the Germans also swiftly occupied Vichy France. Armor, including the Tenth Panzer Division, played a role in the latter.

Tunisia, a land of mountains and valleys, was a different military terrain than Libya but had a similar interplay of positional warfare and maneuver. The emphasis in the German war making there was on mobility, to which armor and the associated doctrine contributed greatly. The doctrine also made use of this capability. The Germans sought to exploit the Axis' central position by mounting a mobile defense and attacking the Allies advancing from Algeria. In contrast, the Italians focused on the Allied forces advancing from Libya.

The Germans also benefited from the difficulty the Allies faced in matching their advance with an adequate buildup of support, a problem that was to recur in 1944.

The German offensive that led to the Battle of Kasserine Pass in mid-February 1943 reflected both the German ability to mount defensive-offensive operations and their superior generalship and fighting quality. Elements of two panzer divisions, including newly arrived Tiger tanks, were launched on February 14 against US infantry who were supported by insufficient armor. As the battle developed, the Shermans and Grants of the US First Armored Division, which had been dispersed in defensive positions, were heavily defeated by the advancing Germans. This also led to the loss of trained crew. After the campaign, the US infantry involved received the relevant training in combined operations.

However, there were important flaws in the planning and execution of the German offensive, and initial advantages were not sustained in part because Rommel did not have the necessary combat power and in part because he wanted to turn to block the simultaneous British advance from Libya into southern Tunisia. In addition, the Americans had rallied, thanks, in part, to the effective use of artillery.[32]

The second German strike in Tunisia in 1943 was launched with three panzer divisions against Montgomery's Eighth Army at Medenine on March 6. Revealed in advance by ULTRA intelligence, this strike was rapidly thwarted, with heavy losses in German tanks (fifty-two tanks), as a result of the strength of the British position, in particular in antitank weaponry. The British 57 mm/6-pounder guns inflicted heavy losses. Montgomery kept his tanks in reserve. Smaller-scale German tank attacks at El Gueltar on March 23 were stopped by US artillery and tank destroyers, although, in turn, German antitank guns halted the advance of the British First and Sixth Armoured Divisions on April 24. The British, having blocked the Germans at Medenine, attacked the Mareth Line unsuccessfully on March 19 only to succeed in outflanking it. The difficulty the Eighth Army faced in breaking through the Mareth Line—a system of concrete fortifications and antitank ditches that had been built to defend the Tunisian border against the Italians by the French before the war—and in forcing the mountainous position at Enfidaville demonstrated that tanks were still vulnerable to well-defended positions with defensive obstacles. One of the surprises of the campaign, however, especially to the Germans, was the ability of Churchill tanks to cope with steep mountain gradients, which resulted in a number of tactical successes for the British.

In a key element of strategic weakness, once the German assaults had been blocked, their position in Tunisia was weakened by the length of their defensive perimeter. This reduced the number of reserves and ensured that the Germans were not able adequately to respond to Allied breakthroughs when they finally occurred, although they checked the US armor-infantry advance in late March. US tanks operating with artillery in support of infantry broke through German positions in late April; the British infantry broke through for their tanks on May 6, and the tanks were able to enter Tunis the following day.

By May 13, 1943, all the Axis forces in Tunisia—possibly 180,000 troops—had surrendered: more men than at Stalingrad. Attempts to evacuate the panzer divisions failed, and over 450 Axis tanks were lost in the Tunisian campaign. The Axis losses in Tunisia were compounded by Hitler's insistence on sending additional reinforcements to the area when it was already apparent that the battle was lost. For example, the use of Tiger tanks prematurely, and in inadequate numbers to be effective, was a case in point. Far from being the Verdun of the Mediterranean, as Hitler had promised, Tunisia became "Tunisgrad,"[33] making the Axis newly vulnerable in the Mediterranean and, as a result, having major consequences for the distribution of German forces as a whole.

THE BATTLE OF KURSK

By then, the Germans were preparing what was to be their last major offensive of the war on a principal theater of the Eastern Front in an attempt to return to the campaigning of the summer and autumn of 1941. Manstein's successful counterattack in February to March of 1943 had left the Germans with a vulnerable front line they could not readily protect. As Hitler did not wish to retreat, this encouraged his support for an attack. A breakthrough of the flanks of the Soviet Kursk salient was seen as a way to achieve an encirclement triumph to match the Soviet success at Stalingrad. Hitler regarded this as a battle of annihilation. However, more mundanely, the attack entailed the elimination of a position from which the Soviets could attack the neighboring German salients in the flanks. Meanwhile, the Soviets had decided to rest on the defensive in order to wear down the Germans by capitalizing on the advantages of doing so and by using the opportunity to destroy the new German tanks. This was Marshal Georgy Zhukov's advice, and it was intended as a prelude to a successful attack. Stavka, the Soviet High Command, adopted that approach.

Had Operation Citadel succeeded, the Germans were considering a further advance to the northeast designed to outflank Moscow from the south and east and thus avoid the direct approach eastward from Army Group Centre against strong Soviet defenses. However, such a follow-up offensive would have faced serious resource problems, not least the replacement of destroyed or damaged tanks and other mechanized vehicles and the availability of sufficient fuel. Germany's failure to sustain and expand its invasion of the Caucasus region the previous summer was significant to the fuel issue.

To prepare for the offensive, Hitler sought to strengthen the tank arm. On March 1, 1943, Guderian, who had been relieved of command on December 26, 1941, for being willing to retreat near Moscow, was appointed to the new post of inspector general of armored troops. As such, he was responsible for overseeing tank design, production, and training. In the last, Guderian sought to incorporate experience gained on the Eastern Front. He held this post until appointed chief of staff of the army on July 21, 1944.

Hitler also focused munitions production on building tanks, and most of those on the Eastern Front were deployed in the battle. To mount the attack, the Germans drew on their greatly increased production of tanks and the introduction of new types, including the Tiger and Panther tanks (although fewer than two hundred of each) and Ferdinand self-propelled guns. The last carried the 88 mm gun and was well protected by armor. However, the size and weight (sixty-five tons) of the Ferdinand ensured that the maximum speed was nineteen miles per hour, and the vehicle required a crew of six. Eighty-nine Ferdinands took part in the battle, but they had serious problems. The lack of any way to train its gun meant that the Ferdinand, a self-propelled gun, was less effective than a tank. It also suffered from a lack of machine guns. The limitations of the Ferdinand were compounded by its tactical employment in the initial stages of the battle. It was used as part of the "break-in" force, for which it was less than ideal, and it proved vulnerable to mines, obstacles, and well-placed antitank guns. When, in contrast, the Ferdinand was pulled back and used in a defensive, tank-destroyer role, it proved extremely effective.

The Soviets were ready for the German attack as they had not been before. Forewarned by accurate intelligence information, the Soviets had prepared a dense defensive system of six belts, appropriately designed to resist tank attack. These belts, which included extensive antitank defenses, field fortifications, and minefields, ensured the terrain was not open and also provided a defense in depth and artillery-support system that inflicted heavy casualties when, against Guderian's advice, the outnumbered Germans attacked on July 5, 1943. Guderian not only objected to the operation on tactical grounds but also on technical ones. As inspector general of armored troops, he knew there were technical and mechanical deficiencies with the new tank designs before committing them to large-scale combat. Guderian also argued that tank numbers should be built up before the battle.

Attrition replaced breakthrough for the Germans. Once the German armor, including the reserves, had been weakened, notably at the hands of Soviet artillery, and the tanks fought their way through some of the defenses, more in the southern than the northern sector, the Soviets were better able to commit their tank reserves against the German pincers. The Germans had Panther and Tiger tanks, which were particularly effective at long range, but the Soviet T-34s were used en masse, which allowed enough tanks to close with the Germans, despite heavy losses, to alleviate the disadvantages. The T-34s could be employed effectively at close range, and the Soviets had more tanks and uncommitted reserves. The Germans, moreover, did not fight well. Aside from tactical flaws, there were many command mistakes. For example, in accepting battle at Prokhorovka on July 12, Lieutenant-General Hermann Hoth, the commander of the Fourth Panzer Army, knowingly gambled on the tactical skills and technical superiority of the outnumbered and unsupported divisions of the Second SS Panzer Corps because he remained committed to his view that the decisive engagement would be fought there.

Although, in a battle the course of which remains contentious, German losses were less than often claimed, and despite some poor Soviet command decisions, including at Prokhorovka, the Germans failed to break through the Soviet lines and close the pocket. Hitler cancelled the operation on July 13.[34] Both sides had benefited from ground-attack aircraft, but not decisively so. The Soviets were greatly helped by the availability of large armor reserves. Indeed, the Soviet management of supply and demand proved important both to production and battlefield capability.[35] Large reserves meant they could take greater losses at Kursk and remain operational while the German losses, although fewer numerically, were greater proportionately and made them less able to advance. The Germans could not afford these losses. The heavy losses of the T-34s indicated that it was, if not obsolete, certainly not cutting edge, but it continued to be used.

The Soviets, having stopped the Germans, were now in a position to counterattack. Their own forces had not been so exhausted in the defensive struggle that they could not swiftly move over to the offensive. The Soviets attacked in the direction of Belgorod and Kharkov, capturing the cities on August 3 and 23 respectively. This achievement reflected the presence of large reserve forces, a particular strength of the Soviet military, and an organizational system that was better able to meet the demands of an offensive than had been the case in the more improvised circumstances at the beginning of the year.

This ability was a matter not only of supplies and maintenance but also of new and effective unit structures.[36] Thanks to a major increase in tank production, the Soviets were able to replace the very heavy losses their tank units suffered, notably in tank-versus-tank conflict and in conflict against prepared defenses. Thus, the 107th Tank Brigade of the Second Tank Army on the northern side of the Kursk salient lost forty-six out of fifty tanks in one day.[37]

Despite their doctrinal emphasis on a delaying resistance, trading space for time while inflicting casualties and preparing for a counteroffensive, the Germans proved less effective in defense than the Soviets, which was an aspect of their more general limitations on the defense. These were apparent both in prepared positions, notably with a lack of adequate artillery support, and also with a shortage of the armor necessary to provide mobile reserves. German tank losses in the Kursk offensive had this dangerous consequence. After the war, Manstein criticized Hitler for his preference for holding positions, as in his stand-fast order of December 18, 1941, rather than turning to mobile defense. However, the latter option posed serious logistical challenges, especially for inadequate fuel supplies.[38] Moreover, both approaches underrated Soviet resilience.

SOVIET ATTACKS IN LATE 1943

The focus on German tank attacks ensures that too much of the discussion about the Eastern Front in 1943 has been devoted to the Kursk offensive. However, this concentration both fails to put the German defeat in the context of a wider Soviet success and also serves to permit an analysis of this operation's failure to offer an explanation of Germany's wider difficulties. This is misleading because Operation Citadel was a failure of the Germans on the offensive, but the wider Soviet success represented a serious failure of the Germans on the defensive.

Before the struggle around Kursk had finished, the Soviets had already launched an offensive further south, overrunning eastern Ukraine. Soviet resources, including the quantity and quality of their tanks and a rate of production far greater than that of Germany, were important. In 1943, their tank production had risen to twenty-nine thousand. Soviet operational skill was also significant. Earlier theories of deep operations advanced in the 1930s were now refined in the cauldron of war. Rather than seek encirclements, the Soviets deployed their forces along broad fronts, launching a number of frontal assaults designed to smash opposing forces and maintain continual pressure, an approach that was most appropriate in logistical terms. Unlike

Britain, Germany, and the United States, the Soviet military did not try to maintain the integrity and strength of their divisions, especially their armored divisions. Instead, they would use them until they were effectively no longer operational or destroyed and replace them with new, formed units with full complements of men and equipment.

The Soviets denied the Germans the ability to recover from attacks, lessened their capacity to move units to badly threatened positions, and searched out the weakest points in their positions. This approach reduced the value of German defensive "hedgehogs," mutually supporting strongpoints that were part of a defense in depth. These "hedgehogs" were less significant in resisting broad-front attacks, especially when they could not rely on armored counteroffensives.

These Soviet successes lessened the availability of German mobile reserves necessary to oppose successfully a Second Front, the proposed Anglo-American invasion of Western Europe. On the other hand, Soviet offensives were not all successful. Thus, that into Belarus in November-December 1943 miscarried. Yet there was a cumulative and effective pressure on the Germans.[39]

THE PACIFIC, 1942–44

Tanks played a far smaller role in the war in the Pacific. Nevertheless, they were deployed, notably by the Americans on the island of Guadalcanal in the Southwestern Pacific in 1942–43, where, on January 22, 1943, a Stuart tank had some success against Japanese defensive positions, particularly destroying pillboxes. The close proximity of the fighting ensured that the tanks required protection, which was provided during that attack. Another Stuart tank, lacking infantry support, had been rushed and set on fire by Japanese troops in the US landing on nearby Tanambogo Island on August 6, 1942. There were also Japanese tanks on Guadalcanal but no tank-to-tank conflict. While very good against the Japanese, the Stuarts were outclassed by the Germans in firepower and armor. The new tank squadron of the New Zealand Third Division operated in the Solomon Islands in 1943–44.

Tanks were used by the Americans in 1944 in Kwajalein, Saipan, and Tinian in the Central Pacific. They encountered not only defensive fire, but also mines.[40] On the first, Shermans defeated Japanese Type 94 tankettes. Allied leaflets dropped on Japanese troops told them, "You Can't Fight Tanks with Bayonets."[41] The Americans also used armed amphibious tractors at least partly operated by tank crews.

ITALY, 1943-45

British and US offensives in Italy faced serious problems. Italy was poor tank country due to the mountainous terrain. Sicily was invaded on July 10, 1943. In its defense, the Italian Sixth Army had few, mostly obsolete, tanks and was not helped by the refusal of the Germans to deploy the Fourteenth Panzer Corps near the coast. When the Allies invaded, the Italian defenders, including their tanks, were overwhelmed, and the German tanks were too far away to offer initial support. Subsequently, when the Allies advanced in Sicily, they found that the Germans took advantage of the terrain, which limited the use of Allied armor.

From September 3, the Allies invaded mainland Italy. Air power was seen as the way to stop German counterattacks,[42] but air power would not ensure success in mounting offensives. In mainland Italy, the density of German forces on the relatively narrow east-west defensive lines hampered Allied advances while Allied firepower stopped German attacks on Allied landing sites at Salerno (1943) and Anzio (1944). In the first case, two German panzer divisions attacked the beachhead in a determined and well-organized attack but suffered from a shortage of fuel as well as from the Allied response, which included heavy naval gunfire and the flying in of reinforcements. At Anzio, the rapid German reaction was led by armored units. There and elsewhere, naval gunfire support, which was chiefly from 6- and 15-inch guns, had a devastating impact on tank armor.

Allied tanks were often used in a fire-support role in support of infantry attacks—in other words, as mobile artillery. Yet armor was still used in large numbers by the Allies. In Operation Diadem, the fourth and last battle of Monte Cassino, the Allies committed two thousand tanks as part of their twenty-five-division-strong force, albeit suffering seriously from German anti-tank guns as in the Liri Valley, where the Germans had built tank obstacles, laid minefields, and cleared lines of fire to ensure killing zones. The static defenses included Panther turrets concreted into the ground. More Allied tanks were knocked out in taking this position on May 23, 1944, than on any other day of the Italian campaign. The action gave an indication of the sort of casualties that could be expected in Normandy when attacking determined and well-prepared defenses. The battle saw the first encounter of a Panther tank by the Western Allies.

At the same time, in Italy there was an absence of relevant Allied doctrine and effective planning. This was particularly the case after the Gustav Line was broken in May 1944. The pursuit of the Germans was insufficiently close, in marked contrast to the Soviet style. In August, Field Marshal Sir Alan Brooke, the chief of the Imperial General Staff, wrote about General Sir Harold Alexander, the Army Group commander:

> I am rather disappointed that Alex did not make a more definite attempt to smash Kesselring's forces up whilst they were south of the Apennines. He has planned a battle on the Apennine position and seems to be deliberately driving the Germans back onto that position instead of breaking them up in the more favourable country. I cannot feel that this policy of small pushes all along the line and driving the Boche [Germans] like partridges can be right. I should have liked to see one concentrated attack, with sufficient depth to it, put in at a suitable spot with a view to breaking through and smashing up German divisions by swinging with right and left. However, it is a bit late for that now . . . very hard to get old Alex to grasp the real requirements of any strategic situation.[43]

Alongside serious US and British command flaws, notably General Mark Clark's concern with focusing on the capture of Rome, rather than fighting the German Tenth Army, there were issues with the terrain. Between Monte Cassino and Rome, the Allies had an uninterrupted chain of mountains on their right side, and many difficult hills between them and Rome. There was only one relatively good road. Moreover, the plain, near the sea, was in origin a marsh, the Paludi Pontine. It had been drained by Mussolini, but soon after the Anzio landing, the Germans had destroyed the many small dams and, thereby, rendered the ground difficult for Allied tanks. In addition, Alexander was short of resources, which were focused on the Normandy (Overlord) and Provence (Dragoon) landings.

The Germans were able to retreat to the Gothic Line, protecting northern Italy. However, near Rimini in September 1944, a combined armor-infantry operation by the Fifth Canadian Armoured Division broke through the defenses, defeating the Germans—a success the division repeated the following year as it fought its way toward Venice.

EASTERN FRONT, 1944

In 1944, the Soviets, repeatedly taking the initiative and determining where the fighting should occur, again used combined forces successfully. They proved adept at developing good cooperation among armor, artillery, and infantry, and, helped by US aid, at making the latter two mobile. At the same time, the Soviet willingness to take very heavy casualties was important.

In early 1944, the outnumbered Germans were driven from western Ukraine. The campaign was less well handled by German commanders than that of early 1943, although the different verdict also reflected an increase in Soviet operational effectiveness and tactical skill, as well as not needing to focus on dealing with the remnants of the German Sixth Army in Stalingrad. As a consequence of Soviet strength and competence and declining German combat, command, and support effectiveness, German counterattacks were less successful than hitherto. The Soviets used their reserves well to maintain the pace of the advance and thwart counterattacks but were greatly handicapped by the difficulties of maintaining resupply. This became more serious as they advanced.[44] The Soviets aimed for synchronized blows in order to deliver a cumulative operational shock (*udar*).[45] In practice, there was less coherence than theory and planning suggested; at the same time, Soviet combined arms expertise increased with experience. However, there were failures, notably the attempts from mid-April to early June to advance across the Dniester River into Romania. In these, the Germans benefited from the logistical strain on the overextended Soviets and the problems created by the spring thaw. At the same time, the bold use of tanks in counterattacks worked in May and June.[46]

Nevertheless, the burden of operational effectiveness was now against the Germans, in particular with Operation Bagration, the attack launched on Army Group Centre on June 23, 1944. In a repeat of the German success against France in 1940, Soviet operational skill was accentuated by the command and intelligence failings of its opponents. In addition, there was striking Soviet superiority in tanks and aircraft. The need for the Germans to defend the entire front against a series of Soviet attacks left them with few resources for staging counteroffensives. Moreover, the Soviets advanced on their flanks, knocking Germany's allies, Romania, Bulgaria, and Finland, out of the war. Soviet operational skill counteracted German tactical proficiency. The latter itself was undergoing strain, both because of Soviet improvements and because the effectiveness of the German army declined as veterans were replaced by poorly trained new recruits. There was also a lack of adequate mobile reserves.

The Soviets not only enjoyed a major advantage in artillery but also continued improvement in their armor to match new German tank types. The T-34/85 was more heavily gunned than its predecessors. The IS (Josef Stalin) 2, introduced in the spring of 1944 and able to take on Tiger IIs, became the best Soviet tank of the war as it proved an effective main battle tank.[47] This was an aspect of the more general enhancement in Soviet fighting capability.

Armor was usually used to the Soviet advantage. However, a German armored counterattack, including Tiger IIs, near Debrecen in Hungary in late October 1944 inflicted heavy casualties on the Romanian Fourth Division (now fighting with the Soviets), which was encircled and forced to surrender on October 20. The Germans remained a formidable force, or at least a potentially formidable force, even though they were losing, which was a contrast between effectiveness at the tactical (high) and strategic (low) levels of war, with the operational level drawing on elements of both.

INVASION OF NORMANDY, 1944

The Canadian attack on the Channel port of Dieppe on August 19, 1942, a raid in force, demonstrated the problems of attacking a defended coast. The planners had intended that nine Churchill Mark III tanks should land simultaneously with the infantry in order to provide close fire support. However, due to a navigational error, the tanks landed fifteen minutes late, which enabled the German defenders to recover from their surprise and put down a terrible fire against the attackers. In the event, twenty-nine Churchills eventually landed, although two were "drowned," and some became bogged down in the sand on the beach. None were able to get past the concrete obstacles blocking the way into the town. The tanks could provide fire support in the subsequent battle, but that was inadequate, and the attacking force was defeated with heavy casualties.[48] This failure indicated the challenge facing the Allies invading Normandy in 1944.

Failure at Dieppe encouraged the British to press, against Soviet demands and US wishes, for the delay of any Second Front into 1944. In the meantime, Allied strength had been built up. This was a matter of scale and quality. Large numbers of tanks were built; new units were constituted, including the US Twentieth Armored Division on March 15, 1943; and relevant training took place. The infrastructure was considerable. The British had calculated that to keep one hundred Churchill tanks going for fourteen days, it was necessary to have 150 tons of spare parts.[49]

Tank availability, dispositions, moves, and conflict played a more major role in the invasion of Normandy on June 6, 1944—D-Day—and in the subsequent conflict than in the invasion of Italy. Allied planners were greatly concerned that the German panzer divisions in France would drive in the beachheads before they could become established and supported by sufficient antitank guns and armor. The German commanders, however, were divided about where the Allied attack was likely to fall and about how best to respond to it. There was particular disagreement over whether the panzer divisions should be moved close to the coast, so the Allies could be attacked before they could consolidate their position, or massed as a strategic reserve, the latter the advice of General Geyr von Schweppenburg. Rommel wanted to defeat the invasion at the waterline. The eventual decision—made by Hitler, who had taken direct control—was for the panzer divisions to remain inland, but their ability to act as a strategic reserve was lessened by the decision not to mass them and by Allied air power. This decision reflected the tensions and uncertainties of the German command structure. These tensions accentuated major failings in German intelligence and planning.

On the invasion day, tanks were used by the invasion force. Responding in part to the problems encountered at Dieppe, the British employed specialized tanks to attack coastal defenses, notably Sherman Crab mine-clearing tanks. There were also Centaurs—95 mm howitzer close-support tanks. The Americans were not keen on these tanks.

On Omaha Beach, there were two American battalions, the 743rd and 741st, each with forty-eight tanks. Landing with the 1st Division, the 741st lost twenty-nine of their Duplex Drive (amphibious) Sherman tanks. These were launched too far offshore—five thousand yards, or nearly four miles from Omaha Beach—in a sea with six-foot waves, and the crews therefore drowned. Only three made it ashore of the thirty-two, but the rest of the 741st landed dry-shod, as did most of the 743rd operating further west with the 29th Division. The Germans had two 88 mm guns at Omaha Beach. They were in fixed bunkers and not mobile. An American tank destroyed the emplacement on the western end of Omaha Beach. There were also mines and antitank ditches on the beach, and the latter had to be cleared by M4 tank dozers. Sixteen were scheduled to land in the early assault, but only six got ashore, and five of those were knocked out. Once the beach was cleared, tanks were able to move inland from Omaha to help clear the town of Colleville.

On Utah Beach, the German resistance was weaker, but only five of twelve expected landing craft tanks (LCTs) landed safely. The decision was made to launch from three thousand yards out, and only a few tanks drowned on the run in. However, the planners had underestimated the effect of the sea state and current on the speed of the tanks through water. As a result, they landed after the initial infantry craft, not before, as had been planned.

The Twenty-First Panzer Division, the sole German armored division in the area and a poorly commanded unit, did not counterattack until the early afternoon. German tanks then approached the Channel between Juno and Sword Beaches, but they were blocked.[50] Far from having division-sized manning and equipment, the Twenty-First had 112 Mark IVs and some old French tanks and lacked the feared Tigers and Panthers. Elements of the division that counterattacked toward the sea were unnerved by seeing follow-on glider forces landing near their position and, fearing being outflanked, withdrew. The Allies, meanwhile, suffered from a shortage of

LCTs, which affected the availability of armor in the crucial early stages of the battle for Normandy.

BATTLE OF NORMANDY

It proved difficult for the Allies to exploit the success and break out of Normandy. The Allies had assumed that the Germans, unable to hold their coastal fortifications, would fall back in order to defend a line, probably that of the River Seine. Instead, the Germans chose to fight hard, both near the coast and for all the territory. This defense obliged the Allies, unexpectedly, to fight in the bocage, the local Norman countryside, with its thick hedgerows and sunken lanes. Although the Caen plain is flat, Normandy was not good tank country. The landscape greatly affected cross-country performance and assisted the defense. Allied armor, doctrine, and tactics were not well-suited to the bocage and, in particular, the opportunities it offered to the defense, although the bocage was also not suitable for the Germans, whose tanks were designed for long-range firing.

Moreover, the German challenge was enhanced not only by their experience on the defense on the Eastern Front but also by the greater strength offered their defense by antitank guns, both self-propelled and not, and by heavy tanks. Resting on the defense, the Germans enjoyed the advantage of firing first, at close range, and from a stable position. Entering open ground exposed Allied tanks to serious risk, which led them to prefer to provide indirect support and, thereby, use dead ground. This situation put a renewed emphasis on infantry-armor cooperation for the attackers, but that is easier in doctrine than in practice, and the bocage made coordination particularly difficult.

With their individual units often lacking adequate training, experience, quality equipment, command, and doctrine, the Allies faced a hard battle and fell behind the anticipated phase lines for their advance. Allied casualty rates were far higher than in the initial landings. Despite air attacks, especially on bridges, the Germans were able to reinforce their units in Normandy, although the delays forced on them both ensured that the Allies gained time to deepen their beachheads and obliged the Germans to respond in an ad hoc fashion to Allied advances, using their tanks as a defense force, rather than driving in the beachheads. When the German armor was eventually employed in bulk on June 29–30, it was stopped by Allied air attack. Another armor counterattack was defeated on July 11.

In the Battle of Normandy, the Germans learned how to adapt in the face of concentrated firepower and air attack, and also adapted well to defending the bocage, whereas the Allies, notably the British and the Canadians, found it difficult to break through and restore maneuver.[51] The Allied tanks failed to achieve what the Americans and British (and Germans) had expected from tanks. This was more than a matter of difficult terrain: the numerous hedges and sunken lanes of the bocage that provided excellent cover for opposing tanks and antitank guns and obstructed observation, movement, and lines of fire, each individually, and even more in combination, affected the capabilities of the attacking armor. Helped by the proximity of the bocage, the Germans also used sticky bombs against tanks. Small unit actions became the norm. These tested the ability to develop new tactics. Both sides did so while having to confront a lack of the necessary experience.

There were also serious operational limitations for tank warfare, not least vulnerability to antitank guns, which had become much more powerful since 1940, and the problems of communications with infantry. The last led to radios being installed in tanks to aid coordination with air power while telephone sets were placed on the backs so infantry could communicate with the tanks. The German antitank weapons included the 88 mm dual-purpose gun, the PaK 38 and PaK 40 antitank guns, the Panzerfaust, and the Panzerschreck. The Germans, however, suffered from a relative shortage of ammunition. Moreover, the Allies had far more antitank guns.

Although the Sherman was effective against opposing infantry, it suffered in tank combat in comparison with the Panther and Tiger but was better than the Mark IV, which remained the most numerous type of German tank. To help in the bocage, some Allied tanks were fitted with steel spikes so they could drive through the hedgerows. These were known as "Rhino" tanks. Sergeant Cullin, who devised the Rhino blades, was a mechanic in civilian life. The blades were iron spikes shaped as cutting blades, fabricated from German beach defenses, and fitted in front of the tracks of Sherman tanks. They proved able to cut through the hedgerows and were quickly approved for introduction to service. It took about a day for a three-man team to make and fit the device to a tank. They were fitted to over 16 percent of the available tanks and made a massive difference, not only to tactical effectiveness but also to the morale of tank crews. The episode, a classic example of US ingenuity and improvisation, reflected the adaptability of tanks as vehicles. This adaptability was also seen in tanks being used in battle to carry infantry, notably so by the Soviets. US adaptability in the Battle of Normandy was also evident in a far more effective tank maintenance practice than that of the Germans. Maintenance by the British and Canadians was also impressive.

The Germans benefited from their fighting quality and experience, although they faced many difficulties, not least poor command decisions. In the eastern sector, the British took heavy casualties in successive attempts to advance near Caen, including the loss of five hundred tanks with the failure of Operation Goodwood on July 18–20, an advance weakened by being from a small bridgehead over the River Orne and on a limited front. This exposed the attackers to fire from both flanks as well as restricted the number of tanks that could be used. Looked at differently, the Allies' failure to break through near Caen in part, at least initially, was also a matter of thwarting the possibility of a German advance in the area most propitious for such a move.[52]

Losses led to questions about the effectiveness of the British armor, as well as about British fighting quality and Montgomery's generalship. Many of the units involved had little combat experience and displayed a formality and rigidity in tactics that left them vulnerable. O'Connor, the commander of the British Eighth Corps, which included part of the British armor, noted that British armored divisions had varied in their fighting quality, adding: "The enemy, particularly the SS divisions, have fought fantastically."[53] O'Connor himself was less successful than he had been against the Italians in 1940–41. There were strains in the morale of some armor units, notably the Seventh Armoured Division and the Fourth Canadian Armoured Division. The overuse of tanks was also a deliberate policy to minimize the continued heavy infantry losses. A lack of sufficient British and Canadian infantry ensured that the Goodwood attack began without adequate infantry support. More infantry to secure the villages that were bypassed in the initial tank advance would have made a major difference in the course of the attack.

The British armor, however, learned rapidly, and it played a greater role in the German defeat[54] than is often credited. Moreover, attacks helped divert German troops, including most of the armor, from the US front further west, which was to be the crucial breakthrough zone. Without these attacks, the Americans would not have succeeded. Thus, the last uncommitted panzer division was sucked into the Caen sector, where the Germans lost tanks and self-propelled guns they could ill afford. Therefore, Goodwood was a tactical failure but an operational success, a contrast also seen on other occasions. Furthermore, of the British tanks put out of action in Goodwood, 231 were quickly recovered and returned to sector.

As so often, it is also necessary to distinguish beyond national characteristics or stereotypes in order to investigate differences between individual units. In Goodwood, the Eleventh Armoured Division did better than the Seventh,[55] although the latter, which was more professional and moved slowly and carefully, had fewer casualties. The Eleventh was helped by being equipped with Cromwell tanks, which were significantly faster and more maneuverable than the Shermans. The same was true of differences, later that year, among US divisions in their willingness to use tanks to support infantry.[56] This was also the case for the German army and its very varied degrees of motorization and fighting quality.

Operation Cobra, delayed by the weather but begun by the Americans on July 25, created a breach, with heavy bombing wrecking the Panzer Lehr Division. Operational flexibility played a part in the Cobra breakout.[57] Firepower and infantry attack were crucial in the initial attack, but the US Second, Third, Fourth and Sixth Armored Divisions played a key role in both the creation and then exploitation of the breakthrough. Coutances fell on July 28 and Avranches three days later.

In turn, Operation Lüttich, a German counterattack by four panzer divisions through the Mortain area, was launched, on August 7, in pursuit of Hitler's hope of wrecking the Normandy landings and, more particularly, pinching that neck of the breakthrough. However, it was thwarted by strong US resistance. Defeat at Mortain prefigured the later German failure in the Battle of the Bulge.[58] The German plan reflected their commitment to a mobile defense. Having cut off the US Third Army, the Germans, who had brought up reserves, planned to turn against the First Army. Thus, the armor was to gain a central position and then use local superiority to defeat the Americans sequentially. However, the Allies had foreknowledge of the plan due to signals interception and destroyed the promised aerial support before the offensive was launched. The Germans suffered by being outnumbered in tanks, with only 190 in their four panzer divisions (divisions in name only), while the US Third Armored had 250. Defeated by US infantry, artillery, and armor, the Germans were also weakened by attacking across the front, rather than focusing on particular points and breaking through. The Germans ended the operation after failing to break through.

Allied ground-attack aircraft also played a role in the failure of Operation Lüttich. The Allies used close air support from the Second Tactical Air Force, notably with a cab-rank system that ensured missions were handled as they arose. In the earlier pattern of the Stuka on Allied forces, the rocket-firing Typhoon had a serious impact on German morale. Germans who were captured in Normandy said the two main differences between fighting in Normandy and on the Eastern Front were, first, the lack of night operations in Normandy and, second, the ever-present threat from "Jabos": British and US ground-attack fighter-bombers. However, these aircraft inflicted less damage in practice. The accurate targeting of unguided rockets was very difficult against tanks—indeed, against anything smaller than a train—and claims of tank kills by aircraft were greatly exaggerated.[59] At the same time, the risk from air attack meant the Germans preferred not to move their tanks by day. Instead, they were employed in defensive positions. Because of Allied air support, the ground-attack aircraft were not often bothered by German fighters, but antiaircraft fire was a serious threat.

ALLIES ADVANCE TO THE FRONTIER, 1944

The much-delayed Allied breakout was followed, from August 10 to August 21, by the battle of the Falaise Pocket, with the nearly trapped German Panzer Group West taking heavy losses to Allied artillery, tank gunnery, and aircraft, but the Allies failed to achieve a complete encirclement. As a result, although much equipment was lost, many Germans escaped and were to provide valuable experience when their divisions were resupplied. The breakout also led to a rapid US armor drive into Brittany, with the Sixth Armored Division advancing to Brest, which was surrounded, while the Fourth captured Vannes, cutting off the German forces in Brittany, on August 5 and took Nantes a week later. This was a mistaken diversion of US armor away from the core target of the German forces moving back toward Germany.[60]

The Allies advanced across France and Belgium to the German frontier. Thus, on August 16, US tanks entered Chartres; on August 24, French tanks of the Second Armored Division, which had disembarked in Normandy on August 1, reached Paris. The US Seventh Armored Division crossed the Marne River at Château-Thierry on August 28 and the Meuse River at Verdun three days later before running out of gasoline. The British Eleventh Armoured Division captured Antwerp on September 4.

However, there was no success in cutting off most of the retreating German forces. Linked to this, the Germans did not experience losses comparable to those suffered at the hands of the far-more-numerous Soviets. In part, this was because it was difficult for amphibious forces to transform themselves rapidly for fast-moving advances. The Anglo-American forces had less experience than the Soviets in large-scale maneuver battles with the Germans and in the exploitation phase of battles and, subsequently, in maintaining the advance when it encountered resistance. It was far from easy to learn how best to use armor for large-scale mobile operations, an issue that remains relevant. The Germans had been doing so since 1939 and still made many mistakes in 1944. US and British commanders had to learn, at many levels, to overcome grave logistical problems and coordinate armor, infantry, and air assets, both before and during combat. At the same time, there were important differences in aptitude in this respect between commanders and units, as had already been shown in North Africa and Italy in 1941–43.[61]

The broad-front approach to the advance across France did not work in cutting off the retreating Germans or in forcing a breakthrough once stronger opposition was encountered. Possibly, a narrow-front approach—for example, a crossing of the Rhine from Alsace by the US Sixth Army Group[62]—would have also failed, but its potential for exploitation was not grasped. The broad-front approach, in part, reflected a "come-as-you-are" tactic, moving forward troops from existing alignments in northern and southern France where Allied forces had landed on August 15. This approach also lessened the burden on particular communication routes. More positively, a broad front was a reflection of the need to maintain superiority over the qualitatively strong German forces. At the same time, this approach represented a needless anxiety about flanks and a major diffusion of combat effectiveness. The resulting lack of concentration of force seen in 1944 was appropriate more for a follow-up advance than for a fighting one. There was no equivalent to Soviet-style "deep battle" or German-style blitzkrieg, neither of which had the same concern about flanks, and no equivalent to what the Germans were to seek to do in the Battle of the Bulge.

Allied operations after the Battle of Normandy, in a chaotic and improvised campaign in which Allied generals failed to display the necessary cooperation, were also affected by supply difficulties, notably the absence of adequate port facilities, damage to the rail system, and a lack of sufficient trucks. In addition, the logistical system was mishandled. Nevertheless, more armor was moved forward. For example, the Twelfth Armored Division, activated on September 15, 1942, left New York on September 20, 1944, and, via England, arrived at Le Havre on November 11, moving to Alsace, where it entered conflict from December 5.

The Germans themselves were vulnerable. On September 15, Field Marshal von Rundstedt complained that Army Group B was covering a front of 250 miles, but with only eighty-four serviceable tanks, assault guns, and light tank destroyers.[63] Two days earlier, the 116th Panzer division had only twelve operational tanks.

The German defense, however, hardened as the campaign of maneuver in the West was forced to a close in the autumn of 1944, with Allied mobility reduced to positional warfare. Explanations solely in terms of Allied failure are inadequate as they fail to focus on German determination, which included an ability to keep much of the war economy going even under destructive

Anglo-American bombing.[64] This meant that more tanks and antitank weaponry were produced. Moreover, fighting for Germany helped motivate the troops, not least due to the unattractive offer of unconditional surrender, although defiance, German nationalism, and military values were all more significant. The German army did not collapse. Its units, both large and small, retained cohesion.[65]

The Germans, indeed, won a series of defensive successes. German success at Arnhem indicated the deficiencies of an airborne assault when confronted by a mobile defense. In addition, the British airborne forces landed there lacked an effective antitank gun, although the PIAT, if not as deadly as the bazooka or the Panzerschreck, did score a number of successes against Tiger tanks. The British armor advancing toward Arnhem faced terrain that was both demanding and dictating: British armor had to move along narrow roads, in a country filled with ditches, canals, and rivers, preventing any wide-front movement of tank units. Instead, they were forced to advance in column and could rarely deploy and use all their firepower.

Further south, against firm German defenses, US tank destroyers and self-propelled guns alike provided the infantry with fire support—for example, in capturing the city of Aachen in October 1944. However, the strength of such positions, protected by well-motivated troops using antitank weaponry, was a formidable challenge. Furthermore, in the hilly terrain of the Huertgen Forest, the Americans took heavy casualties from October as they let themselves get bogged down in forest fighting and failed to break through the German defenses and advance eastwards into better tank country.

In addition, Patton found it difficult to accept that his zeal for movement was stopped by conditions in Lorraine and that it would not be possible to advance speedily to the Rhine. Aside from the German resistance, there were problems with the terrain once the autumn rains had saturated the ground.[66] The infantry bore the brunt of the struggle on both sides, but armor played a role, not least in successful German counterattacks. Moreover, further south, the French Second Armored Division captured Strasbourg on November 23.

GERMAN WINTER COUNTEROFFENSIVES, 1944–45

The Wehrmacht found itself on the defensive, trapped in an attritional war it could not win.[67] German attempts to regain mobility, notably by means of the Battle of the Bulge in December, failed. The Germans had been building up a significant armored force in Germany from September, in order to attack the Americans. However, aside from the political folly of German strategy—the assumption that the United States and Britain could be forced to abandon the war—there was not room for the maneuver warfare the Germans had earlier used so well.

In the Bulge offensive, the tactical and operational advantages of armor when launched against unprepared defenses were clear. The aggressive nature of the surprise assault was impressive, and individual units did not need to be directed from high. The German armor fought well. The strength and novelty of the massed German armor for most of the Allied troops was a problem,[68] as was the German ability to gain and use the advantage of surprise against overstretched defenders lacking adequate reserves. Moreover, the Germans benefited from the impact of bad weather on Allied air operations. A forty-five-mile-long gap was smashed in the Allied front, and, deploying eight panzer divisions, the Germans were able to advance close to the River Meuse.

At the same time, these German tactical and operational advantages were lessened by deficiencies, notably a lack of fuel and some poor training, especially on the part of infantry units, as well as the strengths of the Americans, which included impressive artillery. Initial German successes could not be sustained in part because of the swiftness with which the Americans deployed reinforcements. Once the weather improved, ground-support air attacks proved particularly important against German tanks. The Germans also suffered from supply problems, as well as from the narrowness of the front, the terrain, and the firmness, strength, and eventual success of the US resistance, notably in Bastogne and on the flanks.[69]

To obstruct the German armor advance, US engineers set up roadblocks and mined bridges, delaying the German tanks—for example, by blowing up the main bridges at Trois Ponts on December 17 and that over the River Wiltz the next day.[70] The ability of such moves to affect armor operations was an indication of the problems facing tanks, and not just at the tactical level. Moreover, defensive obstacle-making moves could be accentuated by the use of antitank guns and other antitank weaponry, stationary or mobile. This capability underlined the significance of engineering units as an integral part of armor advances. In addition, antitank mines proved effective against German tanks while US tanks were important to the defense. At St. Vith, the Seventh Armored Division mounted a successful delaying action, while the Combat Command B of the Tenth Armored fought a delaying action at Bastogne. They were also significant to the counterattack, as with the relief of Bastogne by the Fourth Armored Division.

Another German counteroffensive, Operation Nordwind, in Alsace in January 1945, was resisted in part by US tank destroyers. These destroyed many tanks, with the African Americans of the 827th Tank Destroyer Battalion with their M18 Hellcats particularly successful. At the same time, the operation of these tank destroyers revealed serious training and organizational problems, not least in coordination with infantry. The battalion had been trained on the expectation that the gunners would fire only on the instruction of their own officers. Conversely, the infantry officers gave instructions that were suited to tanks rather than the lightly armored Hellcats.[71] As a whole, the operation saw US tank units successful on the defensive, albeit taking heavy casualties.

THE WESTERN ALLIES ADVANCE INTO GERMANY, 1945

US and British forces advancing into Germany in early 1945 took part primarily in infantry struggles, with the armor frequently involved in support, as with the use of tanks to back the US Thirty-Fifth Infantry Division on its advance from the River Poer to the Rhine in March. At the same time, the armor was also involved in tank conflict with German tanks. Moreover, there were divisional-level attacks, as with the US Fourteenth Armored Division breaking through the Siegfried Line and advancing to the Rhine.

In turn, a shortage of gasoline, and being heavily outnumbered in tanks, affected the defense of Germany after the Americans crossed the Rhine on March 7 at Remagan. After the Americans encircled the German forces in the Ruhr on April 1,[72] an operation in which the Third Armored Division played a key role, including overcoming SS panzer training units, they rapidly advanced east and southeast, overrunning much of Germany. On their left, the British, who had developed an effective fighting performance,[73] overran northwest Germany. They benefited there from fighting in far more open country than the Normandy bocage or the waterlogged Lower Rhineland.

These advances still involved much fighting. In this, there was care to keep armor, infantry, and artillery able to offer mutual support. Thus, on April 12, the US Fourteenth Armored Division found the bridge over the River Main at Lichtenfels destroyed. The rifle company accompanying the Twenty-Fifth Tank Battalion forded the river and captured the town under a supporting smoke screen laid down by the battalion's mortar battalion and backed by tanks firing across the river. Three days later, an advance reconnaissance force was cut off in the town of Creussen by a German counterattack that included thirty-five tanks. They blocked a relief force of US armor, but its infantry support was able to advance, and more tanks, supported by frequent air strikes and artillery, defeated the Germans, destroying nineteen tanks. On April 21, west of Allersberg, antitank fire destroyed a US tank and tank destroyer at what they called "88 Junction" from the rounds fired by a Tiger tank. The following day, a US infantry advance on Allersberg, supported by eight medium tanks, two assault guns, and one tank destroyer, met resistance from two Tiger tanks whose armor held up well against bazooka rounds. US attacks were met not only by tanks but also by machine guns, and Allersberg was not taken until April 24.[74] Such campaigning, which involved tough combat until the end of the war, as captured in the film *Fury* (2014), drove home the need for combined operations.

Like the Luftwaffe, German armor was hit by the increasing lack of adequate training. In part, this was a product of the urgent need for tanks for combat, but the crisis in fuel availability was also significant. A lack of training also led to a deterioration in standards of maintenance, which became more serious due to the impact on production standards arising from Allied bombing, which inflicted direct damage, hit the movement of parts and fuel, and put serious pressure on the workforce.

THE EASTERN FRONT, 1945

The final Soviet advance on Berlin in 1945 repeatedly indicated the continued value of tank warfare to the Soviet army. Against bitter resistance, the Soviets were victorious in the Vistula-Oder offensive of January and February. Breaking out from their bridgeheads across the River Vistula, a success greatly helped by plentiful artillery, the rapidly advancing Soviet tank forces then exploited the victory, advancing across western Poland to the River Oder. As with other advances, however, there were growing problems with supplies.

The last stages of the war repeatedly demonstrated the degree to which Allied forces were not only effective but also efficient. This was seen in the continued strength of Soviet operational art, which stressed firepower but also employed mobile tank warfare. Attrition and maneuver were combined in a coordinated sequence of attacks. The Soviets used large numbers of tanks, which were able to exploit opportunities prepared by short and savage artillery attacks. The individual Soviet tank armies gained space to maneuver, and this Soviet maneuverability prevented the Germans from consolidating new defensive positions. For forces that had broken through their opponents, mobility enhanced the ability to prevent their opponents from falling back in order. Mobility replaced the sequence of new front lines seen with World War I advances. Instead, there was now the open battlefield, in which retreating opponents had to rely on defensive "hedgehog" positions that could be encircled if the momentum of the offensive could be maintained. The limit of the new advance was often that of maintaining gasoline supplies, as in the Soviet advance through Poland in early 1945.

With their pronounced tendency to mount aggressive, mobile operations,[75] the Germans themselves launched an offensive in Hungary from Lake Balaton towards Budapest—Operation Spring Awakening—on March 5. Hitler had moved the Sixth Panzer Army from the Ardennes front, but the state of the railways and the weather had delayed the attack. The offensive was expected by the Soviet commanders and fought to a halt by March 15, with the Soviets benefiting from their resources, their ability to create defensive positions hastily, and the impact of mud on the German tanks. As on the Western Front in 1944–45, the German emphasis on maneuver warfare could no longer work even at the operational level.

Deploying about six thousand tanks, including the IS-2, which was designed as a breakthrough tank intended to attack defensive positions, the Soviets used armor extensively in launching the Berlin Operation on April 16. German anti-tank guns inflicted heavy casualties that day, and on the next two, on Soviet tanks that had inadequate infantry support. However, the Soviets, mounting frontal attacks and showing a disregard for heavy casualties, eventually broke through; their tanks reached the major ammunition store at Jüterbog on April 20 and encircled Berlin on April 25. German relief attempts were all defeated. Although they took heavy losses, the Soviets were then successful in overcoming resistance in Berlin; the remaining troops there surrendered on May 2, followed by the Germans as a whole five days later. The campaign, however, showed a flaw in Soviet armor and, more generally, with the use of heavy tanks. They were unable to keep up with the T-34/85s, which hit the cohesion of the Soviet armor.

THE WAR WITH JAPAN, 1945

The war with Japan is not primarily identified with armor warfare. Indeed, from the US perspective, the principal use of tanks was by the Americans as they found the seizure of islands increasingly difficult. This was particularly seen on Okinawa, where the Americans landed on March 26 and where resistance did not cease until June 30. As earlier on the island of Iwo Jima, the Japanese had created a dense network of underground fortifications. This not only vitiated the effects of US firepower, especially air power, but also made a fighting advance on foot difficult, not least because the network provided the Japanese with a myriad of interconnected firing positions. The Japanese had sufficient artillery, mortars, and machine guns to make their defenses deadly.

The Americans made extensive use of tank-mounted flamethrowers in order to clear positions. Although the circumstances were very different to operations elsewhere, the successful use of flamethrower and other tanks depended on effective cooperation with infantry, which provided crucial protection for the tanks.[76] Armored bulldozers were also employed on these islands, not least to close caves that were serving as Japanese positions.

Tanks were used by the Americans in the reconquest of the Philippines in 1945—for example, in the advance on Manila. In turn, Japan employed tanks and 37 mm antitank guns to defend Bataan, although infantry and artillery played the key roles in the defense.

The British also used tanks in resisting the Japanese advance from Burma into India in 1944 and, subsequently, in their advance into Burma. In the former case, tanks and infantry operated closely together as part of the relief force for the besieged British garrison at Kohima. M3 Grants were deployed and outgunned the Japanese. The tanks were then employed in the fighting at Kohima. Bulldozers were also used against Japanese roadblocks.

In 1945, the British employed the 255th Tank Brigade as an armored column to attack the Japanese lines of communication at Meiktila in February and March. Subsequently, the tanks moved south on Rangoon but were badly impeded by heavy rain, and the city instead fell to an amphibious force.

Tanks were used in a very different context, and on a very different scale, in Manchuria that August. On August 8, the Soviet Union declared war on Japan, invading Manchuria at 4 in the morning on August 9. The Soviet forces, deploying 5,500 tanks, were better trained than the Japanese, and many had combat experience from fighting the Germans in Europe. Thanks to the resources available, the troops transferred from Europe to invade Manchuria left their tanks behind and were equipped with new ones in Siberia. This reduced transport burdens on the Trans-Siberian Railway and greatly speeded up the transfer, although there were bottlenecks at the depots because so many troops demanded tanks at once. The system also lessened the demands on the maintenance side. The old worn-out tanks did not require repair.

Aided by skillful deception techniques, the Soviets seized the initiative and advanced rapidly to envelop their opponents. Soviet armored columns concentrated on advancing through the Greater Khingan Range of mountains, where the Japanese were weakly deployed. Their campaign bridged aspects of German blitzkrieg with later Soviet Cold War plans for invasions of Western Europe. Showing an ability to master terrain, the forces of the Trans-Baikal Front crossed the Greater Khingan Range, invading Manchuria from the west. At the same time, the First Far Eastern Front invaded from the east, advancing from near Vladivostok and driving on Harbin. In contrast, the units and commanders from the Far East, who had not seen recent combat and were deployed in the Second Far Eastern Front to the north of Manchuria, operated southward in a more cautious fashion.

Although they were weak, notably in armor, the Japanese fought tenaciously in Manchuria, including using soldiers carrying explosives who detonated them against tanks, a variant on the aerial kamikaze attacks. However, Japanese planning was completely disorientated by the speed of the Soviet advance. The Japanese had failed to appreciate the advances the Soviets had made in 1943–45 in developing and sustaining "deep operations." In particular, the Japanese underrated Soviet mobility and inaccurately assumed the Soviets would need to stop for resupply after about 250 miles, providing the Japanese with an opportunity to respond to the Soviet advance. Indeed, lacking situational awareness, the Japanese were seriously outmaneuvered.

Japanese resistance was greatly affected by the announcement, on August 14, of the Japanese surrender. The commanders in Manchuria nevertheless decided to continue fighting, but, on August 17, a direct order from the emperor ensured compliance. The increasing confusion in the Japanese response helped the Soviets make further advances. They increased the pace of their operations, using airborne detachments to seize important cities and airfields and, against weaker resistance, pushing forward their tanks, many of which were refueled by air. A tank force that had crossed the Gobi Desert joined up with Chinese Communist forces near Beijing. By the time of surrender, over eighty thousand Japanese troops had been killed, compared to fewer than nine thousand Soviets. This was a dramatic display of the effectiveness of rapidly advancing forces making ambitious and successful use of tanks.[77]

CONCLUSIONS

The course of the war amply demonstrated the value of doctrine and training in the use of tanks. Major-General Eric Dorman-Smith, chief of staff for the British Eighth Army for some of North Africa in 1942 and a critic of British performance, saw this as a crucial factor in conflict there the previous year: "In the Middle East Command, during the autumn of 1941, there arose the tactical heresy which propounded that armour alone counted in the desert battle, therefore the British . . . should discover and destroy the enemy's equivalent armour, after which decision the unarmoured infantry divisions would enter the arena to clear up what remained and hold the ground gained."

Dorman-Smith contrasted this with Rommel's Afrika Korps and its tactical preference for a "mixed formation of all arms," and he attributed British deficiencies to the sway of generals with a cavalry background: "the romantic cavalry mystique of horsed warfare" led to "basic tactical fallacies . . . the dichotomy between the unarmoured infantry divisions and the relatively 'uninfanterised' armoured divisions."[78] In a different context, the Soviet Operation Mars, launched on the Central Front west of Moscow in November 1942, suffered from poor armor-artillery coordination and totally failed.[79] So also with the US Twelfth Armored Division in Alsace in January 1945.

In contrast, armored divisions balanced between the arms were effective, rather as the Napoleonic corps had been in the 1800s. On July 1, 1942, Major James Milner MP told the House of Commons that the British had been mistaken in Libya to rush tanks forward, only for them to be wrecked by opposing German artillery. He added: "Never should tanks alone be pitted against tanks, if that can be avoided. To do that means to have a mere slogging match which leads nowhere. All the arms should be used in combination under one command. That is quite clearly what Rommel has done. We, on the other hand, have let our artillery be in the background. . . . Tanks are a kind of cavalry, and they have very definite uses, but alone they cannot win battles, and that is what we have been trying to do with them."[80]

The British eventually adapted their doctrine and closed this capability gap, although the initial doctrine for infantry-armor operations imposed by Montgomery was flawed and required changes after the problems encountered in Normandy in 1944. Combined arms doctrine was affirmed anew. In February 1945, Montgomery argued that close cooperation with infantry was needed in order to overcome antitank guns: "I cannot emphasise too strongly that victory in battle depends not on armoured action alone, but on the intimate co-operation of all arms; the tank by itself can achieve little."[81] That left aside the additional dimension of air land battle.

The world's leading economy, that of the United States, produced eighty-six tanks in 1941–45. US armor was seriously limited at the beginning of 1940, but, on September 8, 1939, President Roosevelt had ordered a protective mobilization designed to strengthen the military. In May 1940, the National Defense Advisory Council was established, a peacetime draft followed in September, and, in March 1941, the Lend-Lease Act added the burden of helping arm Britain. An unlimited national emergency declared on May 27, was followed, after Pearl Harbor, by new production outlines and the establishment of the War Production Board. Productive capacity rose, not least as worker productivity increased, in part due to new plants and techniques.

The major increase in tank production was closely linked to the prominence of armor in the US emphasis on equipment rather than manpower. This prominence was also intimately related to the objective of movement, one also seen in the motorization of infantry and artillery, thus providing a particular quality to US combined arms capability that offered a balanced effectiveness. Movement was intended to allow for "triangular" operations in which the opposing force was frontally engaged by one unit while another turned its flank and a third, in reserve, was poised to intervene where most helpful.

Aside from doctrine, the production of tanks reflected industrial advanced mass-production capacity in the shape, in particular, of forging, casting, cutting, milling, and grinding processes, all aspects of machine-tool work. The Americans benefited from the availability of effective machine tools. The presence of a large auto industry was significant. Thus, the Chaffee was developed by the Cadillac Division of General Motors. Moreover, about ten thousand Stuarts had been built by 1944 at the Cadillac and Massey Harris plants. The ability to fund production was crucial. As with aircraft, the United States' multiple strengths translated into battlefield capability.

US production was supported by those of its allies, notably Britain[82] and the Soviet Union. Each produced large numbers. The Soviets manufactured 98,300 tanks and self-propelled guns. The Soviets proved particularly effective, not only in turning out tanks but also in matching requirements for the necessary equation of quantity with quality. Production processes were enhanced by using newly designed efficient factories that had been carefully located and by focusing on a small number of simple designs with limited updates. Moreover, the Soviets accepted that their tanks would only have a limited life span.[83] They benefited from over fourteen thousand tanks supplied by Allied powers (Britain, Canada, and the United States), including Grants, which saw action at Kursk in 1943.

The war saw a major spread of the use of tanks, including by powers that had not hitherto done so in combat. Thus, there were Canadian, Polish, and South African armored divisions; New Zealand armored regiments; and a Rhodesian armored battalion.[84] From 1941, Romania added captured Soviet tanks and received 218 German ones. Moreover, some Soviet tanks were converted by the Romanians in 1943 into self-propelled guns, with tank destroyers following in 1944. China (the Guomindang, or Nationalist government) received six hundred US CTLS-4TAC and CTLS-4TAY light tanks after Pearl Harbor. They took part in the conflict with Japan.

Production also spread. Developed and manufactured under license from the Swedish company AB Landsverk, Hungary built 202 Toldi tanks in 1939–42. A light tank, the Toldi I, weighed 8.5 tons and had a 20 mm gun. From 1942, the Toldi IIa, which weighed 9.3 tons, was developed. It had a 40 mm gun, and eighty earlier variants were thus rearmed. The tanks saw service against

Yugoslavia in 1941 and the Soviet Union but were vulnerable in frontal engagements with T-34s. The Turán, based on a Czech design, was produced by Hungary from 1940 and weighed 18.2 tons. Initially with a 40 mm gun, it was up-gunned to a 75 mm in 1941 (but only entered service in 1943) in response to the challenge of Soviet tanks. The chassis was also used for the Zrínyi assault gun, which had a 105 mm gun.

In 1943, Australia brought the Sentinel into service. The first tank manufactured there, it used US tracks and engines, British weaponry, and a French suspension system and was built at a new factory at Chullora. However, the tanks never saw action because British and US ones ready for use arrived. In 1941, the Canadian Pacific Railway Company built 1,400 Valentines, most of which were supplied to the Soviet Union where they were popular with tank crew, not least for their maneuverability and interior layout.[85]

Neutrals also sought to develop their tank programs. Spain ordered one thousand Verdeja tanks in 1941, but the tank was not built due to a lack of resources. Instead, in 1943, Spain decided to turn to Germany in order to renew its tank force, launching the Bär Program, which was intended to involve the acquisition of 250 Mark IIIs and 100 Mark IVs. However, the military needs of Germany only allowed the supply of 20 Mark IVs. Spain considered that inadequate and, in 1944, pressed for another 100 Mark IVs and some Tiger tanks. This could, and did, not happen, and, in 1945, the Spanish tank force was largely outdated: 8 FTs, 116 T-26s, 84 Mark Is, 60 CV-33/35, and 20 Mark IVs.

The war also witnessed tank combat in new areas. Linked to this came the determination to make tanks effective that led, for example, to the production of terrain evaluation maps. These major additions to topographical maps were important for both vehicles operating off-road and infantry. German terrain evaluation maps were impressive and effective, and the use of color helped make them readily accessible. The material offered included not just ground suitability but also forest composition (type of tree) and density, slope gradients unsuitable for armored vehicles, important viewpoints with their field of view, and bridge weight limits. The Americans and British produced similar maps. In the former, "trafficability," the suitability of the terrain for cross-country movement, was the key element, and the Americans became adept at producing such material rapidly, as in January 1945 in preparation for what was to be the successful invasion of Germany. The material was made more valuable by being accompanied by charts showing, per month, the expected number of days of "trafficable ground."

The major role of tanks in the conflict on land during World War II helped ensure their greater salience in the postwar world compared to its prewar predecessor. This was true of force structure and planning. In addition, the use of tanks in World War II dominated the public discussion of the war on land—indeed, the future of warfare on land—and helped make an impression of the experience of tank warfare and the war itself normative as an account of the past and a prospectus for the future. This process was encouraged by the very look of tanks. For example, whatever its faults, the Sherman appeared streamlined in comparison to its predecessors. More generally, the increasingly streamlined appearance of tanks and aircraft were parallel developments. Both reflected designers' increasing confidence in an ability to master physical space and technological improvements.

NOTES

1. P. Kennedy, *Engineers of Victory: The Problem Solvers Who Turned the Tide in the Second World War* (New York, 2013).

2. M. T. Calhoun, *General Lesley J. McNair: Unsung Architect of the U.S. Army* (Lawrence, KS, 2015), 234.

3. A. Lewis, *Omaha Beach: A Flawed Victory* (Chapel Hill, NC, 2001).

4. M. E. Haskew, *M4 Sherman Tanks: The Illustrated History of America's Most Iconic Fighting Vehicles* (Minneapolis, MN, 2016).

5. D. Stahel, *Kiev 1941: Hitler's Battle for Supremacy in the East* (Cambridge, UK, 2012), 74, 162–63, 227, 296, 326.

6. K. H. Frieser, *The Blitzkrieg Legend: The 1940 Campaign in the West* (Annapolis, MD, 2005).

7. *HC*, July 1, 1942, vol. 381, cols. 232, 234.

8. *HC*, July 1, 1942, vol. 381, cols. 309, cf 393–94.

9. B. Coombs, *British Tank Production and the War Economy, 1934–1945* (London, 2013).

10. F. M. von Senger und Etterlin, *German Tanks of World War II: The Complete Illustrated History of German Armoured Fighting Vehicles 1926–1945* (London, 1969).

11. Interview with Bernard Kelly, former tanker, May 30, 2019.

12. B. Munro, *The Centurion Tank* (Ramsbury, 2005).

13. S. G. Fritz, *Ostkrieg: Hitler's War of Extermination in the East* (Lexington, KY, 2011), 114–15.

14. P. Mercer, "The Lincolnshire Regiment and the Battle of Caen," *Military History Monthly* 83 (August 2017): 56.

15. D. E. Nash, "Kesternich: The Battle that Saved the Bulge," *Army History* 109 (fall 2018): 43.

16. D. E. Johnson, *Fast Tanks and Heavy Bombers: Innovation in the U.S. Army, 1917–1945* (Ithaca NY, 2013; 1st ed. 1998), 152.

17. D. A. Kaufman, "The 801st Tank Destroyer Battalion," *On Point* 16, no. 1 (summer 2010): 22.

18. H. Yeide, *The Tank Killers: A History of America's World War II Tank Destroyer Force* (Havertown, PA, 2004).

19. O'Connor to Major-General Allan Adair, July 24, 1944, LH. O'Connor papers, 5/3/22.

20. C. J. McInnes, *Men, Machines and the Emergence of Modern Warfare, 1914–1945* (Camberley, UK, 1992), 39.

21. A. Hill, *The Great Patriotic War of the Soviet Union, 1941–45: A Documentary Reader* (Abingdon, UK, 2009), 172, and "British Lend-Lease Tanks and the Battle of Moscow, November–December 1941—Revisited," *Journal of Slavic Military Studies* 22 (2009): 574–87.

22. R. L. DiNardo, *Germany and the Axis Powers: From Coalition to Collapse* (Lawrence, KS, 2005).

23. J. D. Mark, *Death of the Leaping Horseman: 24 Panzer-Division in Stalingrad, 12th August–20th November 1942* (Sydney, 2003).

24. F. W. von Mellenthin, *Panzer Battles: A Study of the Employment of Armor in the Second World War* (New York, 1956); D. M. Glantz and J. M. House, *Endgame at Stalingrad* (Lawrence, KS, 2014); D. M. Glantz, *Operation Don's Main Attack: The Soviet Southern Front's Advance on Rostov, January–February 1943* (Lawrence, KS, 2018).

25. D. M. Glantz, *Zhukov's Greatest Defeat: The Red Army's Epic Disaster in Operation Mars, 1942* (Lawrence, KS, 1942).

26. Wellington, Archives New Zealand, DA 21.1/9/G4/8.

27. J. Fennell, *Combat and Morale in the North African Campaign: The Eighth Army and the Path to El Alamein* (Cambridge, UK, 2011).

28. N. Barr, *Pendulum of War: The Three Battles of El Alamein* (London, 2004); G. Harper, *The Battle for North Africa: El Alamein and the Turning Point for World War II* (Bloomington, IN, 2017).

29. I. Möbius, *Ein Grenadier entscheidet eine Schlacht* [An Infantryman Settles a Battle] (Chemnitz, Germany, 2012).

30. D. M. Glantz, ed., *From the Don to the Dnepr: Soviet Offensive Operations, December 1942–August 1943* (London, 1991).

31. D. V. Sadarananda, *Beyond Stalingrad: Manstein and the Operations of Army Group Don* (Mechanicsburg, PA, 2009).

32. S. Zaloga, *Kasserine Pass, 1943: Rommel's Last Victory* (Oxford, 2005).

33. D. Rolf, *The Bloody Road to Tunis: Destruction of the Axis Forces in North Africa, November 1942–May 1943* (Mechanicsburg, PA, 2001).

34. D. M. Glantz and J. M. House, *The Battle of Kursk* (Lawrence, KS, 1999); S. Newton, ed., *Kursk: The German View* (Boston, 2002); G. M. Nipe, *Blood, Steel, and Myth: The II SS-Panzer-Korps and the Road to Prochorowka, July 1973* (Stanford, CT, 2011); V. Zamulin, *Demolishing the Myth: The Tank Battle at Prokhorovka, Kursk, July 1943: An Operational Narrative* (Solihull, UK, 2011) and *The Battle of Kursk: Controversial and Neglected Aspects* (Solihull, UK, 2017); M. Lak, "The Death Ride of the Panzers? Recent Historiography on the Battle of Kursk," *JMH* 82 (2018): 917–19.

35. J. Barber and M. Harrison, eds., *The Soviet Defence Industry Complex from Stalin to Khrushchev* (New York, 2000).

36. R. N. Armstrong, *Red Army Tank Commanders: The Armored Guards* (Atglen, PA, 1994).

37. I. Nebolsin, *Stalin's Favorite: The Combat History of the 2nd Guards Tank Army from Kursk to Berlin*, vol. 1, *January 1943–June 1944* (Havertown, PA, 2015).

38. M. Melvin, *Manstein: Hitler's Greatest General* (London, 2010).

39. R. M. Citino, *The Wehrmacht Retreats: Fighting a Lost War, 1943* (Lawrence, KS, 2012).

40. K. C. Holzimmer, "In Close Country: World War II American Armor Tactics in the Jungles of the Southwest Pacific," *Armor* 106 (July/August 1997): 21–31; O. E. Gilbert, *Marine Tank Battles in the Pacific* (Conshohocken, PA, 2001); R. M. Neiman and K. W. Estes, *Tanks on the Beaches: A Marine Tanker in the Pacific War* (College Station, TX, 2003).

41. A. B. Gilmore, *You Can't Fight Tanks with Bayonets: Psychological Warfare against the Japanese Army in the Southwest Pacific* (Lincoln, NB, 1998).

42. Alexander to Brooke, January 26, 1944, LH. Alanbrooke papers, 6/2/19.

43. Brooke to Sir Henry Maitland Wilson, Supreme Commander, Mediterranean, August 2, 1944, LH. Alanbrooke papers, 6/3/6.

44. C. J. Dick, *From Defeat to Victory: The Eastern Front, Summer 1944* (Lawrence, KS, 2016).

45. S. Naveh, *In Pursuit of Military Excellence: The Evolution of Operational Theory* (London, 1997).

46. D. M. Glantz, *Red Storm Over the Balkans: The Failed Soviet Invasion of Romania, Spring 1944* (Lawrence, KS, 2007).

47. W. S. Dunn, *Soviet Blitzkrieg: The Battle for White Russia, 1944* (Boulder, CO, 2000) and *Stalin's Keys to Victory: The Rebirth of the Red Army* (Westport, CT, 2006); S. Naveh, *In Pursuit of Military Excellence: The Evolution of Operational Theory* (London, 1997); D. M. Glantz and H. S. Orenstein, eds., *The Battle for L'vov, July 1944: The Soviet General Staff Study* (Portland, OR, 2002).

48. I. McCulloch, "Prelude to D-Day, Dieppe 1942," *Osprey Military Journal* 3, no. 1 (2001): 47–49.

49. P. H. Williams, *War on Wheels* (Stroud, UK, 2019).

50. C. L. Symonds, *Neptune: The Allied Invasion of Europe and the D-Day Landings* (New York, 2014).

51. R. Hart, *Clash of Arms: How the Allies Won in Normandy* (Boulder, CO, 2001); J. Buckley, ed., *The Normandy Campaign 1944: Sixty Years On* (London, 2006); S. Napier, *The Armored Campaign in Normandy: June–August 1944* (Havertown, PA, 2015).

52. M. Milner, *Stopping the Panzers: The Untold Story of D-Day* (Lawrence, KS, 2014).

53. O'Connor to Lieutenant-General Sir Allan Harding, Chief of Staff of Allied Armies in Italy, August 19, 1944, LH. O'Connor 5/3/37.

54. J. Buckley, *British Armour in the Normandy Campaign 1944* (London, 2004) and "Tackling the Tiger: The Development of British Armoured Doctrine for Normandy 1944," *JMH* 74 (2010): 1161–84.

55. C. Dunphie, *The Pendulum of Battle: Operation Goodwood - July 1944* (London, 2004).

56. T. G. Bradbeer, "General Cota and the Battle of the Hürtgen Forest," *Army History* 75 (spring 2010): 27.

57. J. J. Carafano, *After D-Day: Operation Cobra and the Normandy Breakout* (Boulder, CO, 2000).

58. M. J. Reardon, *Victory at Mortain: Stopping Hitler's Panzer Counteroffensive* (Lawrence, KS, 2002).

59. A. D. Harvey, "How Effective Were Tank-Busting Aircraft in the Second World War?," *RUSI* 153, no. 5 (October 2008): 78–82; R. Thun-Hohenstein, "Response to How Effective Were Tank-Busting Aircraft in the Second World War?," *RUSI* 154, no. 1 (February 2009): 92–93; I. Gooderson, *Air Power at the Battlefield: Allied Close Air Support in Europe, 1943–1945* (London, 1998).

60. A. H. Ganz, "Questionable Objective: The Brittany Ports, 1944," *JMH* 59 (1995): 77–95.

61. S. T. Barry, *Battalion Commanders at War: US Army Tactical Leadership in the Mediterranean Theater, 1942–1943* (Lawrence, KS, 2013).

62. As argued by D. P. Colley, *Decision at Strasbourg: Ike's Strategic Mistake to Halt the Sixth Army Group at the Rhine in 1944* (Annapolis, MD, 2008).

63. A. Beevor, *Arnhem: The Battle for the Bridges, 1944* (London, 2018), 62.

64. I. Kershaw, *The End: Hitler's Germany 1944–45* (London, 2011).

65. J. Ludewig, *Rückzug: The German Retreat from France, 1944* (Lexington, KY, 2012).

66. J. N. Rickard, *Patton at Bay: The Lorraine Campaign, September to December 1944* (Westport, CT, 1999).

67. As Eisenhower noted on December 7, 1944, LH. Alanbrooke papers 6/2/35.

68. S. D. Badsey, "The American Experience of Armour, 1919–53," in *Armoured Warfare*, ed. J. P. Harris and F. H. Toase (London, 1990), 42.

69. P. Caddick-Adams, *Snow and Steel: The Battle of the Bulge, 1944–45* (Oxford, 2017).

70. W. C. Baldwin, "Engineers in the Battle of the Bulge," *Army History* 32 (fall 1994): 1–5.

71. N. N. Prefer, *Eisenhower's Thorn on the Rhine: The Battles for the Colmar Pocket, 1944–45* (Philadelphia, PA, 2015).

72. D. S. Zumbro, *The Battle for the Ruhr: The German Army's Final Defeat in the West* (Lawrence, KS, 2006).

73. J. Buckley, *Monty's Men: The British Army and the Liberation of Europe, 1944–5* (New Haven, CT, 2013).

74. J. R. Lankford, "Battling Segregation and the Nazis: The Origins and Combat History of CCR Rifle Company, 14th Armored Division," *Army History* 63 (2007): 26–40, at 31–35.

75. R. M. Citino, *The Wehrmacht's Last Stand: The German Campaigns of 1944–1945* (Lawrence, KS, 2017).

76. P. J. Donahoe, "Flamethrower Tanks on Okinawa," *Armor* 103 (January/February 1994): 6–10.

77. D. M. Glantz, *The Soviet Strategic Offensive in Manchuria, 1945: "August Storm"* (London, 2003) and *Soviet Operational and Tactical Combat in Manchuria, 1945: "August Storm"* (London, 2003).

78. Manchester, John Rylands Library, Special Collections, GOW/1/2/2, pp. 33, 54, 1/2/1, p. 6.

79. D. M. Glantz, *Zhukov's Greatest Disaster: The Red Army's Epic Disaster in Operation Mars, 1942* (Lawrence, KS, 1999).

80. *HC*, July 1, 1942, vol. 381, cols. 408–9.

81. LH. Alanbrooke papers 6/2/37; S. Bungay, *Alamein* (London, 2002), 210–12; C. Forrester, *Monty's Functional Doctrine: Combined Arms Doctrine in British 21st Army Group in Northwest Europe, 1944–45* (Solihull, UK, 2015).

82. D. Edgerton, *Britain's War Machine: Weapons, Resources and Experts in the Second World War* (Oxford, 2011).

83. W. S. Dunn, *Stalin's Keys to Victory: The Rebirth of the Red Army* (Westport, CT, 2006).

84. E. Kleynhans, "The First South African Armoured Battle in Italy during the Second World War: The Battle of Celleno - 10 June 1944," *Scientia Militaria: South African Journal of Military Studies* 40 (2012): 250–79.

85. P. Buttar, *Retribution: The Soviet Reconquest of Central Ukraine, 1943* (Oxford, 2019), 304.

SIX

THE EARLY COLD WAR, 1945–67

US AND SOVIET TANKS FACING OFF IN CLOSE PROXIMITY AT CHECK-point Charlie in Berlin on October 29, 1961, offered vivid evidence of the salience of armored power at what was then a key flashpoint of the Cold War. Captured by photographers and much reproduced, these images were much easier to show, and grasp, than comparable tensions surrounding aircraft or missiles, notably the shooting down of US U-2 spy planes high over the Soviet Union and Cuba. The tank, moreover, was truly one of the key weapons of the Cold War and a counting piece of relative international power.

At the same time, the legacy of World War II long dominated subsequent consideration of tanks and armored warfare. Armies produced studies in order to educate the next generation. This dominance was very much true of popular accounts, not least as the wartime generations remained important and became more so. In addition, armies were dominated by those who had fought in the war. Thus, Creighton Abrams, commander in 1944 of the US Thirty-Seventh Tank Battalion, had played an important role as a successful fighting officer in the Normandy breakout and a key role in the relief of Bastogne that December. After the war, he went on to be head of the Department of Tactics at the Armor School at Fort Knox, to command the Third Armored Division, to command in Vietnam, and to be chief of staff from 1972 until his death in 1974.[1]

Conversely, when the commanders had fought in other branches—for example, the airborne—as with Matthew Ridgway (1953–55), Maxwell Taylor (1955–59), and Lyman Lemnitzer (1959–60), three successive army chiefs of staff in the United States, they did not have a commitment to armor. Ridgway had a corps command opposing the German armor in the Battle of the Bulge. Instead, for these men and others, there was interest from 1954 in the helicopter as a form of airmobile cavalry. The next chief of staff, George Decker (1960–62), had not commanded armor units.

Meanwhile, wartime tanks remained in the lineup of armies, and, in some cases, production as well as use continued. The M24 Chaffee, a US light tank produced in 1944–45, served in the US army until 1953 and in the armies of twenty-nine other states. These tanks were still operating in the 1970s. The Comet was in British service from 1945 to 1960. Use of the Soviet T-34 continued until 1958 while the Sherman was still in use with the Israeli army in the 1973 Yom Kippur War. Tanks were distributed to allies by sale and/or gift. Thus, the Americans gave over two thousand M47 Pattons (a development of the M46) to Italy, which was being grounded in the Western system, while others went to France. This and other American tanks were sent to countries outside the systems of British, French, and Soviet provision.

HISTORICAL ACCOUNTS

World War II left an impression of tank power. This dominance owed much to their being linked to the generals who played a major role in subsequent consideration, notably Guderian, Manstein, Patton, Rommel, and Zhukov. More significantly, there was also the visual overhang, in film, photography, and surviving examples, presented by substantial numbers of tanks from the war. This was on a scale far greater than after World War I. As with aircraft, the relatively simple (by later standards) specifications of the wartime tanks were such that it had been easy to manufacture large numbers. This was particularly so for the victors. Many of these could be seen after the war.

As, for example, with aircraft carriers, the presentation and discussion of the war, both during it and subsequently, played a role in postwar preferences about weapons. In part, for tanks, this presentation was read back onto World War I, but, even more, it was a case of the most recent world war. Assessments by, and of, particular generals contributed to this situation.

Published in 1951, with an English translation the following year, Guderian's *Panzer Leader* considerably exaggerated the author's role in the development of German tank warfare and presented Guderian's politics in a favorable light. Liddell Hart's foreword to the translation was linked to Guderian's willingness to stress how much he owed to the commentator's ideas. Both influenced John Keegan's somewhat naïve biography, *Guderian* (1973), only to be refuted in Kenneth Macksey's *Guderian: Panzer General* (1992). With reason, Liddell Hart was criticized both for the foreword and for his role in the successful "Rommel industry."[2]

That industry proved strong and lasting in Britain, the United States, and West Germany and contributed greatly to often misguided praise for the Wehrmacht, as in Liddell Hart's *The Other Side of the Hill* (1948), which was published in the United States as *The German Generals Talk*. Henry Hathaway's US film *Rommel, the Desert Fox* (1951) was based on Desmond Young's sympathetic 1950 biography, which (like the film) was very popular in Britain, where it went through eight editions in a year. The positive appraisal of Rommel was repeated in another film, *The Desert Rats*, in 1953, the year of the publication of *The Rommel Papers*, which Liddell Hart had edited and greatly forwarded. There was also praise for Rommel from some British generals, including Auchinleck and another field marshal, Archibald Wavell, but this praise was contested—for example, by another general, Brian Horrocks. Rommel, of course, made mistakes, notably but not only in logistics, and was defeated in 1942 and 1944. In both Britain and West Germany, Rommel was more closely linked to opposition to Hitler than was merited. As a result, barracks could be named after him.

In Britain, as part of the active management of reputations,[3] eulogies for Rommel were linked to heated arguments over British generalship in North Africa in 1941–42, arguments that led to bitter disputes that were contested in print and reached the law courts.[4] Moreover, the relative effectiveness of British and German tanks and antitank guns in North Africa was extensively discussed, as were the relevant tactics. With reason, Liddell Hart pointed out that impressions on these heads "are always influenced by the result of a fight, and are far from being scientific evidence."[5]

Praise for the Wehrmacht was also seen in accounts of the Eastern Front. These were stoked by memoirs, notably that of self-adulation by Manstein. Published in 1955, an English translation appeared in the United States in 1982. Alongside his account came a cultural preference, notably in the United States, for the Wehrmacht in its struggle with the Soviet army.[6] The extent to which the German panzer force was increasingly linked to the Waffen-SS, with the latter's Panzer Corps established in 1942, was underplayed or ignored. There were seven SS panzer divisions in 1944–45, and they took a major role in difficult operations.[7] The repeated role of both Waffen-SS *and* army in atrocities was also underplayed or ignored.[8]

The Wehrmacht's emphasis on the attack, as a way both to win victory and counter Allied numerical superiority, proved attractive to many commentators and fed through into the focus on tanks. This affected writing about the war, particularly at the popular level. Thus, for 1943, disproportionate attention was devoted to German offensives, especially at Kursk and the Kasserine Pass, and far too much attention was expended in discussing the Tiger and Panther, rather than concentrating on the overall failure of German armor in 1943–45. "Weapons-envy" was an element.[9]

The myth of decisive armor commanders was also employed to boost the reputation of Patton. Four tanks, the M46, M47, M48, and M60, were officially named after him, the first being christened in 1947 when the first model appeared. The M47 was in service from 1952 until 1959, the M48 (produced from 1952 until 1959) from 1953 until the 1990s, and the M60 from 1960 until it was superseded by the M1A1 Abrams after the Gulf War.

Again, as so often in explaining the US perception of the war, which took place at a distance from home,[10] film played a key role; in this case, *Patton* (1970) was essential to the general's reputation and, indeed, began a Patton cult. For many US men, he became an attractive and important image of masculinity. The Patton film projected misleading implications about the general, the US contribution to the European Theater war effort, and Montgomery, who was usually presented in the United States as an arrogant incumbrance. Coming in the wake of the civil rights movement and the Vietnam War, the film provided respite to the beleaguerment felt by many US men. President Nixon was very interested in the general. It is going much too far to say that watching the film encouraged him to invade Cambodia,[11] but the belief that it did so indicated the significance attached to such aggressive commanders. Patton certainly attracted much attention in historical writing.

A lot of such writing was of high quality,[12] but the emphasis in the popular sphere was scarcely on a balanced account of the weaknesses as well as strengths of armor. This approach drew on the comparable one to air power.[13] More generally, tanks played an important role in the Allied, especially US, presentation of "the good war."

The impact of tanks on discussions of both current and past developments was greatly increased by the growing possibility of illustrations, notably color ones, in books and, even more, in publicity for them. The same was true for magazines, including Sunday color supplements, which began in Britain in the 1960s. British authors wrote at length on the German panzers. Kenneth Macksey (1923–2005), who served in the Royal Armoured Corps during World War II, subsequently produced *Afrika Korps* (1968) and *Panzer Division: The Mailed Fist* (1968), which were published in the United States in *Ballatine's Illustrated History of World War II* series.

On September 3, 1969, the British comic weekly *Punch* put "The War Industry" on its front cover, showing a book and film, television, and theater shots of war. Much of this "industry" focused on World War II, as with Liddell Hart's *The Tanks* (1959) and his last book, a *History of the Second World War* (1970). Liddell Hart himself remained committed to his own view of strategy, armor, and his own significance. Blitzkrieg was presented as the key element in 1940, and the Allied response was castigated: "never was a world-shaking disaster more easily preventable."[14] Paul Kennedy, a research assistant on his 1970 book, noted: "Basil was obsessed by his theory of 'indirect approach' . . . so, Guderian, Israeli tank colonels, etc."[15] This theory of the "indirect approach" readily meshed with growing military interest in the operational level of war and the need, accordingly, for an exemplary and readily digestible history.

Meanwhile, Purnell's *History of the Second World War*, a weekly, had appeared in 128 issues from October 7, 1966; the editor in chief was Liddell Hart, and he took a major role in the work. In addition, the editor, Barrie Pitt, wrote extensively on the Desert War in North Africa. The project cost over eight hundred thousand pounds to produce. It benefited from a major promotion campaign costing ninety-five thousand pounds that included special issue posters. The magazine-style layout and three thousand illustrations helped, and, by 1967, nearly three hundred thousand copies were being sold weekly.[16] Foreign language editions followed, including in France and Italy, and in November 1967 over one million copies of the various editions were sold in Europe in one week. The average weekly sales in Britain were 325,000, and the project made a pretax profit of seven million pounds. A visual impression of the war was consolidated. Moreover, the reputation of the war was important to more general studies, notably with Montgomery's commercially successful book *A History of Warfare* (1968), another heavily illustrated work.

The impression of victory through mobility, with the tank as the means of this success, was firmly established in the popular mind. There was far less of an emphasis on combined operations, let alone the role of artillery. Even if the text referred to both, as with Purnell's *History* and the discussion of blitzkrieg, that was not the impression created by the visuals.

The same occurred elsewhere. Tanks that, when employed in wartime German propaganda, had been images of German strength became, instead, in postwar German films, images of the inexorable Allied strength crushing brave German soldiers. This was seen in *08/15-Zweiter Teil* (1955), in which a heroic soldier is crushed underneath the tracks of a Soviet tank after his antitank gun runs out of ammunition, an idea repeated in the German film *Stalingrad* (1993). Alternatively, as in *Hunde, wollt ihr ewig leben?* (1959), it was Germans on foot bravely knocking out Soviet tanks.[17]

Soviet postwar films made extensive use of mass scenes with T-34s—for example, Yur Ozerov's *Liberation* (five films, 1970–71), *Soldiers of Freedom* (1977), and *Battle of Moscow* (1985). Soviet industrial capacity was thereby emphasized. Newer Russian feature films also put an emphasis on tank warfare, as with *White Tiger* (2012) and *Nesokrushimyy* (*Tankers*, 2018), the latter closer to real events.

COLD WAR

Interest in armor was focused by the Cold War and, in particular, the prospect of a Soviet invasion of Western Europe. This appeared a prospect from immediately after World War II and gathered pace as a threat from the Communist coup in Czechoslovakia in 1948. Helped by the startlingly fast demobilization of US combat forces in 1945–46, as soldiers eagerly returned to civilian society, the Soviet army was apparently well placed to overrun Western Europe. It seemed it could only be stopped by the West's use of nuclear weaponry. When the Soviet Union acquired a matching capability from 1949, that deterrent changed.

In reality, had the Soviet army attacked, its logistical base would have had major issues. Once Truman revoked wartime Lend-Lease aid, the Soviets were no longer receiving spare parts for their military motor transport, which was composed overwhelmingly of Ford and Studebaker trucks supplied by the Americans during the war.[18] The equipment for routine tune-ups, such as batteries, tires, inner tubes for tires, and oil and air filters, were no longer available. Nor were axles, driveshafts, gearboxes, and engine blocks. Tanks alone rolling ahead would not have been enough, and the horses sequestered during the war had to be returned home as Soviet agriculture was in very poor shape. Meanwhile, during any invasion, US and British bombers, escorted by their better fighter aircraft and better fighter pilots, would have been bombing the opposing army front and rear. There is also room for skepticism about the sophistication of Soviet operational art, notably so against a strong and well-resourced opponent,[19] although a lot of intellectual and career investment elsewhere was devoted to building up this sophistication.

Despite these issues, the threat of tank attack apparently increased once the Soviets acquired an atomic capability and weaponized it. The long-term commitment of the United States to the defense of Western Europe, by means of participation in the North Atlantic Treaty Organization (NATO) from 1949 and with the continued location of US troops in West Germany after the occupation ceased, helped ensure the Cold War confrontation long focused on Europe. Land forces were massed and faced each other across the border between West and East Germany. US, British, and French forces continued to be based in West Germany after the occupation ceased, as did the Soviets in East Germany. Moreover, other NATO and Warsaw Pact forces, including armor, were deployed as part of the confrontation. As a result, the North

European Plain appeared the clear cockpit of any future war, with planning accordingly.[20] This encouraged an emphasis on tanks by both sides and the related development of armor-based doctrine.

The buildup of NATO included the provision of tanks, with MDAP (Major Defense Acquisition Program) assistance under the Mutual Defense Assistance Act passed in the United States in October 1969. Denmark, having received a handful of Shermans, then received Centurions as well as US light tanks: M24s followed by M41s. The Dutch army started with Canadian Ram tanks, many of which were already present from the liberation in 1945. Sherman and Chaffee tanks were then provided by the United States. Between 1953 and 1960, 658 Centurions were delivered. In the early 1960s, 131 light AMX tanks replaced the Chaffees (M24s).

Very differently, the (secret) West German Schnez-Truppe (Schnez Organization), formed in 1949 to resist any Soviet or East German attack, appears to have hoped for US tanks to equip the four armored divisions it planned. The organization, which drew heavily on wartime panzer officers, in turn produced key Bundeswehr (West German armed forces) figures, notably Adolf Heusinger and Hans Speidel.

Rearming West Germany, with the foundation of the Bundeswehr in 1955, and bringing it into NATO, also in 1955, both reflected the significance of the Cold War and military balance in Central Europe and set the context for a major expansion in tank numbers due to the particular nature of West Germany as a military power. Not allowed by its allies to develop a nuclear capability, and with no foreign colonies to defend in counterinsurgency struggles but with a potent and threatening neighbor in the shape of Soviet forces in East Germany, West Germany focused on its territorial defense. It was better able to do so due to a rapidly expanding economy that was strong in manufacturing. This encouraged investment in tanks, the production of which began anew in West Germany after the stop at the end of World War II and during the occupation.

Tank attacks were regarded as the key means by which the Soviet army would advance. The Soviets had a major advantage in tank numbers as well as considerable experience from World War II, which led NATO planners to scrutinize the World War II conflict on the Eastern Front. Thanks, in particular, to Soviet advances in 1944–45 and the greater postwar effectiveness of long-range air power, both ideas and practices had to face a very different geopolitical and technological situation to that in the interwar years. This situation was a matter of needs, opportunities, and options.

In the victory parade in Berlin on September 7, 1945, the Soviet Union displayed its latest heavy tanks, the IS-2 and IS-3, with their 122 mm guns, the latter for the first time. These tanks were a product of developments during the war, developments that came to fruition in its second half but that had begun earlier. The first had entered service in April 1944, but the second was too late to see combat in the war. Although the prow-shaped glacis of the IS-3 looked impressive, the tank crews hated it. Its transmission and driveshaft were poor and caused many mechanical problems, and the tank did not have the reliability of the T-34 or even the KV-1 and 2.

The key element was an up-gunning and up-armoring as a main battle tank (MBT) was produced, one that brought together both breakthrough and breakout abilities. This was to be the key requirement during the Cold War and reflected the availability of large tank forces that would need to be defeated in any conflict on land. Kill capabilities were important. In part, this reflected the end of the practice and concept of tank destroyers, which, instead, were absorbed by those of tanks, with the stress in their use on first-hit kills, including at a considerable distance. The latter led to a "sniper" capability.

In response to Soviet armored strength, NATO countries sought to deploy heavy defensive tanks with guns able to penetrate the armor of the heaviest Soviet tank, the IS-3, and its successor, the T-10, which entered service in 1953 and also used a 122 mm gun, although with increased armor. The prime example of the response was the sixty-five-ton Conqueror, with its 120 mm gun and 130 mm armor, that the British deployed in 1955. The heaviest tank in the British army, it remained in service until 1965.

In response to the introduction of the T-54/55 series with its 100 mm gun—the T-54, a medium tank, in service from 1949 and the T-55 MTB from 1958—the US M48 appeared inadequate. This contrast led to the decision to produce what became the M60, which entered production in December 1958. In total about fifteen thousand were built. In many respects, this was a successful tank, notably in terms of firepower (105 mm gun), protection, and cruising range. However, as so often, specifications were not only the product of compromise but also did not incorporate features that were available and seen as desirable. In place of the proposed siliceous-cored armor (a forerunner of Chobham armor), which was deemed too costly and lacked available production facilities, conventional steel armor was the choice. The availability of production facilities was and still is a key element in assessing optional outcomes.

The recommended guided missile system was not incorporated until the M60A2 was introduced in 1973. It could fire both conventional rounds and missiles but was soon phased out due to a preference for high-performance kinetic energy rounds over the missiles, which were ineffective at close range.

Instead, the M60A1 was improved. This led to the M60A3, which had improved range finding including a ballistic computer, thus increasing the probability of first hits, which was the key form of protection. The M60 was provided to allies, including Egypt, Greece, Israel, and Turkey.[21]

In 1956, West Germany and France began a collaborative project to develop a new tank; they were joined by Italy in 1958. For the West Germans, this was to replace the US M47s and M48s with which the Bundeswehr, which had six armored divisions, had been initially equipped. A total of 1,102 of the M47s and M48s were provided, as well as 152 light tanks.[22] After the breakdown of the attempt to codesign a tank with France and Italy, and in response to their concerns about the M60 and the direction of US tank development, the West Germans went ahead on their own and developed the Leopard 1 and, in 1963, when the tank entered service, ordered 1,500 of them. This number reflected the challenge posed by Soviet armor and the capacity of mass-production systems to turn out large numbers. Delivery began in 1965, and the Leopard was soon acquired by Belgium (1968), the Netherlands (1969), Norway (1970), Italy (1971), Denmark (1976), Australia (1976), Canada (1978), Turkey (1980), Greece (1981), and, subsequently, Brazil and Chile. This was a major loss for US and British exporters and a key acquisition by nine NATO powers, providing a degree of consistency.

The Leopard operated contrary to the direction of German tank design in World War II. In place of armor, the emphasis was on mobility as the basis for effective maneuvering. This was achieved, but, at 70 mm, the armor was thin. The forty-ton Leopard was quicker than the fifty-five-ton British Chieftain. The stress on speed—a maximum of forty miles per hour—reflected a doctrine of focusing on maneuverability in defense against any Soviet tank assault, rather than relying on protection in tank-to-tank exchanges or against antitank guns. The Leopard, which also benefited from being highly reliable, was very flexible in its ability to engage with targets. Its name showed a continuity with the late Wehrmacht use of big cat names in Tiger and Panther.

As a rival to the Leopard, the French developed the AMX-30 as a main battle tank, replacing the US M47. Due to concerns about the possibility of providing adequate protection, this tank was designed with relatively little armor but with the emphasis instead on speed and compactness. Delivered from 1966, the tank had a 105 mm gun able to fire a high-explosive antitank (HEAT) projectile effective against tanks at up to three thousand meters. The French emphasis on mobility over protection was also shown with the AMX-13, a light tank into which they put a copy of the German Panther 76 mm gun. France sold these tanks to Singapore, which paraded them through Singapore City in

1969, causing great embarrassment to the allied British armored car squadron there, which was armed only with Saladins.

Looking ahead, West Germany and the United States agreed in 1963 to produce a new main battle tank for 1970. The MBT-70 project failed, however, because of the differing needs of the two powers, notably the US concern for a tank that could operate worldwide, which the West Germans did not require. The design was abandoned in 1969, and the United States turned to what became the Abrams[23] while the West Germans produced the Leopard 2. The same occurred with the joint attempt to create a new armored personnel carrier. When it became clear that the MBT-70 would not be available until the mid-1970s at the earliest, the Dutch tested and compared the British Chieftain and the Leopard, deciding, in October 1968, to buy 468 Leopards, the sort of order that produced valuable economies of scale.

At the same time, there was a continued commitment to self-propelled guns, which offered additional support against any Soviet attack. In 1956, a requirement for a new series was issued in the United States. A key theme was the interchangeability of the gun tube on a common mount, as well as on a common chassis, and a major reduction in weight in order to ease transport. The M107 self-propelled 175 mm gun was the result. It was a tracked vehicle supported by a M548 tracked cargo carrier. The lack of an armored turret, although it increased crew vulnerability, meant the M107 had more working space and could reload faster while, in the pattern of tank destroyers, its speed and maneuverability were intended to provide protection. The M107 saw combat service in Vietnam and was provided to allies including Britain, Greece, Iran, Israel, Italy, the Netherlands, South Korea, South Vietnam, Spain, and Turkey. Subsequently, the M110A2 self-propelled 8-inch (203 mm) howitzer offered greater range: up to thirty thousand meters when firing rocket-assisted projectiles. It was provided to Belgium, West Germany, Italy, the Netherlands, Spain, South Korea, Turkey, Japan, Greece, and Egypt.

Defenses were also prepared to resist Soviet advances in what were seen as armor corridors into West Germany, notably the Fulda Gap (about sixty miles northeast of Frankfurt) and the Hof Corridor.[24]

Other specifications also improved, reflecting the growing sophistication and wealth of economies and the enhanced technological base of armies. Indeed, in his December 1952 Progress Report as secretary general of NATO, Hastings Ismay, a British general, reflected: "Modern war is an affair of whole nations or groups of nations. The armed forces are merely the cutting edge of a mechanism which involves every single national activity."[25]

To cope with supplies, development after 1945 focused on multifuel engines so tanks could run on any fuel. However, these engines introduced a further element of complexity and cost. The development, in the 1950s and 1960s, of complex stabilized gun systems, fast traversing turrets, and good targeting systems provided the ability to aim and shoot accurately while moving, as with the impressive Leopard 1A1 model. This was a key ability if mobility was to be retained and vulnerability lessened. The combination enabled tanks to have high first-shot kill capabilities.

Mobility was also an issue for the Soviet Union, not least as the slower speed of the heavy tanks was an issue in any advance—a concern that bridged World War II and the Cold War. The speed of the T-10 was twenty-six miles per hour. In contrast, the Soviets designed medium tanks that could provide greater speed (T-54/55: thirty miles per hour) but still-impressive armor and armament: T-54/55s, T-62s, and T-72s. As a result, the production of the T-10 ended in 1966, and they were withdrawn from frontline service by 1967; and the development of heavier tanks was cancelled, notably the proposed Obiekt 770, with its 130 mm gun.

Aside from the quality of Soviet tanks, not least their resilience, there were problems for NATO as a result of their quantity. Thus, of the T-54/55 series, over seventy-five thousand, and maybe ninety thousand, were built in the Soviet Union, with another ten thousand in Poland and Czechoslovakia. This series remains the most produced in history. They entered Soviet service in 1949, and production ceased in 1981. The gun was 100 mm, and the tank carried antinuclear radiation equipment as well as fuel drums on the back. To keep a low profile, there was scant care for the crew. The turret was very cramped. The M60 Patton was a response to the T-54/55 series, as was the British L7 105 mm tank gun that was used to upgrade Centurions from 1959 and for the German Leopard 1. In service from 1951, about five thousand PT-76s, a Soviet amphibious light tank used for reconnaissance, were produced until 1969. It weighed 14.6 tons and had a 76.2 mm gun and a range of 300 to 315 miles with its external fuel drums.

Tanks did not develop in an identical fashion. Thus, the Soviet T-62, first appearing in public in 1965, did not employ rifling in its gun but, instead, carried a smoothbore. Differing specifications reflected the perception of requirements in contrasting cultures of tank use. The smoothbore could fire further, but a rifled gun was more accurate. The former was a product of the steppe mentality of Soviet tank doctrine and training—that of wide-open spaces and plentiful numbers. In contrast, Western European use was focused on smaller numbers of tanks and the shorter distances of a more broken-up, and thus confined, battle space. At the same time, technological choice was a product of a range of factors. In particular, smoothbore guns could use rocket-assisted rounds.

The T-62 was also longer and wider than earlier Soviet tanks. Its gun was 115 mm, and its top speed was forty-seven miles per hour. Over twenty thousand were produced, and the tank was supplied to twenty-three countries.[26]

Alongside developments in tanks were others in related vehicles. US antitank weaponry changed as antitank guns were supplemented by improved antitank missiles with a greater range. In 1970, the United States developed a tube-launched, optically tracked, wire-guided (TOW) antitank system. The TOW replaced what had been widely used by NATO previously: the Swiss/German-made Cobra (designed in 1954), a hand-tracked, wire-guided, antitank system penetrating no more than 475 mm RHA (rolled homogeneous armor). Operating TOW was easier and faster than Cobra, and TOW was much more effective, for it had a wider range. Its first version penetrated 500–600 mm RHA, but later its penetration was enhanced to be up to 900 mm. The XM13 Shillelagh Combat Vehicle System, which was used on the M551 Sheridan, incorporated a gun launcher able to fire conventional projectiles or launch the MGM-51 Shillelagh missile. Mechanized infantry represented a way to oppose tanks.

Less impressively than TOW, the British Vigilant, which was launched from Ferret scout cars and deployed from the early 1960s, had a maximum range of 1,500 yards. The British also fielded the long-range Swingfire missile and utilized the French AS11 antitank missile on their Scout helicopters in an antitank role.

At the same time, there was no war in Europe, which meant these tank forces were not used and thus tested. Indeed, a key context for armor, and one to which tanks themselves did not contribute, was provided by the United States adopting the strategy of containment and not "rollback," as some Republican politicians had called for. As a result, there was no intervention in support of the Hungarian uprising in 1956 and therefore no war, let alone forward movement of NATO armor.

The Korean War had revealed that a conventional war, even if limited, would be very costly. Alongside Soviet conventional superiority on land in Europe, this led the United States to press ahead with nuclear targeting. In December 1955, the NATO Council authorized the employment of atomic weaponry against the Warsaw Pact, even if the latter did not use such weaponry.

There was a major fall in the percentage of expenditure on the army, as war by machine now appeared to mean by aircraft, not tanks. In the case of the United States, the army was cut from 38 percent of total military expenditure in 1953 to 22 percent by 1959, with the biggest fall occurring in 1955.

The latter percentage included nuclear weapon systems for the army, which further cut the money available for nonnuclear items. Reflecting the ability to produce more lightweight and compact nuclear weapons, tactical nuclear missiles became a key tool in the Cold War. Tactical nuclear weapons appeared the way to respond to Soviet armor but would have led to the employment of strategic weaponry. The assumption that a subnuclear war, or a tactical-weapons-only nuclear war, could be fought without the feared escalation and that containment in this fashion was possible presumed a congruence in Soviet thinking that was unproven. Indeed, the Soviet Union assumed the use of tactical chemical weaponry in order to maintain the pace of advance on the ground, and from the 1960s they deployed ample tactical nuclear weaponry to the same end. RAND and other think tank studies of the 1960s and 1970s concluded that escalation was unavoidable once fighting had broken out between the Soviet Union and the United States. In short, the US concept of massive retaliation appeared likely.

NATO membership and commitments provided a continuing major role for the US army.[27] Moreover, the political need to protect West Germany, as well as an enhanced commitment to maneuver, led to a greater commitment of US armor and mechanized units to West Germany in the early 1960s. In 1963, the forward defense line was moved to the Iron Curtain.

Meanwhile, in 1959, General Hans Speidel, NATO's commander of Allied Land Forces Central Europe (LANDCENT), introduced an organization for its divisions, the so-called LANDCENT division, according to which the divisions of the Belgian, British, Dutch, and West German army corps, those in NATO's front line, were reorganized. These divisions consisted of two armored infantry brigades and one armored brigade. This structure was adopted, for example, by the Belgian First and Sixteenth Divisions in 1960. The structure most closely matched that of the Bundeswehr. These were organizations for conventional warfare but also thought able to fight under tactical nuclear circumstances. Speidel, having served on the Eastern Front from 1942, had been chief of staff to Rommel in 1944 and in 1950 published a study of Rommel and the Normandy campaign of that year that contributed to the Rommel myth, not least by exaggerating his closeness to the resistance to Hitler.

The first war to which the United States committed substantial forces was, as part of a United Nations (UN) coalition, the Korean War (1950–53). The mountainous terrain (also seen in Italy in 1943–45) and limited infrastructure there were not appropriate for large-scale tank operations. At the same time, North Korea's invasion of South Korea in June 1950 saw the use of T-34/85 tanks. The Soviet Union had provided over two hundred. In contrast, the South Koreans lacked tanks; their antitank weaponry was weak, principally 57 mm towed antitank guns; and there were no antitank mines at this stage.

The North Korean invasion was thwarted by stronger-than-expected South Korean resistance combined with US intervention, which drove the North Koreans back. At Osan on July 5, 1950, an advancing column of thirty-three North Korean–manned T-34/85s was engaged by US artillery in the first battle between the two. Largely equipped with high-explosive, instead of antitank, ammunition, the Americans found it impossible to stop the tanks breaking through. US shells and bazooka rounds bounced off, although the shells were effective when they hit the tank tracks. The Americans then withdrew.[28] In future engagements, they were better armed.

The US tanks in the Korean War included Shermans, M24 Chaffee light tanks, M26 Pershings, and M46 Pattons. Initially, in 1950, the North Koreans used armor in their advance south, outfighting the M24s. The Pusan perimeter was put under heavy pressure from the North Korean T-34s, not least because the US and South Korean forces there were not adequately equipped or trained for antitank combat. Instead, it was necessary to use air support and artillery to help hold the line.[29] However, the arrival of Shermans at the port of Pusan, and later of Pershings and Pattons, ensured that the North Koreans could be checked. In service from 1950 to 1957, the M46 Patton was better than the underpowered Pershing, which was somewhat obsolete. The Patton had a 90 mm gun, providing considerable firepower, as well as a new air-cooled gasoline engine and a sophisticated hydraulic transmission system. Nevertheless, because it was very big, the Patton was an easier target. The British provided Centurion and Cromwell tanks, the former with both an impressive capacity to go up slopes and a gyro-stabilized gun.

By means of a US landing at Inchon outflanking the North Koreans near Pusan, the US-led coalition drove their opponents back toward the Chinese frontier. However, that led to a successful US counteroffensive and then a Chinese invasion in support of the North Koreans, which did not focus on armor. Indeed, setting the pattern for Chinese action, armor was not to the fore in the

Chinese Civil War (1946–49). Thus, the Communist envelopment methods in the crucial Huaihai campaign in 1948–49 did not depend on armor. Success in the civil war had encouraged Mao Zedong to believe that technological advantages, such as those enjoyed by the United States, could be countered while China did not have the manufacturing capacity to produce tanks. In the Korean War, the Chinese attacked frontally in successive waves only to fall victim to US artillery.

Although provided with Soviet 45 mm and 76 mm antitank guns, the Chinese were weak in antitank weaponry. They used long bamboo poles that carried a crude explosive charge. In practice, their frontal attacks in successive waves were more of a threat. These meant that tanks had to rely not on their main gun but on their machine guns for defense. This gave the Patton, with three, an advantage over the Centurion, which had only one. Tank crews referred to "hosing each other down": firing machine guns to kill assailants on each other's tanks.

Once the Chinese had pushed the US-led coalition back in 1950–51, both sides were able to dig in and turn the naturally difficult terrain into even better defensive positions. This put the burden of support for the US positions on artillery and air power. Tanks provided valuable firepower at the tactical level, but artillery was far more significant. This was notably so for the UN forces, both on the defense and, on the offensive, once dug-in troops had to be confronted. There was little room for a mobile armor defense. At the same time, tanks provided mobile artillery for both sides, even in unfavorable terrain. Whereas both sides had impressive artillery, machine-gun rounds fired by US and, from 1952, South Korean tanks proved particularly devastating against Chinese attacks, with the South Koreans using M36 tank destroyers as a source of firepower.[30]

The Korean War was a conflict between regular forces. While it was not so unfavorable for the use of tanks as the brief war between China and India in the Himalayas in 1962, it was nevertheless one in which firepower in the shape of artillery, infantry, and aircraft proved more significant.

TANKS AND COUNTERINSURGENCY

Many conflicts, in contrast to the Korean War, did not see this clash between conventional forces. Revolutionary forces tended not to have any tanks, and the terrain and vegetation of the areas in which they operated were often not well suited to tanks. This was the case, for example, with the Dutch East Indies (later Indonesia) in December 1948, in which the Dutch use of Shermans and

US-supplied light CTLS-4A tanks was far from decisive. Earlier, the British had used tanks there in 1945 in supporting Dutch attempts to reestablish control in the face of nationalist opposition.

The same is true for the Viet Minh's campaigns against the French in Indochina (Vietnam, Cambodia, Laos) in 1946–54. The French used Sherman, Honey, and, later, Chaffee tanks from the United States while the Viet Minh focused in opposition on mines and earthworks. The fighting eventually centered on the heavily wooded interior of North Vietnam in the Dien Bien Phu operation in 1954, in which French troops, who had been parachuted into a valley, were successfully outgunned by Viet Minh artillery and overrun by infantry attacks. France dismantled ten Chaffee tanks, flew them into the valley, and then reassembled them. By then, France had 452 tanks and tank destroyers in Indochina and was using armored groups successfully in combat operations. However, as French support for the war had evaporated, this was of scant significance.

In Algeria in 1956–62, the French used the Chaffee and then the AMX-13, a French light tank produced from 1952. Their guns provided useful support to the infantry. Nevertheless, tanks were largely tangential to the conflict, and armored cars proved more useful.[31]

The British largely relied on scout cars in counterinsurgency struggles—for example, in Malaya, Borneo, and Aden. However, Centurions were used for patrol in the 1960s and in 1964 were deployed from Aden into the Radfan region in order to show the dissident tribes that the government had military force behind it.

In 1959, Allen Dulles, the influential director of the US Central Intelligence Agency (CIA), explained to the Senate Foreign Relations Committee that, in Cuba, "what you need against guerrillas are guerrillas. . . . It is rough country and there is no use sending tanks and heavy artillery up there."[32] The Batista government had fallen there at the start of the year to Fidel Castro's left-wing guerrilla-style insurrection, without the Americans intervening, although they had sent seven Shermans in 1957 while Britain sent fifteen Comets in 1958. Ten of these tanks were used without success by Batista's forces in the decisive battle of Santa Clara at the close of 1958.

By the time of the unsuccessful US-backed exiles' invasion at the Bay of Pigs in April 1961, Castro had 125 Soviet-supplied T-34/85s. At least twenty of them, as well as some Shermans, were used against the exiles' M41 Walker Bulldog light tanks, although five T-34/85s were destroyed in the fighting and others badly damaged.

This was a very different context and target to Hungary, where Soviet intervention in 1956 included the plentiful use of tanks. Over 1,100 were deployed, notably IS-3 tanks and the new T-54. In response, the Hungarians attacked tanks with Molotov cocktails (gasoline bombs), which had only limited effect. The reforming Communist movement was violently overcome. On June 17, 1953, the Soviet Union had used T-34/85 and IS-2 tanks to suppress demonstrations in East Germany, particularly in East Berlin and Leipzig.

Tanks were also used in the West. In 1961, France deployed Shermans on the streets of Paris after the military putsch in Algiers was followed by fear of a parachute assault on the city, which proved groundless. On July 31 1972, in Operation Motorman, the British army ended the "no go" zones the Provisional Irish Republican Army (IRA), a separatism movement, had imposed in Belfast and Londonderry. To help, four Centurion tanks were transported to Londonderry on an amphibious assault ship and landed in landing craft. Adapted with bulldozer blades, fasciae carriers, and a large 165 mm gun able to wreck bunkers, the tanks destroyed barricades, providing passage to the soldiers. Their guns were covered with a tarpaulin and pointed backward in an attempt to lessen tension.

THE SPREAD OF WEAPONRY

A different constraint on the unfettered use of tanks was the spread of weaponry, which ensured that opponents not only had tanks but also antitank weaponry. The major powers that manufactured tanks, however, were not necessarily willing to supply them to other states. Certainly they were not willing to supply the latest models, which affected the combatants in the Arab-Israeli war of 1948–49. Indeed, most of the tanks available then were surplus tanks from World War II. Use spread as tanks were passed on, usually when they were replaced. Thus, the United States provided surplus tanks to Latin American allies such as Brazil and Bolivia.

At the same time, foreign tank sales provided a way to finance domestic production as well as earn foreign revenue and gain influence. Thus, France's AMX-13 went to countries in the former French empire, notably Algeria, Cambodia, Côte d'Ivoire (Ivory Coast), Djibouti, Lebanon, Morocco, and Tunisia, as well as to other powers, including Argentina, Austria, Belgium, the Dominican Republic, Ecuador, Egypt, Guatemala, India, Indonesia, Israel, the Netherlands, Peru, Tunisia, and Venezuela. The AMX-30 was exported to Chile, Cyprus, Greece, Qatar, Saudi Arabia, Spain, and the United Arab Emirates.

Britain provided tanks to its former empire, formal and informal, although not only there. For example, the Comet was exported to Burma, Finland, Ireland, and South Africa. Part of the war debt with Argentina was cancelled with surplus military equipment. The Centurion turned out to be a particularly successful export. Foreign markets included Canada, Denmark, the Netherlands, and New Zealand. Unlike in the 1930s, Italy was no longer a provider of tanks.

Tanks were also provided for strategic purposes. Seeking to engage Yugoslavia, a Communist state that had broken with the Soviet Union in 1949, and fearing that it might be attacked by the Soviets in 1955, thus taking their forces to the Adriatic and the Italian border, the Americans in the 1950s provided 319 M47s and 260 M18 Hellcat tank destroyers, veterans of World War II. In addition, once the occupation of Austria ended and it became neutral, the United States sought to incorporate it into the Western defense system or, at least, to lessen the risk of, or from, a Soviet advance through it in the event of a third world war breaking out. As a result, over 150 M47s were provided. South Korea was provided with 531. The M46 was only supplied abroad to Belgium, a NATO founder member, but the M47 also went to Belgium, France, Saudi Arabia, Spain, and Turkey.

The Madrid Pact of 1953 was used by the United States to fix Spain, which was not a NATO member, into the Western alliance system. The agreement involved the supply of tanks. In 1954, Spain received the first 12 of the 389 M47s it would get in the 1950s and 1960s. Subsequently, 162 M48s were added. The restrictions imposed by the Americans on the use of their tanks in the Ifni War with Morocco (1957–58), however, led Spain to look for new suppliers in Europe. It eventually decided to buy the Leopard 1, with its British 105 mm gun, but, on political grounds, Britain's Labour government was unwilling to agree on the sale to the Franco regime. Other US tanks and tank destroyers were also sold abroad. The M41, a light tank, entered New Zealand service in 1960. M18s also went to Greece and Venezuela.

THE MIDDLE EAST

The situation in the Middle East was very different from 1948–49 by the time of the next Arab-Israeli war—that in 1956 between Egypt and Israel. This was in large part because the diffusion of advanced weaponry became a way to obtain, secure, and support protégés. In 1955, the Soviets, through Czechoslovakia, agreed to provide hundreds of tanks as well as aircraft to Egypt. T-34s and IS-3s were sent. In response, France, because of its endangered colonial position in Algeria opposed to the pan-Arab nationalism of Colonel Nasser of Egypt, armed Israel, providing 180 AMX-13s by 1956.[33]

The Israelis used their armor—AMX-13s and Shermans—more adroitly than Egypt in 1956, overrunning the Gaza Strip and the Sinai Peninsula. The weak resistance put up by the Egyptians reflected Israeli success in gaining the initiative, as well as the poorly trained nature of the Egyptian army and its ineffective use of the numerous weapons it had received. In particular, the Egyptians, who fought well in prepared positions, such as Umm Qataf, suffered from inadequate combined arms training and the rigid tactics of their armor. Israel, in turn, was affected by poor logistics and tank breakdowns.

The Israelis benefited from having numerical superiority in Sinai in part because Nasser focused his forces on the defense of the Suez Canal against British and French attack. The British had landed Centurions, and these tanks repelled Egyptian attacks that used tank destroyers. The British employed their tanks in a slower and more cumbersome fashion than the French AMX-13s, which were lighter, were more maneuverable, and advanced farther. British tanks faced opposition from Egyptian snipers, a classic problem with the prevalent turrets-open style of command. After the campaign, Israel, let down by the failure of Britain and France to sustain their invasion, withdrew from its conquests.

The rivalries of the Cold War ensured the spread of technology even as patrons and protégés changed. In 1965, concerned about rising Soviet influence in Egypt, President Lyndon B. Johnson agreed to sell tanks to Israel, and US support replaced that of France.

At that stage, Egypt was involved in a counterinsurgency war in Yemen that had broken out in 1962 when Egypt backed a successful republican coup in which thirteen tanks played a key role. The Egyptians subsequently deployed a substantial force in Yemen including T-54s: one tank division was present by late 1965. These tanks, however, were inhibited by the effective use of anti-tank weaponry, including mines, that helped lead to Egyptian tactical caution. Egyptian tanks could not successfully protect convoys. Moreover, the terrain was difficult for operations. In turn, this situation fed into a strategic stalemate.

INDIA VERSUS PAKISTAN

In 1965, India fought Pakistan, with each side using large quantities of tanks supplied by the major powers. The Indians, with their British Centurions and US Shermans, fought well against Pakistan's US-made Pattons and Shermans. The much-vaunted Patton failed to live up to expectations as the Pakistani crews found the advanced gun-laying system too complicated to use effectively. That was not the sole factor. In addition, the Indians chose to advance not in Kashmir, as the Pakistanis had anticipated, but, instead, in the Punjab. They were affected by the defenses Pakistan had prepared on the Ichogil Canal Line. An in-depth bank-cum-ditch defense that was ten to fifteen feet deep had been constructed along the canal. The western bank of the canal was made higher by eight to ten feet, and machine guns, pillboxes, artillery, and anti-tank guns were deployed on the bank. If the Indians attacked, Pakistan's plan was that Indian forces would reach the eastern bank only to receive fire from the higher western bank. In addition, the Indian army lacked the equipment required to cross the deep canal. The Indian attack was stopped in this sector. The Indians used tanks to drive on Lahore and Sialkot. The Indian Centurions defeated the 264 tanks of Pakistan's First Armored Division, mostly Pattons, at Asal Uttar on September 8–10: the Pakistanis lost about one hundred tanks, India only ten. However, the Pakistanis subsequently proved more effective at Chawinda on September 14–19, one of the largest tank battles since Kursk; it was brought to a close by the cease-fire.

In the subsequent war of 1971, Pakistani tanks were defeated by Indian counterparts at Basantar: US tanks were beaten by Centurions and T-55s. This was important but not crucial to the outcome. The Indians also used the Soviet-supplied PT-76 amphibious tanks to cross the wide River Megreh in eastern East Pakistan. All the tanks made it across and were a key element in outflanking the fixed Pakistani defenses, along with the extensive use of helicopter operations.

THE SIX-DAY WAR

In 1967, rising regional tension in the Middle East, particularly aggressive Egyptian saber-rattling, led to a preemptive Israeli attack on Egypt. Gaining complete air superiority thanks to a completely successful surprise attack on the Egyptian air bases on June 5 proved crucial, and the Israelis destroyed 286 Egyptian aircraft. Aside from gaining the initiative, Israel also had better training and morale. In Sinai, the Egyptians suffered from a failure to appreciate the caliber of the Israeli military and the nature of Israeli operations and from a lack of adequately trained reservists. Moreover, weakened by cronyism and complacency, the Egyptian command system proved inadequate to meet the challenge.

This very much affected the tank conflict. Soviet T-54 and T-55 tanks used by the Egyptians were beaten by US M48 (Pattons) and (more impressive) British Centurion tanks employed by the Israelis, who showed greater operational and tactical flexibility, not least in successfully searching for vulnerable flanks and thus overcoming the strength of prepared Egyptian positions. The Soviet tanks were not particularly good, and the T-54 was very poor as it lacked even gun stabilization. The US- and British-supplied tanks were far superior. Israel had fitted US engines in the Centurions. However, the French

AMX-13s in Israeli service proved too lightly armored, and its main gun was too weak. Many were destroyed by Soviet tanks. In addition, Egypt had about one hundred Soviet IS-3s, and their thick armor resisted both Israeli bazookas and the Israeli M48s, with several of the latter being destroyed. Yet the IS-3s also took heavy casualties in part due to their poor rate of fire. Seventy-three of them were destroyed.

Having broken into the Egyptian rear, the Israelis ably and rapidly exploited the situation. When, on June 6, Egyptian Field Marshal Amer instructed the army to retreat from Sinai to the Suez Canal, the unplanned withdrawal was chaotic, the cohesion of the army collapsed, and resistance to the Israelis disintegrated. Desert terrain greatly accentuated the vulnerability of Egyptian tanks to Israeli air attacks. The Sinai is devoid of all vegetation and most other features suitable for cover and concealment. Israeli air superiority left Arab forces disorientated and demoralized. This greatly enhanced the impact of Israeli mobility, notably by tanks, while close air support strengthened their firepower, not least in the absence of sufficient artillery support. Retreating columns of Egyptian tanks were attacked in the Sinai passes and destroyed in a manner similar to that of the British air attacks on Turkish forces at Wadi el Fara in 1918 and Coalition air attacks on Iraqi forces in 1991 and 2003. The Egyptians suffered about ten thousand fatalities, and five thousand troops were captured. They also lost much of their equipment: about two billion dollars' worth was destroyed while Israel captured 320 tanks. There was no place to hide in the desert.

The conflict in the Sinai underlined the key role of field maintenance and repair in tank warfare, a role arising from the strain that use put on the machinery, notably engines and tracks. In the case of both field maintenance and repair, the Israelis proved more effective than the Egyptians. Overnight repair of equipment and its return to the battle line proved a crucial element. More generally, nonbattle losses through mechanical failure can be more costly than battle losses. The Israelis then went on to defeat Jordan and then Syria. In each of these conflicts, although far less spectacularly, tanks played a role. Jordan had 90 Centurions and 250 M48s, and Syria had Soviet tanks and dug-in Panzer Mark IVs, but they were defeated. The Israelis also used tank fire as a form of artillery—for example, against Jordan at Latrun and at Nablus Road in Jerusalem. The external fuel tanks on the Jordanian M48s made them vulnerable to Israeli Shermans and air attacks, while Jordanian Centurions were defeated at Hebron.

As with World War II, but far more clearly, the Six-Day War was proclaimed a triumph for armor. Photography very much focused on tanks. Both advancing and in action, tanks were easier to photograph than aircraft and could clearly be presented as seizing territory. The war, which was seen in terms of a plethora of lessons,[34] was presented in the Anglophone world through the prism of Liddell Hart, rather than noting the key significance for Israel of taking the initiative in sequential war making with their opponents. Liddell Hart argued that the Israelis were following his precepts and also drew a line from himself via Guderian and blitzkrieg to Israeli success, a practice already (misleadingly) seen with Israeli operations in 1948 and his idea of the indirect approach.[35]

In 1967, the triumph of the tank appeared both clear and explained. The practical and, indeed, cultural imperative of tanks seemed assured.[36] The symbolic equation of the tank with power was demonstrated with the May Day parade in Moscow in 1965, which saw the first public appearance of the T-62, and, somewhat differently, with a revolutionary French poster of 1968 that depicted a tank above a picture of Charles de Gaulle, then France's president, shown as Hitler, with the caption "Salaires Legers, Chars Lourds" (Light Wages, Heavy Tanks).

NOTES

1. L. Sorley, *Thunderbolt: General Creighton Adams and the Army of His Times* (New York, 1992).

2. David Hunt to John North, April 15, 1963, LH. North papers, III/2/11a; B. Bond, "Liddell Hart and the German Generals," *Military Affairs* 41, no. 1 (1977): 16–22; A. Searle, "A Very Special Relationship: Basil Liddell Hart, Wehrmacht Generals and the Debate on West German Rearmament, 1945–1953," *War in History* 5 (1998): 327–57; P. Major, "'Our Friend Rommel': The *Wehrmacht* as 'Worthy Enemy' in Postwar British Popular Culture," *German History* 26 (2008): 530–45; B. M. Scianna, "Rommel Almighty? Italian Assessments of the 'Desert Fox' During and After the Second World War," *JMH* 82 (2018): 125–46, esp. 138–41. For an accurate account, R. A. Hart, *Guderian: Panzer Pioneer or Myth Maker?* (Dulles, VA, 2006).

3. P. Caddick-Adams, *Monty and Rommel: Parallel Lives* (London, 2011).

4. John Rylands University Library, papers of Major-General Eric Dorman O'Gowan (formerly Dorman-Smith), GOW/1/2–3, 5–7, 11, 16–18, 20–23, 25–29, 36; Liddell Hart to Michael Howard, January 20, 1964, and reply, LH. Liddell Hart papers, 4/27; legal correspondence, LH. North papers, III/2/5a–h; J. Connell, *Auchinleck* (London, 1959); C. Barnett, *Desert Generals* (London, 1960).

5. Playfair to Liddell Hart, February 10, March 11, 1954, Liddell Hart to Playfair, February 12, 1954, LH. Liddell Hart papers, 4/32.

6. R. Smelser and E. J. Davies, *The Myth of the Eastern Front: The Nazi-Soviet War in American Popular Culture* (Cambridge, UK, 2008).

7. B. Wegner, *The Waffen-SS: Organisation, Ideology and Function* (Oxford, 1990).

8. For virulent racism on the part of a non-SS tanker in the Seventh Panzer Division, H. F. Richardson, ed., *Your Loyal and Loving Son: The Letters of Tank Gunner Karl Fuchs, 1937–41* (Washington, DC, 2003).

9. J. Holland, *Normandy '44* (London, 2019), 427.

10. G. Jeansonne and D. Luhrssen, *War on the Silver Screen: Shaping America's Perception of History* (Lincoln, NE, 2014).

11. N. E. Sarantakes, *Making Patton: A Classic War Film's Journey to the Silver Screen* (Lawrence, KS, 2012); D. Milberg, *World War II on the Big Screen: 450+ Hollywood Films, 1938–2008* (Jefferson, NC, 2010).

12. J. N. Richard, *Advance and Destroy: Patton as Commander in the Bulge* (Lexington, KY, 2011).

13. S. Call, *Selling Air Power: Military Aviation and American Popular Culture after World War II* (College Station, TX, 2009).

14. B. Liddell Hart, *History of the Second World War* (London, 1970), 706–8, quote 707.

15. Kennedy to Black, email, March 22, 2019.

16. "History Makes History (and Money)," *Advertisers Weekly*, April 7, 1967, 32–34; LH. Liddell Hart papers, 3/183.

17. J. Lockenour, "Black and White Memories of War: Victimisation and Violence in West German War Films of the 1950s," *JMH* 76 (2012): 183, 187.

18. A. Hill, "The Bear's New Wheels (and Tracks): US-Armored and Other Vehicles and Soviet Military Effectiveness during the Great Patriot War in Words and Photographs," *Journal of Slavic Military Studies* 25 (2012): 204–19.

19. R. M. Citino, "Manstein, the Battle of Kharkov, and the Limits of Command," in *Arms and the Man: Essays in Military History in Honor of Dennis Showalter*, ed. M. S. Neiberg (Leiden 2011), 107, 112.

20. M. Uhl, "Storming on to Paris: The 1961 *Buria* Exercise and the Planned Solution to the Berlin Crisis," in *War Plans and Alliances in the Cold War: Threat Perceptions East and West*, ed. V. Mastsny, S. G. Holtsmark, and A. Wenger (London, 2006), 46–71.

21. P. Feng, "The M60," *On Point* 16, no. 2 (Fall 2010): 14–17.

22. A. J. Birtle, *Rearming the Phoenix: U.S. Military Assistance to the Federal Republic of Germany, 1950–1960* (New York, 1991).

23. R. P. Hunnicutt, *Abrams: A History of the American Main Battle Tank* (Novato, CA, 1990).

24. V. Mastiny, S. G. Holtsmark, and A. Wenger, eds., *War Plans and Alliances in the Cold War: Threat Perceptions in the East and West* (Abingdon, UK, 2006); J. Hoffenear and D. Krüger, eds., *Blueprints for Battle: Planning for War in Central Europe, 1948–1968* (Lexington, KY, 2012); D. A. Carter, *Forging the Shield: The U.S. Army in Europe, 1951–1962* (Washington, DC, 2015); D. Krüger and V. Bausch, eds., *Fulda Gap: Battlefield of the Cold War Alliances* (Lanham, MD, 2018).

25. LH. Ismay 3/21/1.

26. S. J. Zaloga, *Modern Soviet Armour: Combat Vehicles of the USSR and Warsaw Pact Today* (London, 1979).

27. D. T. Fautua, "The 'Long Pull' Army: NSC 68, the Korean War, and the Creation of the Cold War U.S. Army," *JMH* 61 (1997): 116–20.

28. R. E. Appleman, "Reflections on Task Force Smith," *Army History* 26 (spring 1993): 32–40.

29. A. Terry, *The Battle for Pusan: A Korean War Memoir* (Novato, CA, 2000).

30. B. R. Gibby, "The Battle for White Horse Mountain, September–October 1952," *Army History* 89 (fall 2013): 30, 33, 35, 38, 41–42.

31. M. A. Henry, "French Armor in Algeria," *Armor* 81 (November/December 1972): 12–16.

32. *Executive Sessions of the Senate Foreign Relations Committee*, 11, 1959 sessions (Washington, DC, 1982): 125.

33. Z. Levey, *Israel and the Western Powers, 1952–1960* (Chapel Hill, NC, 1997).

34. D. O'Connell, "The 'Lessons Learned' Trap and How to Avoid It: Drawing from the Israeli Armoured Experience, 1948–1973," *Journal on Baltic Security* 2 (2016): 117–28.

35. D. Tal, "Between Intuition and Professionalism: Israeli Military Leadership during the 1948 Palestine War," *JMH* 68 (2004): 908.

36. For this argument with reference to "Star Wars," R. Holloway, "The Strategic Defense Initiative and the Technological Sublime: Fear, Science, and the Cold War," in *Critical Reflections on the Cold War: Linking Rhetoric and History,* ed. M. Medhurst and H. W. Brands (College Station, TX, 2000), 225. See also T. G. Mahnken, *Technology and the American Way of War since 1945* (New York, 2008).

SEVEN

THE LATER COLD WAR, 1968–90

The major war that dominated and continues to dominate US consideration for this period was that in Vietnam. This focused US military and public attention from 1963 to 1973 and drove home the extent to which limited warfare did not necessarily mean a reprise of the European stage of World War II, with the related doctrine and weaponry.

Vietnam is generally seen as a jungle conflict with scant role for tanks. The Viet Cong and North Vietnamese are associated with ambushes and the Americans with air power, notably the use of helicopter gunships. For the US army, the pronounced focus by the air force on the Strategic Air Command, at the expense of the Tactical Air Command, meant that firepower in support of land operations could not be readily obtained from the air. This tendency was further encouraged by the air force's emphasis, even at the tactical level, on interdiction as opposed to close air support. In response to air force pressure, the army, moreover, was limited in aerial roles by the Key West Agreement of 1948, although it sought to circumvent this by using helicopters in ground-attack roles.[1] In Vietnam, where they were available in great numbers, helicopters served as a substitute for tanks. They were slower than fixed-wing aircraft, lightly armored (as well as noisy), and therefore vulnerable, but their mobility was a key compensation.

This account, however, underplays the role of tanks for both sides. They were deployed by the United States and its allies. The main US tank was the M48 Patton medium tank, with its 90 mm gun. Over six hundred were deployed. This tank was also used by South Vietnamese forces, as was the M41 Walker Bulldog light tank. The M67 was a flame-throwing variant of the M48, yet another reflection of the significance of that armament. The Americans also employed the M551 Sheridan Armored Reconnaissance Airborne Assault Vehicle light tank, as well as the M107 self-propelled gun.

Australia and New Zealand employed Centurion tanks in the Australian and New Zealand Army Corps (ANZAC) force in South Vietnam, notably in the face of the 1968 Tet Offensive, when their bases were attacked. These tanks were fitted with additional machine guns in order to deal with rush attacks and counter ambushes. That effectiveness, however, did not mean they dominated the countryside. As a separate issue, Australian training for armor-infantry cooperation was flawed.

Although the Viet Cong had no antitank guns (as opposed to antitank weapons), armored operations were made far harder by the heat, humidity, terrain (hilly or swampy), vegetation, mud, and dust.[2] The limited weight capacity of the bridges was a factor that led General William Westmoreland, the US commander, to press in December 1965 for light, not medium, tanks.[3] He got the fully tracked M113 armored personnel carriers, which were first used in combat in April 1962 and able to operate in the jungle. In total about eighty thousand of all variants of the M113 have been built. The aluminum (and therefore lightly) armored M113 was armed with a .50 caliber machine gun and had a top speed of forty-two miles per hour. Two light machine guns in shields were added in the rear. The M113 proved more effective than the M114 armored fighting vehicles, which were vulnerable to mines, unreliable, and poor at off-road movements. Westmoreland had to accept some M48A3 Patton medium tanks. M132 armored flamethrowers, a variant of the M113, were also provided.

Tanks provided part of the security that enabled the Americans and their allies to hold the cities. The targets provided by urban conflict, notably defended buildings, also ensured that tanks were significant in fighting there with the Viet Cong, as when M48s were used to help retake the city of Hue in 1968. The tanks offered protected mobility and up-close protected firepower. That the tanks proved less useful in the interior of South Vietnam than in the cities did not mean they were without value. They offered key support in ambushes, as they were able to absorb damage and return fire. Moreover, tanks, both US and South Vietnamese, played an important role in the invasion of Cambodia in 1970, providing valuable firepower in infantry-armor assaults on well-fortified Viet Cong bases and thus hitting their supply system. This attack helped secure the Saigon region and buy time for a Vietnamization of the war effort that aided the US withdrawal.[4]

The firepower available to and linked with the US armor was considerable. For example, the First Squadron of the First Cavalry Regiment included three ground cavalry troops, each with three platoons of three M48A3 tanks and seven armored cavalry assault vehicles, plus an air cavalry troop, with helicopters and an aero-rifle platoon, and a supporting 155 mm howitzer battery. This firepower proved effective in battle, but the terrain and vegetation meant it was necessary to leave the vehicles and fight as infantry or require infantry support.[5]

Most of the losses of US and South Vietnamese armor were to antitank weapons, such as the Soviet RPG-7, developed from the German Panzerfaust. This vulnerability led to the fitting of protective screens for tanks.[6] Designed in 1958 and entering service in 1961, the RPG-7 was a portable, reusable, unguided, shoulder-launched, antitank rocket-propelled grenade launcher, with an effective (although not accurate) firing range of 330 meters. As with other Soviet weapons, the RPG-7 benefited from its simplicity and ruggedness. Damage was also inflicted by 57 mm recoilless rifles.

Tanks also played a role for their opponents. The North Vietnamese used captured tanks (just as the South Vietnamese used captured RPG-7s) as well as Soviet tanks—the T-34/85, the PT-76, the T-54—and the Chinese version of the latter, the Type 59, as well as the Type 62. These tanks played a notable role when employed by the North Vietnamese in 1972. This was one of the major offensives of the period, one that stands in comparison, as a military and political move, with the Egyptian and Syrian assault on Israel in 1973. The casualties inflicted on the Viet Cong in, and after, the Tet Offensive of 1968, as well as the inability of US air attacks to destroy North Vietnam's war-supporting capability and logistical system, ensured a greater reliance on North Vietnamese forces, rather than, as earlier, on the Viet Cong, while also creating the possibility for the use of conventional forces in a standard Soviet-style operation. In March 1972, the North Vietnamese launched the Nguyen Hue campaign (or Easter Offensive) across the demilitarized zone between North and South Vietnam. This represented a use of what approximated to a coastal plain. The surprise nature of the attack, and the strong forces deployed, brought initial success. Quang Tri, a provincial capital, was captured, and another, An Loc, was besieged.

A standard view, notably in the United States, emphasizes the role, in the eventual North Vietnamese failure in 1972, of the US Linebacker 1 air campaign, which hit the supply system, and thus the support, of the invasion forces, especially in terms of fuel. The US use of laser-guided bombs was certainly an important enhancement of capability, as was the improved use of radar technology and the vulnerability of tanks to US helicopter-fired wire-guided missiles.

This account, however, underplays the role of South Vietnamese defenders, who held off the invasion, including with antitank guns, and, separately but also related to this, the problems the North Vietnamese confronted in mastering high-tempo maneuverist warfare. Both were also issues for Egypt and Syria when attacking Israel in 1973 and for Iraq when attacking Iran in 1980. The Soviet Union could provide impressive weaponry, particularly tanks, for their allies, and in plentiful numbers, but it proved far more difficult to transfer the doctrine and techniques of effective operational warfare, and notably so if faced by a determined opposition. As more generally, capabilities, both in attack and defense, were focused, accentuated, minimized, or offset by the characteristics of the opponents. Thus, US success in the 1991 Gulf War is not a necessary guide to what would have happened in Central Europe had a third world war broken out.

In 1972, the North Vietnamese failed to make the best use of tanks. This reflected both an operational inability to use them in a maneuverist capacity in order to gain mobility and achieve particular objectives and a tactical failure to get and utilize infantry-armor coordination. Instead, as with the Iraqis in 1980, the tanks were used by the North Vietnamese as an assault force on South Vietnamese positions—indeed, essentially as mobile artillery. This had the effect of squandering the initiative in operational terms while providing targets for US air attack. Precision weaponry was effective against tanks to a degree that "dumb" or free-fall bombs had not been. Moreover, that May, US helicopters mounting new tube-launched, optically tracked, wire-guided (TOW) antitank missiles destroyed North Vietnamese tanks, notably when the latter attacked the city of Kontum.[7]

In 1975, there was a renewed invasion of South Vietnam, this time without US support. Conventional North Vietnamese divisions achieved what they had been unable to do in 1972. They made good use of tanks in 1975 and ably integrated them with infantry and artillery. This was helped by the ability of the North Vietnamese to supply their forces utilizing roads and pipelines down previously contested routes, notably the A Shau Valley.[8] An explanation of North Vietnamese success in 1975 in terms of their tanks not having to face opposition from the air and of the South Vietnamese as cut off from US military aid—an explanation that places the weight of decision on the absence of US intervention—however, is insufficient. In 1975, the South Vietnamese followed an unwise strategy with the abandonment of the Central Highlands, where the North Vietnamese had launched their attack, and focused, instead, on defending the South near Saigon. This strategy gave their opponents a powerful impetus and gravely weakened their own morale and cohesion. North Vietnamese perseverance was also important.[9]

The availability of tanks in East Asia was increased as a result of production in China. From 1958, in response to the support for armor warfare shown by the defense minister, Marshal Peng Dehuai, a practitioner of conventional war, the Chinese produced the Type 59, a version of the Soviet T-54A and China's first generation of main battle tank. This was accepted into service in 1959 and was displayed, advancing in mass, in the Tenth National Day parade that year, and production increased in 1963. Production of this model ceased in 1980, after about 9,500 had been produced. Armed with a 100 mm rifled gun (as well as machine guns), the tank had a speed of thirty-one miles per hour and an operational range of 280 miles. Peng, however, was purged in 1959 by Mao, with whom he had disagreed, and his successor, Lin Biao, defense minister until 1971, followed the Maoist line of political indoctrination rather than military professionalism.

China employed over four hundred tanks in its attack on Vietnam in 1979, including those of the tank regiments that were each attached to Guangzhou and Kunming Military Regions. Both sides claimed to have destroyed many opposing tanks. On February 17, about two hundred Type 59, 62, and 63 tanks advanced as part of the initial invasion of about two hundred thousand troops. In response, the Soviet Union sent aid to Vietnam, much of it by aircraft. This aid included four hundred tanks and armored personnel carriers and eight hundred antitank missiles. In the first battle, that of Dong Dang, Vietnamese defensive positions proved a formidable obstacle until February 23, and the Chinese lost tanks, with twenty-one allegedly being destroyed. In the battle of Cao Băng, which continued from February 17 until March 5, the defending Vietnamese destroyed and damaged Chinese tanks, with one Chinese unit losing tanks on February 20 to Vietnamese antitank missiles and grenades. The two sides produced very different accounts of casualties in this and other battles, with the Vietnamese claiming to have destroyed scores of Chinese tanks in this battle and offering a photograph of the wreckage of one. The Chinese certainly found their vehicles affected by the difficult mountainous terrain of the frontier section of northern Vietnam.

China also provides tanks to allies, including Albania, Congo, North Korea, Pakistan, Sudan, and Tanzania. As such, they were a way to spread Chinese influence. Moreover, the low cost acted to counter the pressures created by higher prices elsewhere. This was also part of the process by which production costs were brought down by export sales.

A year after the US occupation of Japan ended, in a clear show of the contingent impact of politics upon tank development, Japan began a design for a new tank in 1953, aiming to produce a tank of about thirty tons that was equipped with a 90 mm gun and similar to the M47. Trial production of what became the Type 61 tank was finished in 1961, and, by the end of 1975, 560 had been produced. The tank weighed thirty-five tons and had a 90 mm gun and a maximum speed of twenty-eight miles per hour. It was designed to complement the particular nature of Japan, a country with few plains and many hills. As a result, ambush was seen as the principal tactic to be adopted in tank combat. The main strategic concern was with Soviet invasion, particularly of the northernmost main island, Hokkaido. To finance its tank production, wealthy Japan did not rely on foreign sales, which would not have pleased the United States.

The new wealth of the East Asian economies also resulted in tank production in South Korea. Confronted, in the 1970s, with the threat of attack from North Korea, with its T-62s, South Korea sought to replace its M47s and M48s. While the latter were upgraded, plans to produce the Leopard 1 domestically or obtain M60s were not pursued. Instead, like Israel earlier with the Merkava, South Korea decided to focus on producing a domestic counterpart to the newest main battle tanks. The winning design was based on the prototype of the Abrams, notably its main gun, composite armor, fire control system, and laser range finder, but with a more effective hybrid suspension system providing greater stability and ability to range and depress the gun, as well as the tank commander having an independent panoramic sight. What became the K1 was mass-produced from 1985 and entered service in 1987. An upgraded version, with a 120 mm gun and improved armor, entered service from 2001.

In turn, the K2, which was designed by the South Korean Agency for Defense Development, entered mass production from 2013 and was deployed from 2014. It has active protection systems, both soft—electronic—and hard—reactive armor. Each K2 costs more than US $8.5 million. A total of 320 K2s are planned, considerably fewer than the 1,511 K1s produced between 1985 and 2010. South Korea also has 1,700 self-propelled howitzers, of which 1,040 are K55s, which use the US M109 as their base.

Their replacement, entering service from 1999, is the South Korean–developed K9 Thunder. In turn, the latter has been sold abroad, including to Turkey, Finland, and Estonia, and has been considered by many states. This reflects the changing nature of the arms trade. The trade remained a major feature of the world economy, but it altered from the early 1970s as US industrial hegemony was qualified by the relative rise of other economies. However, the United States remained the key producer of arms.

THE YOM KIPPUR WAR

Meanwhile, the effectiveness of tanks had been given greater prominence in the Yom Kippur War (the Ramadan War for the Arabs; also known as the October War), which began with surprise attacks on Israel launched by Egypt and Syria on October 6, 1973. Each had benefited from Soviet assistance in rearming after defeat in 1967—moreover, rearming with more modern weapons—and the conflict was very much part of the Cold War.[10] Furthermore, the Egyptians profited from the end of their onerous 1962–67 intervention in North Yemen, which, albeit in a very different context, was analogous to the Vietnam commitment for the United States and had affected the availability of Egyptian forces when Egypt was attacked by Israel in 1967. The end of this conflict meant the Egyptians could focus again on conventional conflict rather than counterinsurgency operations.

Although an Egyptian deception plan was applied with considerable skill in 1973, the Israelis had received reliable intelligence of Egyptian intentions. Nevertheless, there was a serious failure of analysis and response on their part. As a result, Egypt and Syria, despite massing forces, were able to profit from surprise. Benefiting from the absence of any mobilization of Israeli reserves and from their superiority in numbers, the Arab forces broke through Israeli positions, notably the weakly defended Israeli Bar Lev Line on the east bank of the Suez Canal, which was imaginatively assaulted by the Soviet-trained Egyptians. The strongpoints were strung out, did not cover each other, and were not well defended. Due to a lack of preparedness, the firing positions of the Israeli tanks were empty.[11]

Established, as a result, in new positions on the western fringes of the Sinai Peninsula east of the Suez Canal, the Egyptians then repelled a series of Israeli counterattacks, counterattacks that began on October 6 in an unsuccessful effort by the standing tank division in the area to save the strongholds of the Bar Lev Line, an effort that led to the loss of about 190 tanks on that day. The Israelis were determined not to let the Egyptians consolidate their position. On October 6, and subsequently, the Egyptians inflicted serious damage on Israeli armor, which, in the absence of nearby support, suffered from a doctrine that, based on the experience of 1967, exaggerated the effectiveness of tank attack and failed to provide adequate combined arms capability, especially sufficient artillery support and mobile artillery. There was an overreliance on tanks in the Israeli force structure: Israeli attitudes reflected wishful thinking, notably a belief that they could focus on tank warfare and therefore lessen the risk of suffering infantry casualties, the same choice that contributed to the British army's failure in Operation Goodwood in Normandy in 1944.

There were also serious command and control flaws. The two Israeli reserve tank divisions that attacked on October 8 had poor situational awareness and failed to coordinate their operations, and neither was well commanded. Moreover, the absence of sufficient Israeli tank transporters meant many tanks had been required to drive across the Sinai, which led to mechanical breakdowns.

The Israelis had deployed French antitank missiles in the 1960s and so were aware of their capability, but they did not build on this experience or appreciate the improvements in such weaponry. In 1973, Egyptian infantry units equipped with Soviet Sagger antitank guided missiles and RPG-7 rocket launchers proved deadly and destroyed over eight hundred Israeli tanks and other combat vehicles. The Israelis, whose focus on aircraft and tanks had led to a neglect of artillery, argued, in contrast, that the best antitank weapon was another tank. The success of the Saggers against the Israeli Patton tanks was largely due to the extensive training the Egyptian soldiers had received. Later reports indicated that all the crews had live fired at least two missiles during training. This represented a very expensive, but ultimately successful, investment in the use of the system. The Egyptian confidence in their weapon system was undoubtedly aided by Israeli hubris about the caliber of their opponents.

In a striking illustration of the continuing difficulties of assessing relative capability, claims varied (and still vary) over the effectiveness of tanks and missiles in that conflict. The Israelis claimed their tank losses were overwhelmingly to other tanks whereas the Egyptians stressed the role of their missiles. More generally, there are usually competing accounts of tank losses in conflict. These differences reflect the significance attached to demonstrating proficiency, as well as the strongly competing interests within the military bound up in particular force structures and doctrines. The need for integrity in after-action reports is continually challenged by this factor.

In the Yom Kippur War, the Syrians proved less effective than the Egyptians in fighting the Israelis. As a reminder of the continued relevance of multifactual explanations, this lesser effectiveness reflected, in part, the classic tank trade-offs of arms, armor, and speed. Yet other elements were at play on both sides. In large part, the effective use of tanks, in the shape of doctrine, tactics, and command skills, was crucial, but so was the Israeli focus on the Syrian front, as well as other Israeli advantages there. There were more Israeli tanks near the front line against Syria than against Egypt as well as better infantry. These tanks were used effectively to thwart or delay the Syrian advance.

In addition, there were formidable man-made obstacles to the Syrian advance, including a strong antitank ditch—which, despite the use of bull-dozers and bridge-layer tanks, funneled the Syrian tanks, exposing them to more effective Israeli fire—and large minefields. Both ditch and minefields were backed by hilltop strongpoints that proved more formidable than those on the Bar Lev Line and provided key observation points able to direct fire.

Moreover, in a significant counterpart to the use of tanks, the Israelis had supplemented the defenses with shooting platforms, or ramps, that enabled the hull-down tanks, with only their upper turret and gun visible, to engage more effectively with the advancing Syrian tanks. These platforms offered pre-pared, stable firing positions akin to those enjoyed by well-sited antitank guns or missile launchers. Their use was an aspect of the practice of "tank sniping," which the Israelis had developed in border clashes. They were better than the Syrians in long-range tank duels, which meant they preferred not to engage at close distances when that advantage was compromised.

The Soviet T-54, T-55, and T-62 tanks deployed by the Syrians in 1973, eight hundred on the first day and more subsequently, benefited from being simple to use, thus requiring less training, and easy to maintain and operate; they were also armed with powerful guns and could move a longer distance on a single tank of fuel than the tanks of their Israeli opponents. The last was both tactically and operationally significant. The T-62s were well armored, which made them harder to destroy at long range. Moreover, unlike the Israelis, the Syrians had fully integrated night-vision sights on their Soviet tanks. This was important not only for firing but also in the ambush fighting so important in tank conflict. In addition, the T-62 was the first Soviet tank with an automatic shell extractor, which eased the situation for the crew, although Soviet infantry on maneuvers hated it because the shell extractor sent the spent casings fly-ing out the back, where they hit the supporting infantry.

The compact frames of the Soviet tanks left little space or ventilation for their crew, which tired them out. Combined with thin side armor, this feature accentuated the problem of crew vulnerability to penetrating rounds. The lim-ited depression angle of the main gun also ensured vulnerability as the Syrian tanks could not adopt a hull-down position in order to engage. The limited height also meant the ammunition tended to explode when the turret was hit.

In contrast, the Israeli British-supplied Centurion, an older model, albeit updated, was heavily armed, had a good long-range gun, and could readily depress its barrel, thus exposing little of the tank. In conflict with Pakistan in

1971, the Indians, defending the east bank of the Tawi River, countered this problem with their T-54 tanks by the use of well-prepared defensive positions. The Indians also benefited from the superiority they had won in the air.

Conflict in 1973, as on other occasions, owed much to the impact of the trade-off of different specifications as, crucially, mediated by a training that, in this case, was better for the Israelis. In this conflict, the Syrian tank crews fought less well, not least because of a lack of flexibility. They were also suffering serious sleep deprivation, which delayed their response to the presence of nearby Israeli tanks. Moreover, the Syrians lacked adequate combined arms capability, with poor artillery and infantry support proving key elements. In addition, the Syrians found it difficult to use their antitank missiles and artillery, which put the emphasis on tank-to-tank conflict. Seriously poor tactics overlapped with operational counterparts. A misuse of Soviet operational art by the Syrians was an important element, notably an emphasis not on exploiting breakthroughs by means of an echelon deployment that would thwart counterattacks but, rather, on a mass assault.[12] The Syrians also suffered from the suppression of their surface-to-air (SAM) antiaircraft missile batteries by the Israelis, which enabled the latter to attack ground targets with much greater safety.

In response to urgent Syrian pressure for help, the Egyptians changed their strategy, operational method, and tactics. They moved their armored reserve forward, attacking on October 14 in an attempt to advance to the central passes in the Sinai. This was a mistake as the Israelis, no longer taken by surprise, were strong in defense, not least because the Egyptians advanced beyond the antiaircraft cover offered by the Soviet SAM-ZSU air defense system. In an attack that highlighted the deficiencies of their tactics, the Egyptians lost heavily in what is known as the "Chinese Farm" battle. The Israelis' US-made M48 and M60 tanks had double the rate of fire of the Soviet T-55 and T-62 tanks. The T-62 was not a great improvement over the T-55. The Israelis also used concentrations of artillery fire to overcome the Sagger units. As a result, the Israeli armor could focus on the Egyptian tanks. The Egyptians lost 200–250 tanks, compared to the Israelis' 10–20.

Gaining and using the initiative, the Israelis further took the advantage by outmaneuvering their opponents. Having crossed the Suez Canal on the night of October 15, despite a continuing lack of combined arms coordination,[13] the Israelis overran the Egyptian missile defense units, defeated Egyptian counterattacks, encircled Egyptian forces, and imposed a result on their opponents by the time the conflict was brought to a close. Intervention by the Americans and Soviets, the backers of Israel and Egypt respectively, ensured an end to hostilities. Egypt and Syria lost about 2,250 tanks in the war, and the Israelis lost 840.[14] Competing claims were made about the number, as well as cause, of losses.

Although the 1973 Yom Kippur War proved far less one-sided in its course than the 1967 Six-Day War, it still indicated significant differences in fighting quality that were clearly to the advantage of Israel, particularly when focused by good command. Moreover, these differences suggested, again, that the quantity of resources was less important than their quality and use. This was an interpretation that greatly interested US observers as the Israeli military, with its US tanks, was treated as a representative of what the US army could achieve, as opposed to the Egyptians and Syrians, both of whom used Soviet tanks, doctrine, and training. In practice, the Egyptians and Syrians used these in a way that probably would have been below—indeed, far below—the level of Soviet effectiveness.

A similar pattern of learning was employed by the Americans as far as the air conflict was concerned. These analyses proved mutually supportive as processes and in their conclusions.[15] In turn, Egyptian success with antitank weaponry encouraged commentators to stress its importance. This led to consideration about how best to improve tanks and interest in matching Saggers or developing such weapons further.

ARMORED CONFLICT ELSEWHERE, 1968–79

No other tank conflict in this period had an impact comparable to the Yom Kippur War, but there were other wars in which armor was used. In 1970, armor was extensively employed by Syria when it invaded Jordan. However, the Syrian Fifth Division, with more than two hundred T-55s, after it broke through Jordanian positions, destroying about eighty Jordanian tanks, was hit by air strikes. The Jordanian air force destroyed a large number of tanks, leading to a loss of morale and contributing to the Syrian withdrawal. In 1971, Pakistani M24s (Chaffees) stationed in East Pakistan (now Bangladesh) were lost to attacking Indian forces, whose T-55s were more powerful.

In general, however, mobility was provided by armored personnel carriers—for example, in the Nigerian Civil War of 1967–70, when they were used by government forces against the separatist Biafrans. In practice, the terrain and vegetation posed problems for general forces, as did serious logistical limitations. Such vehicles were not so much an alternative to tanks as a mechanization of the infantry. In its 1971 war with Pakistan, India deployed Polish-supplied wheeled and tracked and Soviet-supplied wheeled armored personnel carriers. In the Yom Kippur War in 1973, the Syrians deployed about one thousand Soviet-provided BMP-1 infantry fighting vehicles and BTR armored personnel carriers. Such vehicles, however, were more vulnerable than tanks, a situation that recurred in Iraq in the 2000s, and also could be less flexible. In 1979, in the conflict that ended with the invading Tanzanians overthrowing President Idi Amin of Uganda, light antitank weapons were used to destroy armored personnel carriers, which were largely road bound.

A warning about Soviet proficiency of a different type to the Yom Kippur War was provided in 1978 when they organized strong military assistance to Ethiopia in its conflict with Somalia. The Soviets provided tanks—over 130 in 1977 alone—BTR-60s and BTR-152s, armored personnel carriers, and artillery, all manned by Cubans, as well as an innovative tank commander, General Vasily Petrov. The East Germans also supplied troops. Petrov adapted cutting-edge weaponry and operational systems devised for war in Europe to the exigencies of Africa and led tank units into battle. Assaults spearheaded by tanks and rocket launchers, and supported by air attacks, parachutists, and helicopter troops, conquered the Ogaden region in 1978. The war enabled the Soviets to test out tactics and equipment, and Petrov went on to serve as commander in chief of ground forces from 1980 to 1985. The Ogaden was similar in terrain, climate, and vegetation to North Africa and much of Southwest Asia—flat, arid, and largely treeless.[16] The Somalis also used BTR-152s, having received many from the Soviet Union in the late 1960s. About half of these were destroyed. The Ogaden, however, did not attract the attention devoted to the Yom Kippur War.

Even less attention was devoted to subsequent Soviet-directed Ethiopian operations in Eritrea. Tanks could be effective, as at Adi Yacob on November 21, 1978, but, when the Eritreans used rugged terrain, as near Keren later in November, the situation proved more difficult.[17] Moreover, the Soviet doctrine of deep penetration and encircling opponents was proved inappropriate in 1978–79 for mountainous terrain where control of commanding positions was crucial and ambushes an ever-present risk.[18] In addition, Ethiopian supply lines lengthened, with implications for troop requirements. Ethiopia lost nearly 180 tanks, 38 of which were captured by the Eritreans, who then used them against the Ethiopians. Thus, the fate of Eritrea did not follow that of the Ogaden, either then or later.

COLD WAR CONFRONTATION IN EUROPE

The Yom Kippur War had been a warning to NATO at a tense moment for the latter.[19] The portable infantry ground-to-tank and ground-to-air missiles were an unwelcome surprise to the Israelis and NATO. The Syrians had new

Soviet tanks. A reading of the war that noted both the threat and the potential offered by new equipment, including the night-vision optics that permitted twenty-four-hour operations, encouraged pressure to upgrade NATO armor. This was the case both for those who saw the war as providing evidence of revolutionary new potential and, more plausibly, for those who emphasized an evolutionary approach.

The Americans were keen to assess the tank battles of that war. Alongside listening to Israeli accounts, they sent commanders to Israel to do so, notably Donn Starry, the head of the Armor Center and School at Fort Knox (1973–75), and Brigadier General Bob Baer. Starry, a protégé of Abrams, had led the Eleventh Armored Cavalry Regiment into Cambodia in 1970 and sought to argue that armor was crucial to the counterinsurgency. He would go on, from 1977 to 1981, to be commander of the new Training and Doctrine Command (TRADOC) and, from 1981 to 1983, to be commander in chief of US Readiness Command. Starry helped develop the doctrine of AirLand Battle, with its concomitant requirements for new equipment, including better tanks and a capable infantry combat vehicle to replace the M113 in the mechanized units.[20]

The challenge from the Soviet Union; the clear limitations of East-West détente by the late 1970s; the lessons learned, or at least derived, from the Yom Kippur War; and the wish of the US army to find a new and/or resumed role after the Vietnam War all encouraged a refocusing of US concern on how best to fight against the Soviet Union in a decisive war in Europe. The range of these causative factors ensured that a number of elements were at play, rather than an either/or situation. Israeli successes encouraged already-existing US and NATO interest in a more flexible practice of land warfare. A focus on Northern Europe was also convenient for the US army, notably with the prominence within it of tank generals[21] and with the stress there on conventional warfare defined in terms of symmetrical conflict focused on tanks. Such conflict was seen as likely to involve fewer casualties and to require less manpower than an infantry war, which was very important given the ending of conscription by President Nixon. The British had already ended conscription. As a result, armies became more professional and relied less on infantry, the average pay of which increased. This further encouraged the emphasis on machinery.

That approach to explaining the focus on symmetrical conflict in Northern Europe can then be taken forward to suggest that, as a result of a mistaken strategy, including a strategic culture, force structure, and doctrinal practice, in which tanks played too large a role, the Americans proved far less prepared for the "wars among the people" that became more significant in the 1990s and more of a problem for them in the 2000s.[22] There is a point to this analysis, but, from the end of US participation in the Vietnam War (1973) to the fall of the Berlin Wall (1989), it would have been feckless for the US (or British) armies to focus on warfare on the model of that in Vietnam or the conflicts in sub-Saharan Africa that occurred in the period. Instead, the strength of Soviet conventional forces in Eastern Europe posed a continuing threat and, indeed, had been an important strategic backdrop element during the Vietnam War. The West German army focused totally on conflict with the Soviet Union.

The motorization and mechanization of infantry further increased the need for tanks to protect, or oppose, such units. Full motorization permitted the development of infantry doctrine that focused on rapid mobility. Thus, along-side the US M113 armored personnel carrier, which was eventually adopted by over fifty countries, the Soviet army, in 1987, introduced the high-speed BMP-3 infantry vehicle, of which over two thousand were built. Capable of carrying eight men as well as a crew of three, it was protected by an air filtration system and armed with a gun, a machine gun, an antitank guided missile, and rifle ports. It was designed to give bite to the expansion in the number of Soviet motor vehicle divisions.[23] The development of armored personnel carriers, starting with the BMP-1 and the Marder, was a key part in the military history of the later Cold War. The Israeli Merkhava tank, with its room for an infantry team, and the Swedish development of a light infantry support tank—the Ikv 91—and a turretless tank served as a reminder that the "grey zone" of defini-tions seen in World War II was present anew. Produced in 1975–78, the Ikv 91 had common components with the Pbv 302 armored personnel carrier but carried a 90 mm gun. The development of this type of vehicle continued after the Cold War.

The same process of motorization also characterized logistics, with the Soviet Union seeing the key development. The horses of World War II were replaced, but the role of rail was also minimized as the truck came to dominate the supply system. A quick advance thereby became a greater possibility and a more urgent threat.

Tank capabilities were enhanced. In part, this was by copying. Thus, the Chinese Type 69 tank was improved in the 1980s by adopting Western tech-nology, notably the L7 105 mm gun. This upgrade, the Type 79, entered pro-duction in 1984 as part of the post-Maoist emphasis on quality over quantity.

The most significant innovation was the production of the M1 Abrams tank by the Americans. Designed in 1972–75, it was produced from 1979, entering service in 1980. Intended to replace the M60, after the 1971 cancellation of the overly expensive and complex US–West German MBT-70 project, and to meet the need for a better tank to oppose the Soviets, the Abrams became the main battle tank of both the US army and marines. Over ten thousand have been built. This was the first vehicle to adopt Chobham armor, an arrangement of metal plates, ceramic blocks, and open space. The Abrams was turbine powered and had a license-built version of the 105 mm British L7 gun. From 1986, the M1A1 version was produced. It had the M256 120 mm gun developed in Germany for the Leopard 2, as well as improved armor. Like the British Challenger, the Abrams was a tank designed to resist the greater numbers of Soviet tanks by having good long-range accuracy and a high-kill ratio, which, indeed, led to them being seen as "sniper tanks," a practice followed by the Israelis in using Centurions against Syrian tanks.[24]

The Abrams, however, did not persuade all purchasers. Instead, in 1979, the Dutch army chose the Leopard 2 to replace the Centurions and the light AMXs: in the early 1980s, 445 Leopard 2s arrived while the older Leopard 1s were improved and modified.

There were also changes in ammunition in response to those in armor. For example, HESH (high-explosive squash head), a projectile containing plastic explosive that flattens on impact before detonating, a 1940s British invention for bunker busting, had been found to be effective against armor. However, it went out of favor in the 1970s as tank armor moved from ever-thicker steel to composite armor.[25]

Encouraging investment, Cold War tensions rose from the late 1970s, notably with the initially successful Soviet invasion of Afghanistan in December 1979. For the US army to have failed to focus on this challenge would have been to invite the charge of redundancy in the face of military and political developments and to have entrusted NATO defenses to nuclear missiles, especially at a time when Soviet missile strength was markedly increasing. Already under President Carter (1977–81), there had been a buildup of US strength and resolve. Both were taken much further under President Reagan (1981–89).

Urgently reconsidering how to defend West Germany and drawing on the new Training and Doctrine Command, the Americans advanced the doctrine of "active defense" in 1976, aiming to win the "first battle,"[26] and then, from 1982, out of dissatisfaction with this doctrine, turned to that of AirLand Battle, with its emphasis on an offensive orientation and winning. Operational-level maneuver was taught at the School of Advanced Military Studies at Fort Leavenworth. These concepts, which affected planning, doctrine, procurement, and careers, led to a more intensive stress on the integration of firepower with mobility. This was a marked development of the process termed ROAD (Reorganization of the Army Division) seen in 1959–63 as a key element of a commitment to "flexible response,"[27] not least because of the emphasis on the coordination of air and land fighting. To give teeth to the process, there was a modernization in the 1970s and 1980s of conventional weaponry and a determination to enhance the capability of what, from 1974, was an all-volunteer army. Moreover, the doctrinal innovation focused on the consideration of how best to direct and win the operational level of war—that between strategy and tactics.

In this, the Americans were advancing concepts that made sense of their own commitment to a maneuverist approach, as opposed to a reliance on fixed defenses for Western Europe, and on a damaging attritional doctrine. Continued attention was shown to the German campaigns in World War II. Thus, the Combat Studies Institute at Fort Leavenworth included, in its 1983 *Selected Readings in Military History: Evolution of Combined Arms Warfare*, Guderian's "Cooperation between Armored Forces and Other Arms."

The Americans were also seeking to match, counter, and overcome the Soviet development of operational art. This development, in the 1960s and 1970s, took forward ideas untried in conflict in the 1930s, but used with great success in 1944–45, in order to sustain an offensive, to overcome the problems posed by the defenders, and to force continual disorientation on them. In part, this process depended on moving forward second- and third-echelon forces in order to replace those in the initial attack and thus sustain the offensive. Under Marshal Nikolai Ogarkov, the perceptive chief of the General Staff from 1977 to 1984, the Soviets developed earlier concepts of "deep battle" thanks in part to the spread of mechanization in the army and the growth of airborne forces. Ogarkov sought a more compact, technologically advanced military, rather than one focused on the techniques of mass conflict.[28] This was very different from the Communist ideas of popular warfare advanced in China under Mao Zedong and widely disseminated elsewhere, notably in Africa, by those who looked to Mao.

The Soviets planned a rapid advance into NATO rear areas, which would compromise the use of Western nuclear weaponry against any attacks. Essentially building on the operational policy of their campaigning in the latter stages of World War II, the Soviets put a premium on a rapid advance. The Eighth Guards Army, which would have assaulted the Fulda Gap (sometimes referred to as the Bavarian Plateau), attacking the US Fifth Corps, was battle ready.

In turn, US AirLand doctrine and strategy proposed the engagement and destruction of the second- and third-echelon Warsaw Pact forces while the main ground battle was taking place along the front line. Stopping the forward movement of Soviet reserves was seen as crucial to winning the struggle along the front line. AirLand became the battle plan in 1984.[29] A flexible defense was called for by Western strategists as the only way to allow Western forces to regain and exploit the initiative, including taking advantage of any use of nuclear weaponry. In addition, the skill of the Israelis against Arab defensive positions in 1967 and, eventually, 1973 appeared to show the vulnerability of forces with a low rate of activity, a point that was certainly to recur in the wars in the Persian Gulf in 1991 and 2003. Alongside learning from the Israelis, West German tactics and operational ideas proved a significant influence for the Americans.[30]

The British were developing similar ideas, notably thanks to the Soviet Studies Research Centre, which was established with government support in 1971 and published on Soviet operational art from then.[31] Mobile defense was becoming an important theme for NATO armor units in the 1970s, and the study of the Yom Kippur War contributed to that.[32] Unlike in the United States,[33] however, there was an early reluctance in Britain to encourage debate. This reluctance changed in the mid-1980s. The key patron of change, Lieutenant-General Sir Nigel Bagnall, commander of the First British Corps in Germany (1980–83), commander of NATO's Northern Army Group (1983–85), and chief of the General Staff (1985–88), was committed to maneuver warfare and an army-wide approach, rather than that of separate corps. In lectures at the British Staff College at Camberley in 1984, he expressed concerns about the threat of Soviet operational maneuver groups (OMGs) launching deep strikes into the rear areas of the NATO front. That year at Camberley, the focus was on Operation Goodwood in Normandy in 1944. The German tactics then were seen as a template for the concept of interlocking defended villages as a way of stopping Soviet armored threats, especially when used in conjunction with highly-mobile antitank helicopters.

Bagnall was in part influenced by Richard Simpkin, a retired Armoured Corps brigadier, veteran of World War II service in North Africa, and author of *Tank Warfare: An Analysis of Soviet and NATO Tank Philosophy* (1979); *Human Factors in Mechanized Warfare* (1983); *Race to the Swift: Thoughts on Warfare in the Twenty-First Century* (1985), which had a foreword by Donn Starry; and *Deep Battle: The Brainchild of Marshal Tukhachevskii* (1987). Bagnall worked with General Hans Henning von Sandrat, inspector of the army from 1984 to 1987 and then head of Allied Forces Central Europe for NATO until 1991, who proved a key German advocate for change.

As chief of the General Staff, Bagnall encouraged doctrine toward maneuver and established a higher command and staff course at the Army Staff College in order to teach operational-level warfare. In 1988, the latter course adopted what became known as the "manoeuvrist approach." Simpkin was influential, as were US texts, notably William Lind's *The Maneuver Warfare Handbook* (1985) and Robert Leonhard's *The Art of Maneuver* (1991). The operational approach was also read back into military history and, notably, that of armor, as with the somewhat simplistic argument that Fuller's understanding of operational art was not appreciated by a hidebound and unscientific British army.[34]

In line with, but not identical to, that of the United States, NATO doctrine changed. Initially, it was that of defending Western Europe as far forward as possible. Step-by-step, this was realized until the Inter-German frontier became the defensive line in the mid-1960s. In turn, from 1967, "flexible response" became the official NATO strategy to make the doctrine credible. In 1985, in addition to defense against Warsaw Pact units at the front, mobile defense became a main task of the NATO armed forces, utilizing follow-on forces attack (FOFA), in which the following waves of enemy forces were attacked before they arrived at the front. This doctrine was adopted to check the Soviets and keep the battle conventional for as long as possible, rather than turning to a nuclear response.

Maneuver was a key element as far as armor was concerned. That, however, was not the sole element of development in army doctrine. Instead, the change in armor was also part of a more general shift toward precision munitions and more sophisticated command, control, and communication systems. These were all designed to confront the offensive capability of the Soviet and allied forces. For example, the changes seen with armor were also seen with field artillery.[35]

What this would have led to had the Soviet Union attacked, including the outcome of probable major tank battles in "pinch points" in Germany—notably the Fulda Gap, which offered lowland routes from East Germany to near Frankfurt and on to the Rhine River—is unclear. This is particularly so due to multiple military and political factors on both sides, including the operation under pressure of alliance systems. Thus, the Soviets had limited confidence in most of their Warsaw Pact allies.

Uncertainty ensured that planning had to address multiple options. It would have been very difficult to prevent such a conflict from becoming nuclear, not least as Soviet forces would almost certainly have used nuclear weaponry from the outset while the United States, Britain, and France would probably have done so had the defense, and therefore their forces, been put under great pressure. There were US atomic demolition munitions (nuclear land mines) in the Fulda Gap, as well as missiles capable of carrying nuclear warheads. France made it clear that it would use its atomic arsenal to stop the Soviet forces in

West Germany as soon as they came within range of its land-based Force de Frappe. This left no room for a classical conventional clash. The idea of fighting a limited nuclear war had scant purchase in reality. There were no agreed-upon conventions on what such a limited war meant, and it would have been difficult to maintain such limits under the pressures of conflict, including the fear of imminent changes in the war making of other powers.[36]

Given this scenario, the planning of both sides for large-scale ground conflict had an air of unreality. There were certainly factors of speed to consider. Although it was widely assumed that any Soviet armor advance would be rapid, it would not be as speedy as a nuclear exchange and, therefore, was unlikely to preempt the latter. The French assumed the Soviets would be so fast that it would be impossible to stop them by conventional means.

Even if these points are accepted, it is still pertinent to look at the issue of likely outcomes. This is particularly so because it is assumed that the combination of Soviet tank strength with Soviet operational art would have proved highly successful. As such, this might have been the greatest tank offensive in history. The evidence cited with reference to Soviet operational art, however, perforce relates to 1944–45, when both Germany and Japan were also facing other opponents, were under very heavy pressure from them, and had only limited air power. Moreover, the German use of tanks made overcoming these tanks a vital aid to the Soviet advance.

The later applicability of Soviet success in 1944–45 is unclear. It is difficult, for the Cold War, to disentangle the advantages stemming, both in World War II and subsequently, from Soviet resources, notably tank numbers, and those arising from Soviet doctrine. It is also unclear how far there was a ready ability to implement the doctrine. Soviet planning could be bold but also formulaic, inflexible, and mechanistic. In addition, as with the German army in World War II, the quality of leading Soviet divisions was not matched across the army or among Soviet allies. In late 1975, shortly after his dismissal, James Schlesinger, US secretary of defense from 1973, declared that, if the Soviet army invaded West Germany, its logistics would give out after ten days.[37] That, however, underplayed the extent to which the Soviets would probably have overrun Continental Europe by then.

WAR IN AFGHANISTAN

The Soviet army was used in conflict from December 1979 until 1989, but in Afghanistan, which did not provide a ready comparison to Europe or Manchuria. This was true not only of the opponent, but also of the role. The Soviet objective became not, as in Western Europe, conquest, for that was rapidly achieved in Afghanistan as far as the cities were concerned, including by tanks crossing the common frontier and advancing southward. Indeed, the Fortieth Army, which did so in 1980, included 600 tanks and 1,500 infantry fighting vehicles.

Instead, the objective soon became a large-scale counterinsurgency operation, one in which armor played only a limited role. Tanks, notably T-62s, BMP-1 and BMP-2 infantry combat vehicles, and the airborne troops' BMDs, helped protect supply routes, notably through the Salang Pass, and cover the cities. This use of tanks was not simply that of providing firepower. In addition, the Soviets employed flail tanks against mines, which the guerrillas actively sowed on the roads. The mines, obtained from the United States, China, Britain, and Italy, provided a cheap and easy antitank technology.

Tanks, however, were not relevant for most of the tasks facing Soviet forces. Neither terrain nor communications routes gave tanks ready access to most of Afghanistan. Instead, the Soviets emphasized the use of air power and armored fighting vehicles rather than tanks, although tanks played a role. The same was true for the opposition. Thus, in 1983, two T-55s, captured by the resistance from the Soviet-supplied Afghan army, were used to protect the resistance base at Zhawar.[38] Increasingly supplied from the West, the Afghan resistance used French Milan antitank missiles in parallel with surface-to-air missiles. More general political, strategic, operational, logistical, and tactical problems caused Soviet failure.[39]

THE IRAN-IRAQ WAR, 1980–88

Instead, the leading war of this period involving tanks was one in which Soviet equipment, but not Soviet troops, played a role. After the fall of the shah in the Islamic Revolution in Iran in 1978–79, Iran was attacked in 1980 by Iraq because its dictator, Saddam Hussein, an inveterate opportunist, sought to exploit the situation. Seeking a quick victory, the Iraqis planned to use the same methods as those employed by Israel against Egypt in the Six-Day War in 1967: a surprise air attack to destroy the opponent's air force, followed by a tank offensive. Although the Iraqis advanced across their long frontier, the main attack was launched into Khuzestan in southwestern Iran, an oil-rich area with a majority Arab population whom the Iraqis hoped would rebel. Three armored and two mechanized divisions were launched in this area.

However well-conceived the operational plan, at least in theory, the Iraqis proved incapable of executing it. They had an impressive Soviet-armed military that was particularly strong in tanks, a product of Iraqi oil money: Iraq then possessed about a tenth of the world's known oil reserves. However, the

Iraqis did not know how to use the tanks well or, in particular, how to produce decisive tactical, operational, and strategic results. Training was poor, as was logistical support: both are crucial for the successful use of tanks. In particular, the Iraqis lacked the mobility and tactical and operational flexibility repeatedly shown by the Israelis in ground combat in 1967 and 1973.

Instead, the Iraqi advance was slower, and their tanks were frequently employed as artillery, downplaying their capacity for maneuver warfare. In place of infantry supporting an armor advance, armor was used to back an infantry one. Iraqi forces also lacked adequate logistics and sufficiently flexible command systems. As a result, they were unable to maintain the initial disorientating advantages brought about by a surprise attack and force their dynamic of warfare onto their opponents. Moreover, tactical flaws and operational limitations were combined with a misconceived strategic assessment of Iranian determination and capability, such that what successes were achieved could not deliver results. This was as pertinent as the particular deficiencies of Iraqi fighting.

In turn, the Iranian armor suffered from a lack of spare parts, as well as from poor training. The provision of spare parts was a key instance of the more general point about the significance of international suppliers of armaments to the continued ability to fight.[40] Both sides were armed by China with Type 59 tanks.

The land warfare proved indecisive; Iraq, throughout, had totally misjudged the strategic situation, underrating the stability and resolve of the new Iranian regime and overrating opposition in Khuzestan. The war continued until 1988, but neither side was able to prevail. After their failure on the attack, the Iraqis were driven back, but their front did not break. The war increasingly involved missile attacks on opposing cities and ended with a compromise peace.[41]

OTHER CONFLICTS IN 1980–88

Meanwhile, in June 1982, Israel invaded southern Lebanon, defeating the Syrians and their Palestinian allies, the Palestine Liberation Organization (PLO). Gaining air superiority, the Israelis relied on air support for their integrated advancing units of armor, infantry, artillery, and engineers. Over eight hundred tanks were used, and Israel's local ally, the SLA (South Lebanon Army), deployed between fifty-five and ninety-seven. The defenders were readily overcome, although Israel had about 30 tanks lost and 100 damaged compared to the Syrians, who had about 300–350 lost. The Israelis advancing along the coast road had lost tanks to PLO antitank weaponry. Other Israeli tanks were brought ashore near Sidon from landing craft. The Israelis advanced as far as Beirut but could not establish a stable situation there and had to withdraw. This was the first conflict in which Israel extensively used the Merkava tank, which had entered service in 1979. Weighing sixty-five tons and with a crew of four, it could carry six troops and was armed with a 105 mm gun (later a 120), as well as three machine guns, a grenade launcher, an internal mortar, and smoke grenades. It had an off-road speed of thirty-four miles per hour and an operational range of 310 miles. The engine was located in front, providing space in the rear to carry troops. In 1982, the Merkava outperformed the Syrians' Soviet-supplied T-62s, stood up well against antitank weapons, and was seen as much better than the Centurion.

In 1980, 1983, 1984, 1986, and 1987, Soviet T-54, T-55, and, from 1986, T-62 tanks and BTR-152s were part of the invasion forces used by the Libyans in Chad. They also employed Soviet doctrine. Tank fire provided mobile artillery, as in the attack on the Faya-Largeau oasis in 1983. However, the Libyans suffered, in the "Toyota War" in 1987, from the greater mobility of their opponents, who used light vehicles adapted to carry French Milan antitank missiles (from 1986) and benefited from a raider's desire for mobility. Libyan units were encircled and defeated, as at B'ir Kora, where ninety-nine Libyan tanks were destroyed or captured. Chad forces also benefited from French ground-attack aircraft, which were particularly effective due to the open landscape.

In the Falklands War of 1982, the British relied on Scimitar and Scorpion armored fighting vehicles (AFVs) while the Argentinians used Panhard wheeled armored cars that could not operate off metaled roads and never got out of the Falklands' capital, Port Stanley. Some of the terrain was suitable for tanks, but the distance of the deployment, the logistical commitment, and the use of British tanks as part of the NATO commitment in Western Europe precluded the British from making that choice. However, the low ground pressure of the tracked armored vehicles employed by the British enabled them to cope with the boggy conditions encountered, and they proved very effective, although they were not used to their full potential in part because commanders were not used to dealing with them. The Scimitars and Scorpions proved extremely successful in a night attack of Mount Challenger, but firepower was largely provided by artillery.

Tanks, however, were employed in the battle of Cuito Cuanavale in Angola in 1987–88, a large-scale conventional battle in the Angolan civil war, with South Africa supporting UNITA and the Cubans backing the government forces. The latter had 182 T-55 tanks while the former had 3 Olifant tanks (upgrades of Centurions) and 4 T-55s. The government forces suffered heavily in failed attempts to cross the Lomba River between September 9 and

October 7, 1988, with sixty-one tanks lost. In turn, the South Africans attacked from November 9, using their own tanks and destroying ten government tanks, while another nine were destroyed in another attack on November 17. The large 90 mm gun on the twenty South African Ratel-90 combat vehicles made it effective against tanks. The government losses led to the dispatch of Cuban reinforcements. There were clashes between Cuban and South African tanks in February 1989, and, the following month, the South Africans lost several tanks to mines while the Cubans established air superiority. South Africa preferred to focus not on tanks but on wheeled armored cars and armored personnel carriers: the Rooikat, Ratel, Casspir, Buffel, and Mamba. Protection against mines was a key requirement. Indeed, tanks were employed in only one operation.

Armor was also used by the Americans when they invaded Grenada in 1983 and Panama in 1989, although tanks did not play a major role. With airborne armor, there was an emphasis on vehicles that were lighter than those transported by sea. Grenada had no tanks and only eight Soviet-supplied BTR-60PB armored personnel carriers and two BRDM-2 scout cars. The latter were part of the resistance at Point Salines International Airport to a parachute landing, but four to five of the BTR-60s were destroyed by fire from US 90 mm recoilless rifles. Elsewhere, the armored personnel carriers mounted effective resistance, but, on the first day, the US force was soon supplemented by a Marine Assault Unit with amphibious assault vehicles and four M60 tanks, which overcame resistance, including destroying a BRDM-2. On the third day, another BTR-60 was destroyed by a M72, a one-shot 66 mm unguided antitank rocket-propelled grenade launcher. In the invasion of Panama, the M113 armored personnel carrier was employed by the Americans.

POLITICAL CONTROL

Tanks played a frequent role in winning and maintaining control in the face of opposition. This was seen in Czechoslovakia in 1968 when a Soviet-led intervention was successful and popular protests failed. The Soviets deployed large numbers of T-55s and T-62s. Most Soviet tanks advanced over the Czech frontier by land, particularly from East Germany. Others, however, were flown into Czechoslovak airports, notably Prague airport, in Antonov-12 and Antonov-22 transport aircraft. First flown in 1965, the An-22 could carry a cargo of 176,000 pounds. Unlike in Hungary in 1956, demonstrators relied on nonviolent protest, such as throwing paint against tanks. Even so, ninety-six Soviet soldiers were killed, as well as about two hundred Czech civilians. The protests had a major impact on international opinion but failed to dislodge the Soviets.

Very differently, in 1989, Communist rule in Eastern Europe collapsed without the use of armies to resist this process in most of the countries. The exception was in Romania, where there was a full-scale anti-Communist revolt in Timişoara, a city with a large ethnic Hungarian population. The regime sent in tanks, which fired on the demonstrators, and deployed factory workers armed with clubs. Nevertheless, in the face of a crowd of over one hundred thousand people, the army changed sides. On December 21, in the capital, Bucharest, a popular demonstration against a public address by the dictator Nicolae Ceauşescu was crushed by the gunfire and armored cars of the Securitate, the Romanian Secret Police, who also used tanks to smash through hastily erected barricades and crush demonstrators. Many were killed, although there is no agreement on precise numbers. However, the following day, renewed demonstrations led Ceauşescu to flee. The army eventually acted in support of the public agitation, providing force sufficient to overawe the Securitate and overthrow the regime. Ceauşescu was shot.

In China, the army, employing Type 59 tanks, enforced control in 1989, providing emblematic photographs of a protestor seeking to block the advance of these tanks in Tiananmen Square in Beijing. These photographs go on being used. Thus, in the London *Evening Standard* of April 17, 2019, and the *Economist* two days later, an advertisement for *Chimerica*, a new television drama about a photojournalist accused of doctoring an award-winning photograph, carried a copy with the caption, "How Far Would You Go To Stand Up For The Truth?"[42]

Tanks were also extensively used in coups in non-Communist states. In Chile, *El Tanquetazo* or *El Tancazo* (tank putsch) are the terms employed to refer to a failed military coup of June 29, 1973, against the left-wing government of Salvador Allende. Six Shermans and ten other armored vehicles took part, with the tanks firing on La Moneda—the presidential palace, and the Ministry of Defense. Loyal troops suppressed the rising. A successful coup, by far larger forces, followed on September 11, 1973. Air support enabled the armor and infantry launching attacks on La Moneda to advance again after initially retreating in the face of snipers. Allende's government was overthrown and replaced by a junta headed by General Pinochet.

Tanks were used in Valencia in Spain on February 23, 1981, by those in the military who unsuccessfully sought to mount a coup against the civilian government. Fifty M47s were ordered onto the streets there in order to give force to the coup supporters' declaration of a state of emergency. An armored column was sent to the local Manises airbase, but it retreated in the face of a threatened attack by aircraft with air-to-ground missiles. The failure of the

coup in Madrid, an operation mounted by the Civil Guard, led to its abandonment in Valencia.

OTHER STATES

Mention of Spain, which had acquired 299 AMX-30s from France between
1970 and 1983, serves as a reminder of the number of states that had tanks
and the problems created by focusing only on the leading powers. Any focus
on leading powers can lead to disregarding important developments in technology. For example, the disadvantage of a fixed gun was only really solved
with the Swedish S-tank (Stridsvagn 103) as its sophisticated, fully automated
transmission and suspension system aided engaging with the target. At the
same time, this turretless tank, which was a response to the vulnerability of
turrets and the high profiles of the previous model, had operating problems
due to its low profile. As a result, it proved better as a tank destroyer. Designed
by Sven Berge in 1956, the tank was produced by Bofors AB in 1967–71 and was
in service from 1967 to 1997. Being the first main battle tank to use a turbine
engine helped in the very low-profile design. It had an extended-length 105 mm
gun, and its speed of thirty-seven miles per hour reflected the need in Swedish strategy and tactics to be able to launch counteroffensives against a possible Soviet invasion. The Swedes also (secretly) planned to oppose any Soviet
advance by, in turn, advancing into Finland and fighting the Soviets there. The
lack of a turret meant that tank companies were matched with similar numbers of mechanized infantry companies equipped with Pansarbandvagn 302
armored personnel carriers. In attack, their turreted 20 mm machine cannon
could protect the flanks of the tanks.

The use of tanks by second-rank powers included their effective handling by
Turkey when it invaded Cyprus in 1974. However, of the initial twenty-three
landing craft, only one was for tanks. The Greek Cypriots deployed T-34/85
tanks against the landed force but lost five in a counterattack on the first day.
The Turks used antitank rockets—for example, a day later against a Greek
Cypriot counterattack employing Soviet BTR-152 armored personnel carriers.
On the third day, in turn, the advancing Turks lost five M47 tanks to Greek
short-range antitank weapons. Subsequently, Turkish advances using about
two hundred tanks, including M48s, made successful advances, overcoming
Greek Cypriot defenses with the help of air attacks. The Greek Cypriot use of
outnumbered T-34/85s was unable to stop the advances.[43]

More generally, tanks served as the key display of force for most states and
continued to be acquired by states happy to see them as crucial adjuncts to
power. Thus, at the end of the 1960s, seeking to lessen reliance on the United

States, Argentina developed the "Europe Plan" to buy weaponry there, including French AMX-13 and Panhard tanks. In the 1970s, an agreement was reached with the Germans for the construction of armed vehicles of the TAM (Tanque Argentino Mediano) family in Argentina. In addition, some SK-105 Kürassiers were purchased from Austria at the time of the 1978 crisis with Chile.

The tank trade was important to the economics of production. Thus, an improved Chieftain was designed for the Iranians under the name Shir 1 in 1974. In 1979, in the aftermath of the Islamic Revolution in Iran, the order was cancelled. In turn, that year, Jordan ordered a modified version named the Khalid. In turn, the sixty-two-ton Challenger 1 was originally designed by Britain for Iran after the Chieftain order was cancelled. However, the link between the two countries fell victim to the Iran-Iraq War. The Iranian tanks were completed as Challenger 1s and saw service in the British army from 1983 to 1992. At this stage, the oil wealth of the Middle East led to tank purchases from abroad and not, as in East Asia, the development of indigenous production. Iran was not to follow this course of production until later, and, hitherto, the other oil-rich states, lacking the necessary industrial capacity, have not done so. The same is true with armored cars. Thus, the six-wheeled Brazilian EE-9 Cascavel, which entered service in 1974 and was produced until 1993, was purchased by Iran, Iraq, Libya, and Qatar, as well as Bolivia, Burkina Faso, Chile, Colombia, Cyprus, Congo, Ecuador, Gabon, Ghana, Guyana, Morocco, Nigeria, Paraguay, Surinam, Tunisia, Uruguay, Venezuela, and Zimbabwe.

Alongside interest in armored cars and personnel carriers, the focus on heavy tanks in this period affected the market for light tanks. Thus, the US-made Stingray, an air-transportable 22.6-ton tank with light armor but a 105 mm rifled tank gun, was only purchased by Thailand, which ordered 106.

Most states sought to acquire current models of tanks but also made do with older ones. Thus, in 1990, Yugoslavia had two thousand tanks, most elderly T-54 and T-55s, although there were about three hundred M84s. This was the Yugoslav version of the T-72 that had entered service in 1984 and also been sold to Kuwait. From the late 1940s, Yugoslav forces had focused on defense against Soviet invasion and therefore had modern antitank missiles.

CONCLUSIONS

Some of the earlier ideas about armored warfare only became viable in the 1970s and 1980s, but, at the same time, interacting capabilities created fresh problems alongside the opportunities realized. The idea of one-shot kills at long range became viable in the late 1970s with stabilized guns and accurate means to measure range (which required the use of a laser). At the same time, the development of armor reduced the effectiveness of tank fire against other tanks as well as the effectiveness of antitank guns. As a result, from the 1980s, the Americans developed the M93 Hornet WAM (wide area munition) mine. It uses acoustic and seismic sensors to detect a tank and fires an infrared-detecting submunition about ten meters above the target, which establishes its position, before firing an EFP (explosively formed penetrator) down on the tank to hit its less well-armored area. However, problems with the effect of wind restricted deployment.[44]

The Cold War is usually seen as the background to a threatened third world war, perhaps one that would have focused in land conflict on combat between large tank forces. Much was made at the time of the potential of these forces. Yet this argument underplays the considerable limitations of the tanks of the period. Maintenance was a key issue across the spectrum of tanks, by type and nationality. Indeed, to maintain armored units, it was necessary to cannibalize others, and the same process took place at the level of individual tanks. Visiting armor stores in logistical bases made this readily apparent. Had a third world war broken out, both sides, to a degree, would have stuttered into action, alongside impressive levels of combat readiness in some units—for example, of the East German army. However, this conflict would have been superseded rapidly by the nuclear exchange.

NOTES

1. J. J. McGrath, *Fire for Effect: Field Artillery and Close Air Support in the U.S. Army* (Fort Leavenworth, KS, 2010).

2. W. C. Haponski, *One Hell of a Ride: Inside an Armored Cavalry Task Force in Vietnam* (The Villages, FL, 2009); D. A. Starry, *Mounted Combat in Vietnam* (Washington, 1978).

3. J. M. Carland, "Armor Goes to War: The 11th Armored Cavalry Regiment and the Vietnam War, December 1965 to December 1966," *Army History* 99 (spring 2016): 7.

4. J. M. Shaw, *The Cambodian Campaign: The 1970 Offensive and America's Vietnam War* (Lawrence, KS, 2005).

5. K. W. Nolan, *Search and Destroy: The Story of an Armored Cavalry Squadron in Viet Nam, 1/1 Cav, 1967–1968* (Minneapolis, MN, 2010).

6. D. A. Starry, "A Report on the 11th Armored Cavalry in Southeast Asia 1969–70," *Armor and Cavalry Journal* 3 (March–May 2010): 49–54.

7. D. Andrade, *America's Last Vietnam Battle: Halting Hanoi's 1972 Eastern Offensive* (Lawrence, KS, 2001); J. Willbanks, *The Battle of An Loc* (Bloomington, IN, 2015).

8. T. R. Yarborough, *A Shau Valor: American Combat Operations in the Valley of Death, 1963–1971* (Havertown, PA, 2016).

9. G. J. Veith, *Black April: The Fall of South Vietnam 1973–1975* (New York, 2012).

10. I. Ginor and G. Remez, *The Soviet-Israeli War 1967–1973: The USSR's Military Intervention in the Egyptian-Israeli Conflict* (Oxford, 2017).

11. U. Bar-Joseph, *The Watchman Fell Asleep: The Surprise of Yom Kippur and Its Sources* (New York, 2005).

12. J. L. Young, "The Heights of Ineptitude: The Syrian Army's Assault on the Golden Heights," *JMH* 74 (2010): 852–70.

13. A. Ezov, "The Crossing Challenge: The Suez Canal Crossing by the Israel Defense Forces during the Yom Kippur War of 1973," *JMH* 82 (2018): 481–82.

14. E. Sakal, *Soldier in the Sinai: A General's Account of the Yom Kippur War* (Lexington, KY, 2014); D. Asher, ed., *Inside Israel's Northern Command: The Yom Kippur War on the Syrian Border* (Lexington, KY, 2016); D. Rodman, "A Tale of Two Fronts: Israeli Military Performance during the Early Days of the 1973 Yom Kippur War," *JMH* 82 (2018): 208–18.

15. S. Bronfeld, "Fighting Outnumbered: The Impact of the Yom Kippur War on the U.S. Army," *JMH* 71 (2007): 465–98.

16. P. B. Henze, *The Horn of Africa from War to Peace* (New York, 1991).

17. A. T. Weldemichael, "The Eritrean Long March: The Strategic Withdrawal of the Eritrean People's Liberation Front (EPLF), 1978–1979," *JMH* 73 (2009): 1252–55.

18. Weldemichael, "The Eritrean Long March": 1253.

19. D. A. Ruiz Palmera, "The NATO-Warsaw Pact Competition in the 1970s and 1980s: A Revolution in Military Affairs in the Making or the End of a Strategic Age," *Cold War History* 14 (2014): 533–73.

20. L. Sorley, ed., *Press On!: Selected Works of General Donn A. Starry* (Fort Leavenworth, KS, 2009).

21. L. Sorley, *Thunderbolt: General Creighton Abrams and the Army of His Time* (New York, 1992).

22. D. Fitzgerald, *Learning to Forget: US Army Counterinsurgency Doctrine and Practice from Vietnam to Iraq* (Stanford, CA, 2013).

23. W. B. Haworth, *The Bradley and How It Got That Way: Technology, Institutions, and the Problem of Mechanized Infantry in the United States Army* (Westport, CT, 1999); J. A. English, *Marching through Chaos: The Descent of Armies in Theory and Practice* (Westport, CT, 1996), 154.

24. B. I. Gudmundsson, *On Armor* (Westport, CT, 2004).

25. Ex inf. Anthony Saunders.

26. H. G. Gole, *General William E. DePuy: Preparing the Army for Modern War* (Lexington, KY, 2008).

27. I. W. Trauschweizer, *The Cold War U.S. Army: Building Deterrence for Limited War* (Lawrence, KS, 2008).

28. D. M. Glantz, *Soviet Military Operational Art: In Pursuit of Deep Battle* (Totowa, NJ, 1991).

29. J. L. Romjue, "The Evolution of American Army Doctrine," in *The Origins of Contemporary Doctrine*, ed. J. Gooch (Camberley, UK, 1997), 70–73; B. Jensen, *Forging the Sword: Doctrinal Change in the U.S. Army* (Stanford, CA, 2016).

30. I. W. Trauschweizer, "Learning with an Ally: The U.S. Army and the *Bundeswehr* in the Cold War," *JMH* 72 (2008): 497–508.

31. C. Donnelly, "The Soviet Concept of Desant," *RUSI* 116, no. 3 (September 1971): 52–56; C. Donnelly and P. H. Vigor, "The Soviet Threat to Europe," *RUSI* 120, no. 1 (March 1975): 72.

32. A. Jackson, "The Evolution of the Division in British Military History," *RUSI* 152, no. 6 (2007): 80.

33. A. Clarke, ed., *The Defense Reform Debate* (Baltimore, MD, 1984).

34. J. Kiszely, "Thinking about the Operational Level," *RUSI* 150, no. 6 (2005): 39. At that point, Lieutenant-General Sir John Kiszely was director of the British Defence Academy.

35. B. L. Dastrup, *Modernizing the King of Battle: 1973–1991* (Fort Sill, OK, 1994); J. B. A. Bailey, *Field Artillery and Firepower* (Annapolis, MD, 2004).

36. J. Hoffenaar and C. Findlay, eds., *Military Planning for European Theatre Conflict during the Cold War: An Oral History Roundtable Stockholm, 24–25 April 2006* (Zurich, 2007).

37. Referring to questions after a speech at the University of Chicago, Pete Brown to Jeremy Black, email, May 12, 2019.

38. R. Braithwaite, *Afgantsy: The Russians in Afghanistan 1979–89* (2011; repr. London, 2012), 214.

39. L. W. Grau, *The Bear Went Over the Mountain: Soviet Combat Tactics in Afghanistan* (Portland, OR, 1998).

40. M. Carver, *Twentieth-Century Warriors* (London, 1987), 442.

41. D. Hiro, *The Longest War: The Iran-Iraq Military Conflict* (New York, 1991).

42. *Evening Standard*, April 17, 2019, 12–13.

43. J. Hughes-Wilson, "The Forgotten War," *RUSI* 156, no. 5 (October–November 2011): 84–92.

44. Ex inf. Anthony Saunders.

EIGHT

SINCE 1990

WIDELY USED AS A TERM IN THE 1990S, THE "REVOLUTION IN MILI-
tary Affairs" (RMA), the grandly named claim for a paradigm shift in military capability, was more rhetoric and intellectual market share than sound
analysis. The RMA fulfilled, however, the wish to gain a "peace dividend"
after the end of the Cold War, as well as to maintain a war-winning capability,
and mirrored the continuous US quest for high-tech "silver bullets" to solve
political-military problems. Helped by this quest, as also after World War II,
the struggle for resources was won in the United States by the air force, and not
the army. Indeed, on October 10, 2007, in his address to the annual Conven-
tion of the Association of the United States Army, Robert Gates, the secretary
of defense, noted that the army's share of total defense investments between
1990 and 2005 was only about 15 percent. In this context, there was only limited
support for a transformation in tank power, capability, and doctrine. Instead,
the emphasis was elsewhere. This was also the case increasingly for the US
army as the emphasis after the Iraq War in 2003 shifted to counterinsurgency.
The same was true for other armies.

THE GULF WAR, 1991

The Cold War was speedily followed by a dramatic display of armored power
in the shape of the major role of tanks in the US-led attack on Iraqi forces in
Kuwait in 1991. The Iraqis had conquered Kuwait the previous year using two
armored divisions and two mobile infantry ones. Outnumbered Kuwaiti Chieftain tanks fought delaying actions, notably the battle of Jal al Atraf, known as
the Battle of the Bridges, on August 2, in which advancing Iraqi mechanized
and armored columns that had not expected resistance took heavy casualties before the Kuwaitis, who, in danger of encirclement and running short

of ammunition, retreated to neighboring Saudi Arabia. In response, in 1991, a US-led coalition drove the Iraqis out.

There had been many predictions in early 1991 that Iraqi entrenchments would be difficult to capture and that the Iraqis would force attritional warfare on the coalition, causing heavy casualties. These fears were a throwback to the world wars, especially World War I, and to the strength of the defensive, and they drew on an overestimation of Iraqi capability based on an idea that its army was battle hardened after its long war with Iran in 1980–88. There was also an overestimate of the capability of Iraqi equipment, much of it recent Soviet weaponry, including T-62s and T-72s. At the same time, the Iraqis clearly hoped that it would be possible to lure the Americans into a Stalingrad-type situation, which was a reflection of the power of that image or, at least, its use.

These fears and hopes proved quite unfounded as the US-dominated coalition forces were greatly superior, with their superiority compounded by mistaken Iraqi moves. Displaying, in a very different context, the positional preference they had frequently shown during the Iran-Iraq War, the Iraqis had dug themselves in, believing this would protect their tanks from air and tank attack. However, they failed to appreciate the capabilities of both precision munitions and up-to-date tank gun technologies, including infrared viewing devices for nighttime, that ensured a high first-shot kill capability even when only part of the turret was visible. In terms of weapon use, tactics, organization, and doctrine, the Iraqis fought as if fighting Iran in the recent war of 1980–88. This was a serious mistake as the terrain and, far more, the opponent were both different. The Americans showed that Iraqi tanks could be engaged at a range that invalidated Soviet "kill-zone" tactics.

While the Iraqis were attacked on the coast on the direct route to Kuwait City, their right (on the coalition forces' left) was outmaneuvered by a rapid and successful US advance to the west. This advance put tremendous pressure on the Iraqis as the outflanking US forces then turned in to attack them and swiftly destroyed much of the Iraqi army. Forcing Iraqi opponents to retreat exposed them to US armor and air attack, a prime aspect of cooperation between means of attack in order to force opponents into a condition of vulnerability. In this context, remaining static led to destruction, but so did mobility. In one hundred hours of nonstop combat, the Iraqis lost nearly four thousand tanks and up to fifty thousand troops, as well as eighty-one thousand troops taken prisoner.

The coalition forces benefited not only from superior technology but also from their ability to maintain a high-tempo offensive in executing a well-conceived plan that combined air and land strength. Both air and land forces could deliver precision attacks. Deep maneuver was important, as was massed joint fire: the Iraqis discovered that the composite armor that provided protection from other tanks and antitank weapons fired on the ground proved less effective when tanks were targeted by aircraft. Allied, particularly US, fighting quality, unit cohesion, leadership, and planning, and Iraqi deficiencies in each of these areas, all played a major role in ensuring victory. The key US tank was one introduced to fight the Cold War, the M1A1 Abrams tank, which was first used in combat in this war. British Challengers, French AMX-30Bs, Kuwaiti M84s, Saudi AMX-30s and Pattons, and Qatari AMX-30s (which destroyed T-55s) also played a role. The flat desert of western Kuwait, with its sand a problem for engines, was not as good tank country as the North European Plain, but it was better than the mountainous and marshy terrain on which Iraq had fought Iran.

The success of tanks in the Gulf War attracted much attention, but it was overshadowed by that of aircraft. Nevertheless, the coordination of satellites, aircraft, and tanks in land campaigning helped enhance the effectiveness of tanks in acquiring targets. This provided a key advantage to the Americans. Interacting with US satellites in a Global Positioning System (GPS), tanks successfully employed precise positioning devices. Accurate targeting was required if precision weaponry was to be effective. This "network-centric warfare," a highly integrated and digitally linked information system, relied on semi-automated weaponry. Tanks and aircraft were seen as the key platforms in such warfare. Moreover, GPS guidance meant that US forces could operate in areas considered unnavigable by Iraqi forces (which lacked GPS) and therefore left undefended by them.

In addition, US tanks were more effective than those of their Iraqi opponents. In 1991, only nine Abrams tanks were destroyed, and none due to enemy fire: instead, seven were destroyed by friendly fire and two to prevent capture. With an effective range of more than 2,500 meters (8,200 feet) compared to the Iraqis' of fewer than 2,000 meters (6,600 feet), the Abrams enjoyed a key advantage. Moreover, the tanks went on being more effective, notably in the 2003 Iraq War.

In the 1991 Gulf War, US aircraft inflicted considerable damage on Iraqi tanks using the doctrine, training, and equipment prepared for dealing with Soviet tank advances. The Americans deployed A-10s (Warthogs, Thunderbolt IIs) with Maverick missiles and an armor-piercing GAU-8/A Avenger rotary cannon, which fired depleted uranium rounds at 3,900 revolutions per minute, AH-64 Apaches with Hellfire missiles, and F-111s operating as deep-interdiction aircraft, carrying out what became known as "tank plink-ing," the laser-guided attacks on individual tanks, one by one. B-52 bombers were also directed against tactical targets.

Thus, tanks, at least Iraqi tanks, had to cope with the increased lethality of antitank weaponry. Since the Vietnam era, tanks had proved to be highly vulnerable to helicopter gunships firing antitank missiles. In the Iran-Iraq War, the Iranians benefited from the use of missiles against Iraqi tanks, with helicopters firing missiles. The range of antitank weapons increased both then and subsequently. They included, on the part of the United States, the A-10, an aircraft that that entered service in 1977 as an inexpensive antitank platform for missiles, and the Vulcan cannon, a very effective antitank weapon that entered service in 1959.

The sophistication of antitank missiles had improved. As with other tech-nological developments, this improvement was a matter of enhancements in existing types, as well as the introduction of types. Thus, there were improve-ments in wire-guided missiles, from the Soviet Sagger model, introduced in 1963, to the more accurate Soviet Metis-M, introduced in 1978. There was also the addition of laser-guided antitank missiles, such as the Russian Kornet-E, introduced in 1994.

A very different use of tanks occurred later in 1991 when, on August 19, a group of hard-line Communists, organized as the State Committee for the State of Emergency in the USSR, or the Gang of Eight, attempted a coup in Moscow. In street fighting, three protesters were killed by the army, but the tanks were unable to overawe the crowds, and the coup failed. Trolleybuses and street-cleaning machines had been used to construct antitank barricades, but the key factor was an unwillingness to use the army to crush the opposi-tion. The same happened in Vilnius, where the Soviet army again did not choose to act decisively and thus effectively. These differing contexts for the use of tanks can be readily amplified. Contrasting tasks and results were more generally instructive for the varied effectiveness of tanks.

THE IRAQ WAR

In the Iraq War in 2003, "smart" (guided) bombs were used far more than they had been in 1991. They and the A-10 destroyed many of Iraq's Russian-built tanks, despite sandstorms affecting aerial operations and reconnaissance. The integration of air power and land maneuver generated an overwhelming tempo that provided the Iraqis with problems to which timely response proved impossible. The US tanks obtained most of their indirect fire capability and support from aircraft rather than artillery. An attacking force far smaller than in 1991, and with far more terrain to cover, took relatively few casualties in achieving its goals, despite not enjoying the conventional margin of numerical advantage of attackers over defenders. The Soviet-supplied Iraqi T-55s, T-62s, and T-72s that were not destroyed by air attack could not prevail against the M1A1 Abrams. The Iraqi tanks, notably the T-55s, were old, and there was a shortage of spare parts.

As in 1991, the static, or at least less mobile, nature of the defenders provided exposed flanks the Americans could exploit. Moreover, by holding back key units to defend Baghdad, Saddam Hussein helped the Americans advance to the city and thus created an atmosphere of defeat there. Thanks to the speed and firepower of their armored and mechanized forces, the Americans were able to advance on Baghdad without having to devote much concern to rear or flank security.

In Basra, the 120 mm guns of British Challenger 2 tanks outranged opposing T-55s and destroyed numbers of them, both dug in and mobile. Tanks cooperating with Warrior military fighting vehicles transporting infantry then overcame resistance within the city. Entering service in 2000, the Challenger 2 had second-generation Chobham armor, fired depleted uranium ammunition, and could accurately engage two targets in rapid succession. It proved effective and reliable, as did the Warrior and the 155 mm self-propelled AS90 gun.

Subsequent resistance in Iraq posed very different challenges: those of urban control. These challenges were in part faced by tanks that had been upgraded. Thus, the basic M1A2 tank, introduced in 1993, had a System Enhancement Package that included GPS, digital terrain maps, crew-compartment cooling and air-conditioning, and provisions for an underarmor auxiliary power unit.

The urban conflict in Iraq, with tanks facing ambushes and resistance using rocket-propelled grenades, indicated the fortress-like value of tanks. In the town of Fallujah in 2004, combined arms training, to which the mobile firepower of the Abrams tanks contributed greatly, played a key role. Moreover, the multiarmament capability of the tanks was significant. The flex-mounted machine gun served to protect tanks from envelopment while the gun engaged with targets. The machine gun also offered help against enemies on the rooftops above and could penetrate masonry as could the tank's main gun. At the same time, it was clear that the tanks required the backing of effective infantry, as well as close air support that provided a vertical envelopment and thus challenged enemy ability to dominate the rooftops, as well as overcoming the tanks' inability to acquire and kill beyond the neighboring block.[1] Tanks faced not only attack but also the problems posed by hard conditions, including plentiful rubble that acted as a cover for improvised explosive devices

(IEDs), heavy use, a shortage of spare parts, and the difficulties of operating in narrow streets and around tight corners. Tanks are not that good in urban conflict because they can be stopped by their own size.

Protection was a key issue for all elements of the US army, from soldiers, who were equipped with individual body armor, to vehicles that were provided with improved armor, including reactive armor tiles. The Abrams tanks offered protection for crew compartments while armored personnel carriers were provided with screens against rocket-propelled grenades, as were the rear of tanks. Survivability was a key background to firepower and mobility.[2] The Abrams tank force casualty rate was about 5 percent.

The British philosophy of high levels of armor to ensure survivability, albeit at the expense of mobility, was largely vindicated in the particular circumstances of the Iraq War and urban warfare in Basra. The Challenger strength in Iraq was reduced to a squadron of fourteen tanks after the initial invasion. Although small in number, they were deployed on a virtually daily basis for several years and were continuously attacked. One tank was destroyed in a "blue on blue" incident during the invasion, and two were badly damaged in 2006–7. The new Iraqi army established by the Americans, meanwhile, was initially organized with T-55s and T-72s because they were available.

FORMER YUGOSLAVIA

Tanks played a role in the conflicts in former Yugoslavia, including in the unsuccessful campaign by the largely Serb forces of the Yugoslav People's Army against Slovenia in 1991 and in the fighting in Croatia, Bosnia, and Serbia in 1991–95. Intervening in Slovenia, Yugoslav tank columns were blocked by truck barriers, and T-55s were destroyed by antitank rockets near Nova Gorica. Subsequently, Yugoslav tanks were captured and became part of the Slovenian army. At least one hundred Yugoslav tanks played a key role in the fighting for the town of Vukovar in Croatia in 1991 but found the urban operation difficult due to a lack of training and infantry support and the skillful Croat use of antitank weapons, including mines. The Serbs, instead, turned to artillery.

Tanks were also employed by the Western forces that intervened, but United Nations (UN) Rules of Engagement were highly restrictive. Twice, a squadron of Danish Leopards—1A5s—deployed to Bosnia in 1994 as part of a Danish-Swedish United Nations Protection Force (UNPROFOR) battalion successfully engaged Bosnian Serb forces in defense of the UN Protected Area of Tuzla, the latter at the extreme range of around three miles.

Aircraft were much less effective in the North Atlantic Treaty Organization (NATO) air campaign launched against Serbian forces, including tanks, in Kosovo in 1999 than they had been in the Gulf War. In part, the Serbs made effective use of camouflage. The weather also had a severe impact on air operations, a large number of which were cancelled or affected as a result. Laser-guided weapons require largely cloud-free skies in order to lock-on and work. Thus, supposedly all-weather aircraft proved, in practice, to have more limited capability. In part, however, this was a comment on misguided expectations of accuracy, prediction, and effectiveness. These were a recurrent issue, indeed problem, with modern armaments and, most particularly, with views on airpower. Moreover, although the Serbian high- and medium-altitude anti-aircraft systems proved ineffective, shoulder-fired missiles affected NATO's willingness to mount low-altitude flights and thus to be effective in ground attack. The Serbs had used their tanks against Kosovars, but there was no ground conflict with NATO forces.

Confrontation and conflict in the former Yugoslavia saw former Warsaw Pact and NATO tanks involved. That was part of the overhang of the Cold War. The same was true with the situation elsewhere, as in the Caucasus. There, in 2001, Armenia had 110 main battle tanks, Azerbaijan 262, and Georgia 90. This reflected the plentiful numbers of ex-Soviet tanks. In addition, at that stage, Russia, which had continued to supply Armenia with arms in the 1990s, had a base in Armenia with 74 main battle tanks.

OTHER CONFLICTS

Tanks faced limitations and problems. Thanks to missiles, they increasingly appeared vulnerable in close combat, especially in urban areas, although four Pakistani M48s and Malaysian German-made Condor armored personnel carriers played a key role in Mogadishu, Somalia, in October 1993, helping rescue trapped US Rangers. The Somali warlord Mohamed Farrah Aidid had Italian-made Type 6616 armored personnel carriers, as well as improvised fighting vehicles. A Somali rocket-propelled grenade (RPG) killed a Malaysian soldier in a Condor. In 2000, when Ethiopia invaded Eritrea, the Ethiopians benefited from better armor (Russian T-72s), as well as superior air power and greater numbers, only to find that the Eritreans fought well.

In Lebanon in 2006, Hezbollah's mines and laser-guided Russian Kornet antitank guided missiles challenged the Israeli armor advancing in heavy Merkava tanks, which, despite losses to mines in the Gaza Strip in 2002, had hitherto provided a key capability advantage over Israel's opponents on land. The missiles were able to breach the tank armor. Five tanks were destroyed and many more (thirty-seven) rendered unserviceable. Sixteen Israeli tank crewmen were killed, which was a heavy loss for the Israelis. However, more would have been killed but for the tanks and their design. Hezbollah's well-built bunkers were also a serious problem, but there were also broader questions about Israel's relative effectiveness.[3]

After the 2006 war, Merkavas were reequipped from 2010 with the Trophy Active Protection System. As a result, in 2014, the tanks were better protected in the Gaza conflict with Hamas, and none were damaged. With their strong armor, they acted as effective armored personnel carriers. In 2013, the decision was made to resume production of the Merkava.

Across the world's conflicts, there was a role for tanks, however limited, as in the Aceh region of Sumatra, where tanks were used as part of a conventional warfare response by the Indonesian military in 2003–5 against the GAM (Free Aceh) separatist movement. In practice, neither side could prevail. Tanks were also used in Afghanistan in the 2000s and 2010s. NATO forces did so—for example, the Danes and Canadians who employed Leopard 2s—although far less than other armored vehicles, and Australia did not judge it appropriate to send its Abrams tanks. The British made much use of Scimitar armored vehicles with upgraded armor, the Americans used Strykers, and the Italians also deployed wheeled armored vehicles. Their crews, and those of the tanks, faced great heat, of over 122°F, but also, when the tanks were open, snipers. Ex-Soviet tanks were employed by local forces, notably Abdul Rashid Dostum, the "strongman" in northern Afghanistan, who had tanks supplied by Russia and Uzbekistan.

The impact of tanks was greatest when deployed against another state in a limited conflict and for a restricted goal. This was seen with comparisons in Russian attacks. In the 1990s, under President Boris Yeltsin (1991–99), the Russian army had very little funding, and training was nugatory. Tanks were not maintained well, and morale was low. The army did not perform well in Chechnya in 1994–96. The Russian use of tanks in the attack on Grozny, the capital of Chechnya, in 1995 suffered from a lack of relevant experience, training, doctrine, and tactics, as well as from poor cooperation with the infantry, inadequate communications, and the strength of the resistance. In the end, artillery played a key role in suppressing opposition.

In contrast, under Vladimir Putin, who became president in 2000, there was a buildup in Russian capability, although it was very uneven across the military. Professionals replaced conscripts, and there was an attempt to address competence. Training improved. In 2008, in support of local separatists as part of a dispute with Georgia, Putin sent hundreds of T-72s into neighboring South Ossetia. Georgia was not in a position to mount effective resistance, and the Russian goal was limited. However, the 2008 war also revealed problems.

Many Russian tanks broke down, and they lacked the night-vision equipment on the Georgian T-72s, which had been improved with US help. The Russians, nevertheless, benefited from greater numbers and the experience of fighting in nearby Chechnya.[4]

OTHER ARMORED VEHICLES

The weaknesses of tanks, as well as the desire for a peace dividend after the Cold War, led to a revival of interest in both armored cars and armored personnel carriers. The two indeed have overlapped in function. By 2010, the United States had 6,302 main battle tanks and 6,452 armored fighting vehicles, and the latter were seeing more use. The US-made M113 remained in use around the world, in some cases with upgrades, such as the M113A2 (1979), which included armored fuel tanks, and the M113A3 (1987). Relevant states included Afghanistan, Albania, Argentina, Australia, Bahrain, Bolivia, Bosnia, Brazil, Canada, Chile, Colombia, Denmark, Ecuador, Egypt, Germany, Greece, Iran, Iraq, Indonesia, Israel, Jordan, Kuwait, Lebanon, Lithuania, Morocco, Macedonia, Normandy, Pakistan, Peru, the Philippines, Poland, Portugal, Saudi Arabia, Singapore, South Korea, Spain, Switzerland, Taiwan, Thailand, Tunisia, Turkey, Uruguay, Vietnam, and Yemen.

The revival in interest in armored fighting vehicles was apparent with the US development of the Stryker eight-wheeled medium-weight armored vehicle. In the late 1990s, the Americans advanced the Army After Next project, focusing on a new generation of weapon systems able to respond rapidly to all circumstances. The systems were designed for expeditionary warfare, as opposed to the fixed deployments represented, for the Americans, by West Germany and South Korea in the late 1980s. Instead, there was an emphasis on nimbleness, speed, and multipurpose flexibility all within a context of lower expenditure.[5] This capability entailed airlift, which encouraged the development of smaller, lighter fighting vehicles that could be used to equip light infantry units. The plan was to be able to field a combat-ready brigade anywhere in the world in 96 hours and a division in 120 hours. This was a key enhancement in capability compared with the situation in 1990 when Iraq invaded Kuwait and the distant Western forces had been greatly dependent on transport to Saudi Arabia by sea.[6] Such a dependence was particularly the case for heavy tanks.

The Stryker became the platform of choice for a while, providing a mobile, armor-protected combat system, and each vehicle was able to connect with all the information systems serving the unit. A sense of greater effectiveness was derived from the comparison between the difficulties experienced by the Americans in Mogadishu, Somalia, in 1993,[7] when trying to rescue two downed helicopters and the far less costly experience of a Stryker unit facing a similar task in Iraq in September 2004.[8]

The Russian T-15 Infantry Fighting Vehicle series and the French VBCI are counterparts to the Stryker as armored infantry fighting vehicles, making infantry more mobile, and the vehicles are protected notably against ambushes and mines. A key producer of such vehicles, the Swiss-based company Mowag, produced Piranhas, with independent suspension for all the eight wheels. Versions of the Piranha carried 105 mm guns or 120 mm mortar systems or transported troops and were manufactured for Belgium, Canada, Denmark, Ireland, New Zealand, Sweden, Switzerland, and the United States. In 2006, Belgium ordered 240 Piranhas.

Such vehicles were aspects of the attempt to replace a dichotomy of light and heavy forces and vehicles by producing "medium" ones. At the same time, medium vehicles were made more attractive by arguing that they could be multipurpose and able to operate at different levels of intensity. That was the logic, for example, behind the German Puma Infantry Fighting Vehicle, mass production of which began in 2009. With a unit cost of 8.85 million euros; a main armament of a 30 mm gun and a secondary armament of a machine gun, an antitank guided missile, and a grenade launcher; a weight of 31.45 tons; an ability to carry six infantrymen; and a modular composite armor, this offered much of what a "light" tank might be assumed to have and reiterated the German commitment to the names of wild cats. The first two serial vehicles of the projected 405 (from 2012, the order was reduced to 350) were handed over to the German army in 2010, with full operational readiness to be achieved by 2024, and an upgrading to include communications technology able to work alongside that of fighter aircraft.

Similarly, the Chief of the Italian Defence Staff Strategic Concept, issued in Italy in 2005, focused on the creation of suitable expeditionary forces and argued that armored wheeled vehicles would offer an improved balance between mobility and protection, the emphasis being on an increase in the former. In place of a focus on tanks would come a family of armored vehicles based on the Centauro platform, each equipped with a gun and able to transport an entire rifle section of eight personnel. The acquisition process for the first three prototypes of the VBC 8x8 armored combat vehicle began in 1999, and the first was delivered to the army in 2005.[9] The Centauro is a fast antitank armored car that is cheaper than a tank but as well armed. Currently, it is used by Italy, France, Spain, Jordan, and Oman. In 2008, the Dutch acquired twenty-five Bushmasters for their force in Afghanistan, and they were delivered by air. It is a four-wheeled armored vehicle equipped with a .50 caliber machine gun.

Many armored fighting vehicles include characteristics of tanks. For example, the Warrior, which started life as the MCV-80 (Mechanized Combat Vehicle for the 1980s), was brought into service by Britain in 1988, moves on tracks, and has the commander and gunner stand in a turret. The Warrior has a 30 mm cannon, a 7.62 mm chain machine gun, and an external camera fitted with night vision. Designed for conventional warfare, the Warrior was still in service in the 2000s in Afghanistan. It is now the subject of an expensive life extension program that is not going particularly smoothly. Designed to extend service life to 2040, this program will provide improved protection, as well as "electronic architecture" and, for many, a new turret and a 40 mm cannon.

The improved armor of vehicles operating in Iraq and Afghanistan in the 2000s and 2010s, for example British Warriors and Land Rovers and Canadian armored 4x4s, was also instructive. Such armor was necessary in order to deal with the challenges of RPGs, IEDs or roadside bombs, and suicide bombers. The Americans moved from wanting up-armored High Mobility Multipurpose Wheeled Vehicles to seeking Mine Resistant Ambush Protected vehicles, which were also used. The lack of metal content in IEDs made detection harder, as did the constantly changing nature of the devices. It was estimated that, whereas 9,300 roadside bombs were laid in Afghanistan in 2009, 16,000 were laid by 2011. Strykers, initially effective in Afghanistan, proved inadequate against IEDs as their armor was too thin and their wheels too easily blown off. This underlined a value of tracks. IEDs were used by jihadists against Malian armored fighting vehicles from 2013.

The need to provide protection in mobility has led to reevaluation, with the emphasis now more on the protection than the firepower side of the equation. In Iraq, some of the Abrams tanks had an armor upgrade in the shape of a Tank Urban Survival Kit (TUSK). New combat vehicles, such as the improved Piranha 3, were built with more protection against mines. The concept of a protected crew cell was important, and V-shaped hulls specifically designed to project outward the kinetic energy of an exploding bomb were important features. A key element of armor was provided by the fitting of a blast plate. However, in a form of arms race, the creators of IEDs have made them more powerful at the same time that they remain cheap to produce and flexible in use, not least by being carried by both people and vehicles.

Alongside protection and mobility; deployability, reliability, and supportability were key elements for vehicles, with weight for protection challenging the factors of mobility and deployability. Software sophistication, reliability, and robustness were also of much greater significance than in the past.

Such vehicles are very much used for security purposes. Policing missions in politically difficult environments were, and are, frequently supported by armored personnel carriers, as with the Chinese response to ethnic discontent in western Sichuan in 2011. In 2017, the army of Zimbabwe mounted a successful coup against President Robert Mugabe, making much use of its Chinese-supplied Type 89 armored vehicles, notably the armored personnel variant with its heavy machine guns.

Tanks and heavy artillery, in contrast, have become relatively less significant. Thus, the 2010 British Strategic Defence and Security Review proposed the loss of 40 percent of Challenger 2s. Instead, under the plans for Army 2020, the British focused on the acquisition of 589 Ajax tracked forty-two-ton armored fighting vehicles, which were designed to be a weaponry focus for Strike Brigades.[10] In some respects, these were tanks, and they were certainly well-protected, but they lacked the lethality of tanks and in some respects are really a reconnaissance vehicle.

Following the 2015 Review, Britain proposed to be able to deploy 112 Challenger 2s and, to that end, to upgrade 148 out of the 227 available via the Life Extension Program, which aims to extend the service span of the tanks to 2035. However, there is a lack of sufficient tank transporters, which would be a major issue if tanks have to be sent to oppose Russia in the Baltic Republics. More generally, the British approach left unclear whether the priority was for heavy or medium platforms, and the emphasis placed on present, as opposed to next-generation, capabilities is also problematic.

The Dutch, who had had between seven hundred and one thousand tanks throughout the Cold War, decided in 2011 that, as a result of ongoing cutbacks from the 1990s, they could not sustain their fully fledged armed forces any longer—with a "complete" navy, army, and air force. The decision was taken to dissolve and dismantle the tank units, with the Leopards being sold to Finland and Chile. From then, they have utilized a close cooperation with German tank units in order to retain the relevant tactical and operational knowledge. The Dutch handed over their last sixteen tanks to the Germans, leasing, in return, eighteen German tanks that are used by a Dutch tank squadron that together with three German tank squadrons have formed, since 2016, the German 414 Panzer Battalion. This is part of the Dutch Forty-Third Mechanized Brigade, which is under the command of the German First Panzer Division, providing a clear example of a very far-reaching integration and the degree to which neither state has any real mission where the partner would either have to accept one country's political decision unwillingly or block the use.

DEVELOPMENTS IN TANK DESIGN

There have been attempts to lessen the tank's vulnerability to antitank weapons, notably with improvements to armor so it responds better to being hit by missiles and the use of jamming devices. There has been significant progress in both directions: for example, by the use of composite armor; explosive reactive armor, which, in effect, is pads on the outside of tanks that detonate incoming rounds on impact, rather than letting these rounds penetrate; and electronic shields. A British experimental vehicle of 2000, the Advanced Composite Armoured Vehicle Platform, was the first complete monocoque composite armored vehicle to be built. It was formed from a glass fiber and resin composite structure. However, developments instead focused on explosive reactive armor. Because the explosion of the incoming antitank projectiles occurs before penetration, its effects are mostly lost. However, no matter how effective the reactive armor, damage occurs. The best protection (if any) against such projectiles is to be hull down with the main body not visible, but that is dangerous due to the wide use of IEDs, as in Afghanistan.

Some projects for new tanks did not attract lasting investment, which ensured that older models continued in service. As part of a broader pattern of problems in weapons acquisition, alongside plans for new versions of the Abrams, the Americans considered the tracked M8 Armored Gun System in the early 1990s only to cancel the program, as they did the Future Combat Systems XM1202 Mounted Combat System, but they introduced the eight-wheeled M1128 Mobile Gun System to supplement Strykers.

Tanks, nevertheless, continued to attract investment. In 1993, the T-90 entered service in Russia. A modern variation of the T-72B, and incorporating many of the features found on the T-80U, it could go thirty-seven miles per hour, had an operational range of 340 miles without fuel drums, and used a 125 mm main gun as well as explosive reactive armor, a jamming system, and thermal imaging. In turn, the T-90A entered service in 2004. This tank was used in Dagestan (1999), Ukraine (2014–), and Syria (2015–). With extra horsepower, the T-72B3 entered service from 2010.

Russia, however, was denied many former markets by political change. Instead, former Communist states upgraded their Soviet-era tanks, with the Polish T-21 being developed into the PT-91, which entered service in 1995 with additions, including reactive armor. A total of 233 were delivered, and another 48 were sold to Malaysia in 2007–9. T-72s were also upgraded by the Czech Republic, Georgia, and India. Having broken politically from the Soviet Union, Romania had already produced its own tanks. In place of the Soviet T-55 came the TR-77, a medium tank that in part drew on the T-55, but with major differences. Developed between 1974 and 1980 and produced between 1979 and 1985 in a new factory built in Bucharest in 1979–80, this tank had serious design and production flaws, including with the fire control system. After that came the TR-85, a fifty-ton main battle tank with a 100 mm gun that was developed from 1978 to 1985 and produced from 1986 until 1990.

There have also been developments in tank ammunition. For Britain, the modern version of the APDS (armor-piercing discarding sabot) is a KEP round (kinetic energy penetrator), CHARM (Challenger armament), and an APFSDS (armor-piercing fin-stabilized discarding sabot). The L23 British APFSDS round used in the Iraq War had a monobloc tungsten nickel copper long-road penetrator; later versions employed depleted uranium. These have muzzle velocities in excess of 1,500 meters per second. In contrast, a modern HESH (high-explosive squash head) round has a muzzle velocity of about 670 meters per second and is used against structures instead of high-explosive rounds.[11]

THE TANK TRADE

The end of the Cold War did not stop the tank trade. Indeed, tanks now judged surplus to requirements were more plentiful as a result. For example, Lebanon acquired former Belgian Leopard 1s, and Ecuador acquired Leopard 1s from Chile in 2008. In 1995, Italy bought surplus Leopard turrets from Germany and mounted them on reworked hulls. In 2000–2006, Germany transferred 361 M113s to Lithuania. Between 2003 and 2008, Spain acquired 239 Leopard 2s, mostly manufactured in Spain, which increased the acceptability of the deal.

India purchased versions of the T-90 from Russia from 2001 for a total of 248 tanks. Others were delivered to Algeria. Countries that expressed interest in purchasing the T-90 included Cyprus and Peru. Abrams tanks were produced by the United States for Australia, Egypt, Iraq, Kuwait, Morocco, and Saudi Arabia. Britain sold 254 Warriors to Kuwait.

Important production for domestic markets was seen in both Japan and South Korea. The latter was a rapidly developed new industry that produced high-specification tanks that have both thermal shields and explosive reactive armor. Germany is increasing its tank numbers but in 2018 had fewer battle-ready tanks than Poland.

Copying is another form of diffusion. In 2017, Iran began to mass-produce the Karrar (Striker), a battle tank similar to the Russian T-90. The Iranian tank, with a top speed of thirty-seven miles per hour, has a 125 mm gun with a laser range finder for a computerized targeting system, as well as a 14.5 mm heavy machine gun, the capability to fire missiles, armor to thwart antitank weapons, and rear slat armor against rocket-propelled grenades. Such investment will continue, not least due to the appeal of using tried-and-tested platforms as well as to different elements of conservatism in the military.

CONFLICT IN THE 2010S

In 2017, Iraqi forces recapturing Mosul from the Islamic State (IS) found that the city's alleyways made it difficult to use tanks and, separately, employ them safely. Instead, alongside heavy bombardment by artillery, the Iraqis made plentiful use of "Toyota tanks"—pickup trucks armed with a medium heavy piece of equipment—to obtain mobile firepower. These were also extensively used in conflict within Libya in the 2010s, just as they had been used by Chad against Libya's Soviet tanks in 1987. This variety captured the very different equations of mobility and firepower in ground warfare in the late 2010s as well as more general questions of effectiveness. Tanks could prove militarily important at the point of contact, as when deployed by the Americans in Fallujah, Karbala, and Kufa in Iraq in 2004.[12] That capability did not, however, necessarily bring the military and political outcomes sought.

Thus, in August 2011, in order to overcome resistance in the city of Hama, a major center of opposition to the Assad government of Syria, the government used about 270 tanks. Having been deployed to blockade the city, contributing to the dislocation of opposition, the tanks broke through barricades, which lighter-weight armored vehicles would have found more difficult. The tanks' machine guns subsequently proved more effective than the Molotov cocktails and stones thrown at them. Yet this use of force did not stop the Syrian opposition, and, by the close of the year, tanks were pulled back, albeit still located on the edge of cities ready to be moved in. On February 17, 2012, the journalist Marie Colvin in the *Sunday Times* referred to buildings "pockmarked after tank rounds punched through concrete walls" in the rebellious city of Homs. Long a close Soviet ally, Syria had plentiful tanks, including, at the start of the civil war in 2011, about 2,000 T-55s, 1,000 T-62s, and 1,500 T-72s, as well as 100 PT-76Bs. Syrian tanks, however, were destroyed in urban fighting by antitank weapons, notably when not protected by infantry. In turn, extra armor was added to then.

More modern tanks entered local conflict in the shape of Russian and Turkish interventions from 2015, with Russia supplying Syria with about thirty T-90s from late 2015, as well as modern T-62s and T-72s, and the Turks deploying Leopard 2s, which were used to drive the Kurdish YPG (People's Protection Units) militia from the Afrin region of Syria in 2018.

The Americans permitted their allies, from the spring of 2014, to provide the Syrian rebels with TOW2A missiles, a version aimed at tanks using reactive armor, and directly supplied antitank missiles to the rebels from 2015. The TOWs were important in defeating Syrian tank attacks in the spring of 2015, notably attempts to raise the siege of government troops in Jisr al-Shugour and again in northern Hama that October. As of 2019, Syria still has maybe 5,035 tanks, 5,170 armored fighting vehicles, and 500 self-propelled guns.[13] However, a large number of armored vehicles have been destroyed, not least 1,400 tanks, including even T-90s.[14] Moreover, Turkey has lost several Leopard 2s to antitank missiles and vehicle-borne IEDs.

In February 2012, twenty tanks were among fifty vehicles used when the Ethiopians captured the city of Baidoa, a major center of the al-Shabaab militia movement in Somalia. Again, tanks were important to output, in the form of military activity, but this could not determine outcome. Antitank weaponry was certainly less expensive and easier to acquire. Thus, in 2007–8, when the Mexican government deployed close to forty thousand troops against the drugs cartels, the cartels' weaponry included antitank rockets.[15] Yet the deployment of tanks was seen as a way to demonstrate purpose, as by Egyptian forces in Sinai from 2013.

The wider Middle East continued to be a testing ground for tanks. In October 2017, French-provided Milan antitank missiles were used with great effect by Kurdish militia opposing the advance of Abrams tanks, both of the Iraqi army and those of the Iranian-officered Iraqi Shia militia. The Abrams tanks had been seized from the Iraqi army by the militia in an earlier clash: the Americans had equipped the army with the tanks, agreeing to supply 315 in total. In 2017, the Americans were disturbed by the success of the Kurds' antitank missiles. The Kurds themselves had T-64 and T-72 tanks they had earlier captured from the Iraqi army.

Antitank missiles were also used effectively in Yemen in the late 2010s, with the Houthis destroying Abrams tanks used by Saudi Arabia. The intervening forces in Yemen included the United Arab Emirates with its Leclerc tanks.

In Ukraine, where conflict began in 2014, the separatists in the Donbass seized tanks from the army and were also supported by Russia, including with the modernized T-72B3. Ukraine used T-64s—for example, in the battle for Debaltseve in 2015. To pressure Ukraine, Russia deployed large numbers of tanks, particularly in late 2018, near the border, and their presence became an issue in politics and propaganda. The presence was both affirmed and denied.

COUPS

Tanks were also used in coups, both by those who sought to mount them and their opponents. Thus, in 2016, tanks were deployed by the army during its unsuccessful coup in Turkey. As a result of such action, tanks were a key image of power, one juxtaposed by critics with that of the people. Tanks were not alone as armored cars were used by the Zimbabwe military to help overthrow President Robert Mugabe in 2017 and by the government of Venezuela to suppress opposition in Caracas in April 2019, while police with armored personnel carriers and water cannon suppressed protests in Istanbul in 2013. To a degree, police force use of armored personnel carriers, and indeed armored fighting vehicles, provides an indication of the nature of future counterinsurgency war.

PUBLIC IMPRESSIONS

The technological trend appeared to be against armor as advanced electronic engineering was better adapted to aircraft and missiles. Nevertheless, tanks continued to play a prominent role in public interest. Thus, in Britain, the major military history publisher, Osprey, had a series, Osprey Modelling, that responded to the range of model kits available and the continued popularity of modeling. Works such as Geoff Coughlin and Neil Ashby's *Modelling the M3/M5 Stuart Light Tank* (2003) also offered much information on the tanks. In such works, tanks always appeared as effective.

More generally, armor in World War II continued to dominate the coverage of tanks. *Desperta Ferro Contemporánea*, the leading Spanish military history magazine, in its 2016 coverage of the Battle of the Bulge noted that the image of the Tiger II was emblematic of the battle.[16] Such can be said as well of the effectiveness and dominance of tanks in many films, notably *Fury* (2014), an account of a US tank up against tough odds in the closing stages of the war in Germany. The Sherman tank from that film is at Bovington. At the same time, brave infantry-defying tanks, the theme of *Battle of the Bulge* (1965), continued to be important, as in *Saving Private Ryan* (1998), a US classic. All three films were about the last year of World War II.

For other periods and subjects, there was also a practice of emphasizing tanks. The dominant image of armor was shown by news photographs of the war as well as book covers, even the cover of Jim Lacy's *Takedown: The 3rd Infantry Division's Twenty-One Day Assault on Baghdad* (2007). A picture of tanks parading in Moscow was put on the front of Mark Galeotti's *The Modern Russian Army, 1992–2016* (2017).

Tanks were popular items in military museums. One of Britain's most popular museums is the Tank Museum at Bovington in Dorset, and it has received generous National Lottery grants. The 2019 anniversary of D-Day included the opening of a restored landing craft tank by the National Museum of the Royal Navy, with another big Lottery grant.

Moreover, tanks were left on display at prominent tourist sites, and not only in Europe—for example, at Sevastopol. Thus, in Rabaul in New Guinea in 2019, a damaged Japanese tank rests outside Admiral Yamamoto's wartime headquarters, which is such a site. In popular writing on military history, furthermore, there was a fascination with the combination of mobility and firepower offered by tanks.[17]

The period produced an iconic photo, not the one for the previous period of the power of the Chinese tanks in Beijing in 1989 but one resonant of the link between tanks and the strength of rulership. President Putin of Russia posing on a tank served as an image of threat as a revived Cold War was discussed from 2014. Thus, the image appeared on the front page of the *Economist* of March 28, 2014, under the title "The New World Order," the tank clearly the image of a reliance on force.

NOTES

1. B. R. Simms and C. D. Taylor, "The Battle for Salem Street," *Army History* 65 (fall 2007): 4–15, esp. 13–14; J. S. Brown, "Thoughts on the Future Force," *Army History* 60 (winter–spring 2004): 24.

2. P. R. Mansoor, "Spears and Ploughshares: Equipping the Force for Operations in Iraq," *RUSI Defence Systems* 7, no. 3 (spring 2005): 64–65.

3. M. van Creveld, *The Sword and the Olive: A Critical History of the Israeli Defense Force* (New York, 1998).

4. R. Thornton, "A Bear with Teeth? The Russian Military in 2008," *RUSI* 153, no. 5 (October 2008): 48–52.

5. J. S. Brown, *Kevlar Legions: The Transformation of the U.S. Army, 1989–2005* (Washington, DC, 2011).

6. W. M. Donnelly, *Transforming an Army at War: Designing the Modular Force, 1991–2005* (Washington, DC, 2007), 19–25.

7. M. Bowden, *Black Hawk Down: A Story of Modern War* (New York, 1999).

8. R. J. Reardon and J. A. Charlston, *From Transformation to Combat: The First Stryker Brigade at War* (Washington, DC, 2007).

9. F. Cecchi, "Medium Forces: The Italian Army Point of View," *RUSI Defence Systems* 9, no. 1 (summer 2006): 72–73.

10. P. Antill and J. Smith, "The British Army in Transition: From Army 2020 to the Strike Brigades and the Logistics of Future Operations," *RUSI* 162, no. 3 (June/July 2017): 50–58; M. Clark, "Strike Unsure? Clarifying the Role of Armour in Joint Force 2025," *RUSI Defence Systems* 18, no. 1 (2016).

11. Ex inf. Anthony Saunders.

12. K. D. Gott, *Breaking the Mold: Tanks in the Cities* (Fort Leavenworth, KS, 2006).

13. http://globalfirepower.com, accessed May 3, 2019.

14. J. Janovksý, "Seven Years of War—Documenting Syrian Arab Army's Armoured Vehicles Losses," http://www.bellingcat.com, accessed May 3, 2019.

15. M. Joyce, "Mexico's Security Crisis and Implications for US Policy," *RUSI* 154, no. 1 (February 2009): 66–70.

16. Cover Image explanation, *Desperta Ferro Contemporánea*, no. 15 (2016): 4.

17. R. M. Citino, "New Gang in Town: The Rise of the German Panzer Division: How Mobility Came to Define Warfare in the 20th Century," *MHQ: The Quarterly Journal of Military History* 28, no. 2 (winter 2016).

NINE

INTO THE FUTURE

"IF THERE IS ONE LESSON FROM THE VOTE IT IS THAT FORCE ALONE does not work in the internet age. One knitting old lady can stop a whole line of tanks." This reflection, by a senior Spanish politician in 2017,[1] when the Spanish government sought to prevent an independence referendum in Catalonia, captured one crucial aspect of the relative effectiveness of tanks—that of the very contexts within which force operated. In practice, such issues were handled very differently in particular countries and in specific contexts. In most countries, there would be no such stop, whether in peacetime or wartime. For example, without reference to tanks, Gandhi might have been effective against the British in the 1920s and 1930s, but he certainly would not have been against the Japanese, the Germans, or the Soviets.

Focusing on the performance of the tank as a machine is not the whole story, but it is obviously significant.[2] In this respect, looking to the future, secrecy about developments is an element in assessing capability. Thus, the true effectiveness of current tank armor is, for those outside the military, a matter of speculation. Moreover, the performance of tank armor has greatly affected other specifications, such as weight and cost. Despite improvements to tank protection in the shape of better protective systems, particularly new material and better sensors,[3] there are still serious vulnerabilities. For example, the Russian T-90 has, as part of its Shtora-1 active protection system, automatically triggered infrared dazzlers to jam laser-targeting systems on missiles as well as an infrared-obscuring aerosol cloud and explosive reactive armor. Nevertheless, at least five or six were knocked out in Syria in 2016 and 2017.[4] Tanks are vulnerable to nonelectronically traceable weapons or devices, such as bazookas. Finland has prepared to resist a Russian invasion by purchasing Panzerfaust 3s, which have a simple optical targeting device and no electronics that can be jammed.

This point can be illustrated by the Israeli-designed Trophy system, which in 2019 was adopted by the Americans to improve their Abrams M1A2, equipping up to four tank brigades. A counter antitank system, it is based on four sensors covering the four sides of a tank and releasing information to the tank radar, which orders the central system to react with radar-guided weapons that fire Multiple Explosive Formed Penetrators to destroy the incoming weapon within seconds. Designed for urban warfare, this also works on open ground. This is a major tool in tank protection and effectiveness electronically, but lacks effectiveness against dull-ammunitioned antitank weaponry from the APFSDS (armor-piercing fin-stabilized discarding sabot) down to Molotov cocktails. As a result, a hull-down station remains the best kind of tank defense, which, however, itself poses issues of vulnerability.

Moreover, even if destruction can be avoided, damage, as from the outset of tank warfare, remains a central problem. The cost of replacing damaged tank tracks is formidable, let alone that of dealing with engine problems. More seriously, damage is a key issue because, due in part to cost but more to other commitments, the number of available tanks has fallen. While antitank, like antiaircraft, weaponry continues to indicate the effectiveness and importance of antiweapons, their impact is increased by the fall in the number of tanks and aircraft. The growing sophistication of armor electronic systems and cyberattacks means tank operations are likely to be part of cyberwarfare.

At the same time, the place of the tank in modern conflict has declined, a point underlined in both procurement and doctrine. Thus, Russian rearmament from the mid-2010s has focused on air, naval, and missile weaponry, especially nuclear weaponry. The army has received attention, but only within this context and one in which the Russians have been developing what the West has named "hybrid warfare," below the level of overt use of regular military units but including the use of the threat of nuclear or conventional forces, information warfare and cyberwarfare, and the actual employment of special operations forces.[5]

In 2015, in the Victory Day celebrations in Moscow, air defense missile launchers and intercontinental ballistic missiles were displayed alongside tanks, including the new T-14 Armata. This was presented by the Russians, keen to boost prestige and foreign sales, as superior to Western rivals, such as the US Abrams and the British Challenger 2. Weighing forty-eight tons, the T-14 has a speed of fifty to fifty-six miles per hour and a 125 mm gun.

However, during the rehearsal, the T-14 on display stalled for fifteen minutes. Similarly, although there was initial talk of 2,300 tanks for the army, production and fiscal issues led to a major reduction. The unit cost was estimated at $3.7 million. Nevertheless, the T-14 was now part of the display culture of the Russian military as seen, for example, in the Victory Day celebrations in 2019, alongside 152 mm self-propelled howitzers.

Of the current leading tanks in service throughout the world, most are not at the technological cutting-edge. Two clearly representing investment in new systems are the Russian T-14 and the Japanese T-10. The latter has reduced its weight by one ton to forty tons, compared to its predecessor, by utilizing lightweight nanocrystal steel and modular ceramic composite armor. The T-10 also has a hydropneumatic suspension system, a 120 mm smoothbore gun, and a speed of forty-three miles per hour. Automatic loading enables the T-10 to operate with a crew of only three.

From 2014, Russia deployed tanks in an effort to intimidate Ukraine and, in 2017, in the Zapad-17 military exercise, to intimidate the North Atlantic Treaty Organization (NATO) in the Baltic sphere. At the same time, although the Ivan Gren–class of landing ship, tanks (LSTs) that Russia was then building was large and impressive, there were only two of them. In contrast, China, by 2011, had twenty-six LSTs of over four thousand tons. These were a threat to Taiwan, and on June 6, 2019, the Taiwanese defense ministry announced that it had asked the United States to sell it 108 M1A2 Abrams, 1,240 TOW missiles, and 409 Javelin antitank missiles as part of a two billion dollar order including 66 F-16 fighters and 250 Stinger antiaircraft missiles. The tanks, TOWs, and Javelins would all represent upgrades on existing weaponry. However, Chinese tanks posed less of a threat to Taiwan than that coming from the development of Chinese missile systems.

Given the costs, it is not surprising that many states prefer to buy tanks from low-cost producers, as with Thailand, a traditional US ally, receiving Chinese VT-4s from 2017, or seek armored vehicles, which are not only cheaper but simpler to maintain and multipurpose. Armored vehicles are also easier to manufacture, which is highly important for "offset" deals, those in which reciprocal investment plays a role, with local production proving part of the process. The more complex the system, the harder to employ a low skill base and respond to a lack of high-quality production capacity. At the same time, purchasers seek such agreements, both to lessen costs and help local defense industrialization. The particular requirements of sophisticated tanks pose a major problem to this equation.

Changing force structures were an issue for the United States, which dramatically reduced its military presence in Europe after the Cold War in part due to the redeployment to the Middle East but also as a result of the run-down in the army. The last US tank stationed in Europe departed in 2013. In turn, in response to the Ukraine crisis beginning in 2014 and the Russian threat to the Baltic Republics (Estonia, Latvia, Lithuania), NATO built up its forces. Initially, the NATO Stabilization Force was equipped with only light vehicles and no main battle tanks, but it had an antitank capability.[6] Nevertheless, as a key element, heavy equipment was soon stockpiled in Western Europe, with the equipment to be used for units that were to be airlifted in from the United States in the event of crisis. In 2015, the United States and NATO developed plans to pre-position military vehicles, including heavy tanks, in Eastern Europe. The troops to use them were to be flown in, which was an important adjunct to the use of air power to help armor.

There is certainly a NATO vulnerability in the event of war. Russian forces suffer from undermanning, poor morale, inadequate maintenance, and the dependence of public finances on the price of oil, which contributed to a fall in military spending in 2018. The operations against Ukraine were only sustained by drawing on units from across Russia. Yet the Russian army has been configured for high-tempo attacks, which increases the threat it poses.[7] The Russian VOSTOK exercise in 2018 demonstrated that military investment over the last decade, but especially since 2015, had had a favorable impact on manning, morale, and maintenance concerns.

Moreover, the Baltic Republics, vulnerable to attack and weak in air power, lack the capacity to stop a Russian tank advance, and it is unclear that appreciable NATO forces could be rapidly deployed other than to provide a "tripwire deterrent." There has been talk, indeed, of a new "Fulda Gap" between Russia's ally Belarus and its Kaliningrad enclave on the Baltic, with the Russians thus advancing, through southern Lithuania, to cut off the Baltic Republics from reinforcement by land. The Suvalki Gap, the sixty-mile-wide Lithuanian strip of land between Belarus and the Kalingrad region, is NATO's weak spot. NATO has stationed troops there to deter a Russian attack. In 2019, NATO also decided to fund a new $260 million weapons store at an airbase close to Plowditz in central Poland to be better able to equip reinforcements that were flown in. However, the scale and speed of the necessary NATO action are both significant issues.

More generally on the world scale, tanks will have to face the greater share of the population that lives in cities and the particular military environment this focus creates. This environment brings together conventional combat with asymmetrical operations—a range also seen in other environments but with particular characteristics in cities.[8] In this setting, infantry requires protection in the form of armored personnel carriers and tanks and the assistance of armored bulldozers. If operating in the narrow streets of many cities, it will be important to have smaller tanks. That does not mean, however, a comparable need for fleets of tanks. Separately, cities can be cut off and isolated. Siege by means of stopping power, fuel, water, and food supplies will lead to a breakdown of urban life.

At another scale, there is the question of whether the West's military dominance is coming to an end,[9] with consequences for the weapons particularly associated with it. Alternatively, to maintain that dominance, does there need to be a change in weapons and/or their use?

Although the demise of the tank has been predicted since it was invented,[10] technical responses, if not solutions, to the continuing problems of firepower, mobility, and armor suggest the tank is here to stay, at least until there is a major change in the parameters of land conflict. As with unmanned aircraft, there may be unmanned tanks, and the same for antitank weapons.

At the same time, aside from improvised explosive devices (IEDs), cut-price precision weapons using off-the-shelf components are a threat to existing tanks and their use. This is not only a possibility for nongovernmental organizations (NGOs) and others involved in asymmetrical warfare, such as terrorist organizations. Most prominently, the US Army Research Laboratory's Aeromechanics and Flight Control Group is examining the potential of what it terms the Cooperative Engagement Capability program. This rests on guiding "dumb" weapons by means of radio messages from smart munitions. Thus, a swarm of submunitions would be given a guidance system, increasing effectiveness and replacing indiscriminate fire. Precision and speed will be delivered at lower cost than at present and thus will be able to hit dispersed targets. The nature of artillery would change, and individual soldiers would have maneuvering munitions with a type of video game console. The devolution of responsibility to such combatants offers a dramatically new version of that offered by the idea of decentralized command. The latter is generally held up as a means to success, notably providing necessary flexibility.[11]

In looking to the future, the comparison with changes in naval warfare is arresting. Tanks were intended originally by the British as armored ships on land. The force structure of navies, however, from the late 1940s saw battleships replaced by aircraft carriers. In contrast, tanks remained armed with guns as their size allowed no similar transformation to that seen at sea. In contrast, drones and similar unmanned land vehicles will allow a vehicle of the scale of a modern tank to carry and control a number of those vehicles and will turn the tank into a kind of carrier, including of unmanned land vehicles (ULVs): unmanned little tanks.

Flexibility is certainly necessary at all levels of military activity.[12] This is particularly so with rapid troop advances. In these cases, mobile combat and uncertain supply produce both tactical and operational strain. Effective combat reconnaissance, and a willingness to reformulate goals and means and reorganize battle groups, are all important in confronting that strain.[13] However, employing an argument in favor of flexibility (and notably mobility) in order to advance the case for particular weapon systems, including the tank, is less appropriate. In part, this is a consequence of the very unpredictability of the tasks that may be confronted. Flexibility at the systemic level does not necessarily mean such flexibility at that of individual units and vice versa.

Indeed, this issue becomes more of a problem with costly items that are available in limited numbers, with their use therefore being a problem. As with aircraft, the peak numbers of World War II cannot be repeated. The rising cost per unit raises questions of obsolescence and also affects the flexibility of tanks. Sir Peter Luff, British minister of defense procurement from 2010 to 2012, has observed, "My prejudice about tanks is that they are only really valuable if they are available in mass. If you can't afford mass, stick to attack helicopters."[14]

At the same time, their capabilities and roles are different, and in missions other than the conventional high-intensity battle, tanks—protected weapons platforms with good sensors and considerable resilience—are most welcome, even if large numbers are not available. Furthermore, attack helicopters, which were initially designed to stop massed tank attacks, are costly and require more training and infinitely more logistical support and maintenance.

Another aspect of compromised flexibility arises from the complex logistical burdens posed by tanks, notably in terms of providing fuel and maintenance. Modern tanks can have a large fuel capacity. Thus, the British Challenger 2 has a fuel capacity of 350 gallons. However, tanks can use up to a gallon per mile. Moreover, resupplying their needs not only is a formidable burden involving much manpower but also requires dumps that need protection. Such issues, in particular, compromise the viability of heavy tanks.

Yet it was not only heavy tanks that faced problems as the Americans and British discovered in Iraq after their success in the 2003 invasion. British Challenger 2s took damage from IEDs. The threat to all vehicles from ambush, notably by IEDs, car bombs, and suicide bombers, is such that it is important to prevent the enemy from approaching and engaging.[15] To this end, armor can only achieve so much. Instead, surveillance, firepower, command, and tactics are all important—both by the armor and by cooperating units, including not only infantry but also aerial.

The vulnerability of vehicles to ambush, and thus the relative compromising of effectiveness, has important tactical consequences, notably so if the number of tanks is limited, as was the case in 1916–18 and is again today. Moreover, that will probably remain the case unless there is a process of miniaturization. Yet, just as the antitank gun did not make tanks obsolescent, so also with antitank missiles, IEDs, and other modern weapons. Indeed, there are remedies against the effectiveness of antitank weapons, notably electronic countermeasures, as on the new Polish PLO-01 stealth tank, a fifth-generation MBT; as there were not on behalf of cavalry against machine guns, bar transferring to tanks. Separately, there is also a greater range of armor thanks to the opportunities provided by lighter-armored vehicles, whether tracked or wheeled. These opportunities include those of cost, but they do not negate the value of main battle tanks as a component of an effective system for land fighting, especially if enhanced with new capabilities, notably autonomous systems.

These points revive some of the debates about tank use in the 1920s and 1930s, as well as underline the adaptation seen in the history of the tank. At the same time, broader questions of doctrine, usage, and the cultural dimensions involved in both, especially the latter, are highly significant in effectiveness and, thus, capability.[16]

Current developments continue to underline the problematic future of the tank. In February 2020, General David Berger, the Marine Corps Commandant, told a Congressional committee "we are designed for a competition behind us, not in front of us," and soon after it was announced that all the Marines' 170 battle tanks were to be phased out and the bridging units required for fast tank advances scrapped as the Marines focused instead for expeditionary warfare in the Pacific with a greater reliance accordingly on lightness and missiles. China meanwhile announced that its HJ-12 antitank missiles were capable of destroying any battlefield tank.

NOTES

1. *Financial Times*, October 10, 2017, 4.

2. R. S. Cameron, "Pushing the Envelope of Battlefield Superiority: American Tank Development from the 1970s to the Present," *Armor* 107 (November/December 1988): 8–14.

3. "The Armour Strikes Back," *Economist*, June 4, 2011, https://www.economist.com /technology-quarterly/2011/06/04/the-armour-strikes-back; C. K. Bartles and L. W. Grau, "New System Preserves Armor Dominance of Future Battlefield: BMPT 'Terminator-2,'" *Armor* 125 (April/June 2015): 46–52.

4. S. Roblin, "Russia's Deadly T-90A Tanks are Dying (Like Everyone Else's) in Syria," *The National Interest*, July 12, 2018.

5. Rod Thornton, "The Russian Military's New 'Main Emphasis': Asymmetric Warfare," *RUSI* 162, no. 4 (August/September 2017): 18–28.

6. R. D. Hooker, "Operation *Baltic Fortress, 2016*: NATO Defends the Baltic States," *RUSI* 160, no. 3 (June/July 2015): 29–30.

7. I. Sutyagin and J. Bronk, *Russia's New Ground Forces: Capabilities, Limitations and Implications for International Security* (London, 2017).

8. L. A. Di Marco, *Concrete Hell: Urban Warfare from Stalingrad to Iraq* (Oxford, 2012).

9. M. Urban, *The Edge: Is the Military Dominance of the West Coming to an End?* (London, 2015).

10. S. C. Crist, "The M1A2 Abrams: The Last Main Battle Tank?," *Armor* 106 (July/August 1997): 14–16; K. Elmonairy, "The Tank Is Dead! Long Live the Tank!," *Armor* 125 (January/March 2015): 121–27.

11. E. Shamir, *Transforming Command: The Pursuit of Mission Command in the U.S., British, and Israeli Armies* (Stanford, CA, 2011).

12. M. Finkel, *On Flexibility: Recovery from Technological and Doctrinal Surprise on the Battlefield* (Stanford, CA, 2011).

13. R. H. S. Stolfi, "A Critique of Pure Success: Inchon Revisited, Revised, and Contrasted," *JMH* 68 (2004): 505–26.

14. Luff to Black, email, April 27, 2019.

15. S. M. Speakes and G. M. Martin, "Modernising the American Army in an Era of Persistent Conflict," *RUSI Defence Systems* 10, no. 3 (February 2008): 43.

16. K. M. Pollack, *Arabs at War: Military Effectiveness, 1948–1991* (Lincoln, NE, 2002).

TEN

CONCLUSIONS

THE SCENE OF THE BEATLES DRIVING ACROSS SALISBURY PLAIN IN a Centurion tank, in their 1965 film *Help*, is not generally regarded as part of the cultural impact of the tank, and neither is James Bond commandeering a T-55 (with some additional armor) in what purports to be St. Petersburg in *GoldenEye* (1995). Indeed, tanks are regularly portrayed as images of state power, as with the depiction of President Putin atop one. Margaret Thatcher in the turret of a Challenger 1, scarf flowing, goggles on, while visiting British troops in West Germany in 1986 was one of the most iconic pictures of her and clearly underlined the cultural connection between tanks and power in the British popular imagination. She fired a practice shell using laser targeting to hit the target (an old tank) directly. Thatcher was accompanied by West German chancellor Helmut Kohl, who also test-drove a Leopard and fired a shell. Running for the US presidency in 1988, in contrast, George Dukakis got it totally wrong when he posed, at a campaign stop at the General Dynamics Land Systems' plant in the Detroit suburb of Sterling Heights, in a M1A1 Abrams tank pretending to be something he was not.

References to tanks are widely diffused. The phrase "parking tanks on the lawn" in Britain means bringing undue influence to bear and has been used frequently since the 1960s. As Labour prime minister and then in a bitter dispute over trade union legislation, Harold Wilson, in 1969, allegedly told Hugh Scanlon, president of the powerful Amalgamated Union of Engineering Workers, to "get your tanks off my lawn."[1] The London *Times* of May 4, 2019, referred, in an article headlined "Crowing Lib Dems Park Their Tanks on Rees-Mogg's Lawn," to local council results that led to the Liberal Democrats representing, at the local level, the Conservative parliamentarian Jacob Rees-Mogg. There was no reference in the article to tanks.

And not only that phrase and image. In a comment piece in the *Sunday Times* on April 14, 2019, Niall Ferguson, a prominent historian, argued, "The present danger to free thought and speech is not Red Army tanks pouring through the Fulda Gap in Germany; it is the red army of mediocrities waging war on dissent within academia and the media."

There is always a danger in reading too much from isolated mentions and episodes and still more from a particular vision of the present character, and future trajectory, of modernity. To argue the obsolescence of the tank from the growing success of antitank weaponry, or the primacy of unarmored or less armored vehicles, is possibly to draw too much from the present situation. Separately, it is clear that it is necessary to have a broad definition of the capability not only of tanks but also of less armored military vehicles. Aside from the specifications of the weapon, it is instructive to consider the degree to which an effective industrial base is significant for their manufacture and availability and also to assess the availability of oil necessary to permit the deployment and use of this type of weaponry. Moreover, technological reliability and competence in its use are crucial to the effective utilization of any military technology. Reliability includes the provision of supplies, notably gas and oil. Tanks were not alone in this, but mechanization accentuated, as well as transformed, the logistical demands of war. A key element of the Cold War was that both sides were able to provide plentiful supplies of fuel, and this ability underpinned the gigantic tank fleets. The United States and the Soviet Union were among the world's leading oil producers.

In contrast, during World War II, the Germans were heavily reliant on horses.[2] However, for propaganda reasons, they did not wish to show this.[3] This is not emphasized by most popular historians. Instead, the theme of German quality continues to be offered by some writers—notably, in Britain, Max Hastings—who generally do not devote comparable attention to German failings.[4]

Such points are not simply "academic" but have an obvious present-day (and historical) policy relevance. This is understandable given the tendency to use military history as a building block for doctrine. Moreover, in a less focused, yet still highly influential, fashion, there is the establishment of a military culture and organizational coherence based on experience or at least on an account of the past—particularly, in terms of current weapon systems, of the recent past. The latter characteristic has been very much the case with tanks, although there is no inherent reason why a deeper history of mobile warfare should not also be relevant.

The focus on tanks has resulted in an emphasis on the experience, or rather perception, of World War II and the Arab-Israeli wars. The former led the US army from 1945, confronting the prospect of facing apparently imminent and large-scale Soviet attack in Western Europe, to consider the example of the Wehrmacht when defending itself against the Soviet Union in 1943–45, and the US military repeatedly sought advice from German generals.[5]

That was not the sole experience of significance. Indeed, some of those offered at the time of World War II remain of general relevance. The draft report of 30 Corps, part of the British Eighth Army, dated November 21, 1942, reflected on the recent victory over the Germans and Italians at El Alamein: "The operations proved the general soundness of our principles of training for war, some of which had been neglected during previous fighting in the desert. In all forms of warfare, new methods should never disregard basic principles. The operations involved a reversion, with the difference due to the developments in weapons, to the static warfare of the war of 1914–18. This reversion should not be regarded as an isolated exception unlikely to recur . . . our organisations and weapons must remain suitable both for mobile and periodical static operations."[6]

Thus, alongside their value, tanks could not transform the context or, indeed, nature of conflict. They could play a role in "static operations," notably providing firepower in the attack and offering support for defending forces, including in the shape of counterattacks. However, tanks were clearly better suited to the role of mobile operations, at the same time depending on artillery and infantry support in the latter. Indeed, on September 27, 1950, Stalin complained about failures on the part of the North Korean army and its Soviet advisers, notably, "erroneous and absolutely inadmissible tactics for tank use in combat . . . you have used tanks in combat without preliminary artillery strikes aimed at clearing the field for tank maneuvers. As a consequence, the enemy easily destroys your tanks."[7]

More generally, tanks contributed to effectiveness, rather than transforming it, and, more particularly, provided a new dimension of mobility to the notion, seen in World War I and used with great effect by the Allies in late 1918, that all maneuver was to be determined by and linked to the fire plan. A very different dimension of mobility was provided by aircraft.

At the same time, there were important general-purpose advantages in the use of tanks, notably in the shape of the force and presence in part available from the equation of force equals mass times acceleration. An observer of the unsuccessful 1944 Warsaw uprising noted the effective German use of tanks:

"The first barricades, temporary, wooden, weren't worth anything. The tanks rode right over them . . . barricades. And right away those tanks rode over them . . . the Germans were arresting people and herding them in front of the tanks against the partisans."[8]

Tanks are part of the more general synergy between resources and fighting quality. More and better weapons themselves are not sufficient to obtain victory. They can increase fighting quality, including by enhancing confidence and morale. Conversely, such weapons can also compromise this quality, notably by encouraging a misguided confidence in the weapons themselves or by leading to tactics in which there is a reluctance to close with the enemy for fear of affecting aspects of the weapons' performance. Indeed, the relationship is that, instead of more resources increasing fighting quality, better fighting quality can make a more effective use of resources. This implies that forces with superior fighting quality will benefit disproportionately from enhanced (in both quality and quantity) resources. In the absence of such resources, nevertheless, forces with superior fighting quality can use this fighting quality to lessen, indeed sometimes close, the capability gap.

Yet, whether or not there are superior resources, it is highly important to put a strong emphasis on training, for that is the crucial basis for the successful use of tactics, the implementation of doctrine, and the development of fighting quality. Thus, for the British in World War II, the training regime in 1941–44, notably on Salisbury Plain, focused on differing assumptions about tank doctrine, including that gained from combat in North Africa, and was important to subsequent performance, particularly once France was invaded in 1944.

At the same time, capability gaps owe much to tasking and to whether it was appropriate and/or viable in a context made dynamic by the strength and intentions of others, including allies as well as enemies. Thus, the state of the British army vis-à-vis Germany in 1939–40 was in part due to the British government's hesitation about confirming that land forces would be sent to the Continent until soon before the war began. In part, this hesitation reflected the highly dynamic character of British strategic commitments in this period, a dynamic character that was a consequence of a rapidly changing and unpredictable international context.

Tanks themselves have many limitations, and these remain the same ones that have existed from the outset. They face particular problems with reliability and vulnerability. In the former case, despite their cross-country capabilities, tracked vehicles tend to be less easy to operate and maintain than their wheeled counterparts and require more maintenance and fuel. Moreover, the tracks provide a ready area of vulnerability to attack. This vulnerability, part of the more general issue of exposure to weaponry, including in ambushes, has become more pronounced as more people live in cities, which have become a more significant area of operations. As a consequence, the potential for antitank weaponry is enhanced. The latter continues to evolve and is far less expensive and easier to use than armor. In the 2010s, more tanks were destroyed by anti-tank weapons than by other tanks. Emphasizing combined arms operations as a means to protect tanks does not, however, deal adequately with the challenge of this environment.[9] As another aspect of this challenge, tanks continue to play a key role in infantry support, which also exposes them to antitank weapons.

From a different direction, given the potential for antitank tactics and weaponry, tanks can be seen, in one light, as another version of cavalry and as similarly anachronistic or, at least, vulnerable to developments in firepower. Separately, cavalry ideas in the shape of the organizational and tactical structures and practices were long significant to armor, including in Britain and the United States, with an emphasis on reconnaissance and armor in a maneuver role, not a combat-support one. The latter issue was very much seen in the debate over new challenges, tasks, and capabilities after the end of the Cold War.[10] Complicating it was the question of cost, which is far greater for tanks than for other armored fighting vehicles, whether in terms of purchase, maintenance, or supply.

Tanks provide firepower and protection, but the last has been lessened by the ease of the relevant antiweaponry. That critique, however, is not a reason to dispense with tanks. This is not only due to the value of existing capabilities but also because the nature of conflict is unpredictable, and, as with battleships in 1941–45 in the face of air power, while other powers have tanks, it is sensible to have them as a form of tank killer. They will also continue to provide protection for infantry, protection that is necessary in both urban and nonurban contexts.

The lightness of many US wheeled units, notably armed with Strykers, including those up-gunned with a new 30 mm automatic gun, indicated that the US army hoped the next war would be in an urban environment with light units, rather than a "tank war." However, the experience of 2004 on, whether in Iraq, Afghanistan, Lebanon, Syria, or elsewhere, made clear the value of more strongly armored vehicles. Moreover, choices are in part more effective by the acts of opponents, both in terms of this particular environment and with reference to others—for example, rural Eastern Europe, where Russia has to be confronted. Aside from standard protection issues, the Stryker also faces other issues as, like other "connected" combat systems, its processes can be hacked.[11]

Yet if you put a big gun on the top of a light armored vehicle, as with the German-Dutch Boxer, in service since 2011 (and with Britain rejoining the program in 2018), there is a question of whether tracked tanks are required. Such a vehicle cannot give you protection anywhere near that of a tank, but it is still pretty good, and the vehicle can have great tactical mobility and, therefore, operational and strategic value. The six-wheeled Boxer has remarkable off-road mobility. An earlier instance, the Brazilian Engesa EE-9 armored car, with its 90 mm gun, was an effective and inexpensive vehicle produced between 1974 and 1993 that was widely sold and is still in use.

The discussion of current options certainly casts a harsh light on J. C. Fuller's sweeping optimism in his *Tanks in the Great War* (1920), which was not a slim essay or printed lecture. Fuller was a deep thinker, an excellent writer, and a skilled military historian, but, like many other theorists, he could be overly confident in his predictions. Written the previous year, the book had closed with a chapter forecasting what tanks might do. After arguing that the introduction of the tank "entirely revolutionises the art of war," not least by replacing muscular energy as the motive force, a point he frequently made, Fuller claimed that weapons were the key element, indeed, "99 per cent," in victory. He argued that tanks' cross-country capability made the land an isotropic surface for conflict "as easily traversable in all directions by a tractor as a sheet of ice is by a skater"—a parallel, not that he brought out the point, with aircraft. Fuller also claimed that the potential would greatly and rapidly improve. Fuller predicted a speed and maneuverability for tanks they have not yet reached and, more seriously, thought little of the prospect of opposition.[12]

Just as modern commentators and the modern public look back in order to ground the discussion, the same was true for those considering the situation, including the future, in 1920. While focusing on World War I, Fuller also considered British failures in 1879–85: the battles of Isandhlwana (1879), Maiwand (1880), and El Teb (1884) and the failed relief of Khartoum (1885), defeats at the hands of the Zulus, Afghans, and Sudanese respectively. Fuller (wrongly) claimed that a tank could have covered in two days the 180 miles to Khartoum that took twenty-one days in 1885 and that "One tank would have won Maiwand, Isandhlwana, and El Teb . . . one tank, costing say £10,000 can not only win a small war normally costing £2,000,000, but render such wars in the future highly improbable if not impossible." Fuller had similar views on a successful invasion of Afghanistan from Peshawar on India's North-West Frontier, which would have been a major commitment, and not only in the nineteenth century. Such an invasion was an option for Britain in the Third Anglo-Afghan War, that of 1919:

Armour, by rendering flesh impervious to bullets, does away with the necessity
of flank guards and long straggling supply columns, and our punitive expedition
equipped with tanks can reach Kabul in a few days, and not only reach it but abandon
its communications, as they will require no protection . . . tank supply columns . . . are
self-protecting. . . .

From small wars to internal Imperial Defence is but one step. Render rebellion hopeless
and it will not take place. In India we lock up an unremunerative army 75,000 British
troops and 150,000 Indian. Both these forces can be done away with and order maintained,
and maintained with certainty, by a mechanical police force of 20,000 to 25,000 men.

. . . war will be eliminated by weapons.[13]

From the perspective of 2020, Fuller's prediction appears naive, and doubly
so due to the problems that faced first Soviet and then US-led interventions in
Afghanistan (the country of Maiwand as well as Kabul) from 1979, as well as
the difficulties of controlling Sudan (the country of El Keb and Khartoum).
Aside from exaggerating the developing capability of tanks, Fuller, like many
commentators, seriously underplayed that of antiweapons. Capability became
in part a matter of confronting and overcoming the latter, but the initiative and
advantage were far less with the tank than had been anticipated. Although the
antitank potential of other tanks is significant, it is less than that of other weapons, a situation that has developed greatly due to the use of "smart bombs."

The major problem with Fuller's analysis and projections, however, was
not so much the specifics, seriously misleading as they were, but rather the
developmental assumptions away from people and toward machines. This was
a repeated theme of Fuller's; indeed, he suggested that, eventually, one man
might win a war as their controller.[14] Linked to this was his clear idea that the
future brought change to a degree that the past was redundant.[15] This is an
instance of the notion of a paradigm shift or, phrased differently, a "Revolution in Military Affairs." The emphasis on modernity and modernization was
that also seen with air power, but the comparison does not demonstrate the
validity of Fuller's approach, and, certainly, antitank weapons and methods
proved more viable than their antiaircraft counterparts.

Viability is related also to cost and flexibility. The extent to which the limitations of heavy tanks on both accounts reduced, and still reduce, their value
was and is not always brought out by the discussion of specifications, let alone
considerations of combat effectiveness. Moreover, Fuller was seriously flawed
in his pursuit of misleading parallels and analogies: "The cross-country tractor, or tank, widened the size of roads to an almost unlimited degree. The
earth becomes a universal vehicle of motion, like the sea, and to those sides
which relied on tanks, naval tactics could be superimposed on those of land
warfare."[16]

That claim might be regarded as simply an exaggeration if the perspective was the Kuwaiti desert, but it was wrong as far as most terrain was concerned and remains so. There was also Fuller's misleading pseudoromantization of the Tank Corps: "the modern knights in armour . . . his horse now a petrol engine and his lance a machine gun."[17] Again, there was a parallel with aircraft pilots.

Although deeply flawed, Fuller's arguments continue to resonate with advocates for armor. Thus, a 2011 *RUSI* article, considering how "radical technological change has revolutionised warfare," provided an excerpt from Fuller's 1919 Gold Medal (Military) Prize—"we stand on the threshold of a new epoch in the history of war—the petrol age . . . we see that the tank can replace infantry and cavalry, can supplement artillery." The anonymous note from the journal claimed that Fuller had "quickly grasped the possibilities. . . . Ultimately it would be German officers . . . who would most swiftly adopt many of the ideas Fuller developed, and use them to devastating effect in the Second World War."[18]

So also with the claim, often made, that Fuller's understanding of both the tank and operational art were not appreciated by a hidebound and unscientific British army.[19] This was, and remains, a misleading characterization of a force that, having played a key role in the defeat of the German army in 1918 (akin to the Soviet role in 1944–45), was then translating to a range of distant and difficult commitments, from Russia and Ireland to British Somaliland and Iraq.

None of the argument by, or on behalf of, Fuller helped with a balanced assessment of the achievements and potential of armor, whether at the tactical, operational, or strategic levels. That remains the case, even if the fascination with the tank is generally now more circumscribed as the constraints within which it can act are better appreciated and the relative cost-benefit attraction of other weapon systems are considered. These shifting contexts provide a background for the need to bring into balance defense (armor), offense (gun), and mobility while, additionally, as for all weapon systems, effective mass production and easy maintenance and operability are also important, as in the T-34. Yet other specifications were also important. Thus, the Israeli Merkava emphasizes defensive ones because Israel can ill afford using tank crews. At the same time, the military restructuring plan approved by Israel's Knesset (parliament) in 2013 proposed a reduction in tank numbers as part of a move toward a lesser reliance on ground forces and a shift toward operations from the air.

However defined, the tank is far more than simply a legacy system of the 1910s or, indeed, World War II. Nevertheless, the future of the tank is unclear, and its limitations, vulnerabilities, and costs are readily apparent.

NOTES

1. Scanlon later claimed that he never heard this from Wilson's lips. See also N. Farage, "UKIP: We Are Parking Our Tanks on Labour's Lawn," *Guardian*, September 27, 2014; C. Arthur, "Why Google Is Parking Its Tanks on Microsoft's Lawn," *Guardian*, July 8, 2009.

2. R. L. DiNardo, *Mechanized Juggernaut or Military Anachronism? Horses and the German Army of World War II* (Westport, CT, 1991).

3. G. L. Weinberg, "Some Myths of World War II," *JMH* 75 (2011): 718.

4. For example, review in *Sunday Times* of book by Jonathan Fennell on March 31, 2019.

5. K. Souter, "To Stem the Red Tide: The German Report Series and Its Effect on American Defense Doctrine, 1948–54," *JMH* 57 (1993): 658–88; R. W. Hutchinson, "The Weight of History: Wehrmacht Officers, the U.S. Army Historical Division, and U.S. Military Doctrine, 1945–56," *JMH* 78 (2014): 1345–46.

6. AWM. 3 DRL/6643, 3/9, p. 1.

7. *Cold War International History Project Bulletin* 6–7 (winter 1995–96): 109.

8. M. Bialoszewski, *A Memoir of the Warsaw Uprising* (New York, 2015): 7–8, 10–11.

9. K. D. Gott, *Breaking the Mold: Tanks in the Cities* (Fort Leavenworth, KS, 2006).

10. R. S. Cameron, *To Fight or Not to Fight? Organizational and Doctrinal Trends in Mounted Maneuver Reconnaissance from the Interwar Years to Operation IRAQI FREEDOM* (Fort Leavenworth, KS, 2010).

11. T. Rogoway and J. Trevithick, "Commandos Ride Black Hawk Helo and Stealth Boats during Shadowy Exercise in Miami Port," The Drive, December 13, 2018, https://www.thedrive.com/the-war-zone/25458/the-u.s.armys-new-up-gunned-stryker-armored-vehicles-have-been-hacked, accessed April 8, 2019.

12. J. F. C. Fuller, *Tanks in the Great War* (London, 1920), 308–21, quotes 308–9, 313.

13. Fuller, *Tanks in the Great War*, 317–18.

14. Fuller, *Tanks in the Great War*, 310.

15. Fuller, *Tanks in the Great War*, xix.

16. Fuller, *Tanks in the Great War*, 306.

17. Fuller, *Tanks in the Great War*, ix, 306.

18. J. F. C. Fuller, "The Application of Recent Developments in Mechanics and Other Scientific Knowledge to Preparation and Training for Future War on Land," *RUSI* 65 (1920) and Anon., "Military Technology and the RUSI Journal," *RUSI* 156 (2011): 114, 118.

19. J. Kiszely, "Thinking about the Operational Level," *RUSI* 150, no. 6 (2005): 39. At that point, Lieutenant-General Sir John Kiszely was director of the British Defence Academy.

SELECTED FURTHER READING

There is a welcome mass of relevant literature. The focus here is on recent works as earlier ones can be pursued through their notes and through the footnotes in this book.

Buckley, J. *British Armour and the Normandy Campaign 1944.* London: Frank Cass, 2004.

Citino, R. M. *Blitzkrieg to Desert Storm: The Evolution of Operational Warfare.* Lawrence: University of Kansas Press, 2004.

Coombs, B. *British Tank Production and the War Economy, 1934–1945.* London: Bloomsbury, 2013.

Corum, J. S. *The Roots of Blitzkrieg: Hans von Seeckt and German Military Reform.* Lawrence: University of Kansas Press, 1992.

Fuller, J. F. C. *Tanks in the Great War, 1914–1918.* London: John Murray, 1920.

Gale, T. *The French Army's Tank Force and Armoured Warfare in the Great War: The Artillerie Spéciale.* Farnham, UK: Ashgate, 2013.

Gat, A. *British Armour Theory and the Rise of the Panzer Arm: Revisiting the Revisionists.* London: Macmillan, 2000.

Glantz, D. M. *Colossus Reborn: The Red Army at War, 1941–1943.* Lawrence: University of Kansas Press, 2005.

Gott, K. D. *Breaking the Mold: Tanks in the Cities.* Fort Leavenworth, KS: Combat Studies Institute Press, 2006.

Gudmundsson, B. I. *On Armor.* Westport, CT: Praeger, 2004.

Habeck, M. R. *Storm of Steel: The Development of Armor Doctrine in Germany and the Soviet Union, 1919–1939.* Ithaca, NY: Cornell University Press, 2003.

Harris, J. P. *Men, Tanks and Ideas: British Military Thought and Armoured Forces, 1903–1939.* Manchester, UK: Manchester University Press, 1995.

House, J. M. *Combined Arms Warfare in the Twentieth Century.* Lawrence: University of Kansas Press, 2001.

Read, B. H. *Studies in British Military Thought: Debates with Fuller and Liddell Hart.* Lincoln: University of Nebraska Press, 1998.

Searle, A. *Armoured Warfare.* London: Bloomsbury, 2017.

Searle, A., ed. *Genesis, Employment, Aftermath: First World War Tanks and the New Warfare, 1900–1945.* Solihull, UK: Helion, 2015.

Simpkin, R. E. *Tank Warfare: An Analysis of Soviet and NATO Tank Philosophy.* London: Brasseys, 1979.

Stone, J. *The Tank Debate: Armour and the Anglo-American Tradition.* Amsterdam: Harwood, 2000.

Wright, P. *Tank: The Progress of a Monstrous War Machine.* New York: Viking, 2000.

INDEX

JEREMY BLACK is Professor of History at the University of Exeter. He is the author of many books, including *A History of Britain: 1945 to Brexit, War and Technology,* and *Warfare in the Western World, 1882–1975.* Black is a recipient of the Samuel Eliot Morison Prize from the Society for Military History.